W9-AFM-335

ERASMUS, TYNDALE AND MORE

Desiderius Erasmus
From the picture by Holbein

ERASMUS, TYNDALE AND MORE

by

W. E. CAMPBELL

" For as the sea shall never surround and overwhelm the land, and yet hath it eaten many places in, and swallowed whole countries up, and made places now sea that sometime were well-inhabited lands, and hath lost part of his own possession in other parts again; so though the faith of Christ shall never be overflowen with heresies, nor the gates of hell prevail against Christ's Church, yet in some places it winneth in new people, so may there in some places by negligence be lost the old."

More, *Apology* (1533), *English Works*, p. 921.

" Men recognised in Erasmus some quality larger, sweeter, riper, nobler than in their own minds."

Prof. J. S. Phillimore, *Dublin Review*, July 1913, p. 9.

THE BRUCE PUBLISHING COMPANY
MILWAUKEE

PRINTED IN ENGLAND

TO
MY WIFE
1907–1948

Acknowledgments

I WISH I could acknowledge by name all those to whom I am indebted for what I have tried to sum up in this volume. That, however, is obviously impossible within the compass of a single page. But first, and before all, I cannot estimate my indebtedness to my friends the late Professor R. W. Chambers and Professor A. W. Reed, with whom I have been privileged to collaborate in editing the first two volumes of a new folio edition of the *English Works of Sir Thomas More*. Nor can I sufficiently thank the Abbot and Community of Downside Abbey for the almost daily use of their great Library when working upon these pages, and for many years before. I was also greatly indebted to the late Monsignor Hallett for his kindness in reading through my typescript and for his criticisms and most valuable suggestions; to the Editors of the *Dublin Review* and the *Catholic World* (America) for their kindness in allowing me to use matter printed in those periodicals; and, at the very last, after the galley-proofs were in my hands, the added *Note on the Death of Erasmus* owes its important information to Rev. R. G. Villoslada, S.J., embodied in an article of his entitled *La Muerte De Erasmo*, published in Spanish by the Vatican Press so late as 1946. Other indebtedness I have gratefully to acknowledge to Rev. J. F. Mozley, for new information about Tyndale, and to the late Dom. R. H. Connolly and Mr. John Todd for valuable help.

Contents

Illustrations

1

Introduction

AN IMMENSE amount of exact and profound scholarship has gone into the study of the lives of Erasmus, Tyndale and More, particularly in our own country during recent years. But such studies have
dealt for the most part with one or other of these famous men. In the
pages which follow they will, of course, be considered individually,
but also in their relationships with one another and with the beginnings
of the Reformation movement in its English phase, though not without
reference to continental happenings.

It may be well to remind ourselves that all three of them were
Catholics in the pre-Reformation sense of that word, and that while
Erasmus and More remained what they had always been, with Tyndale
it was not so; for when he had passed the third decade of his life he left
his own country, and, going to Germany, came under Luther's influence
and forthwith embraced the Protestant religion. Subsequently he engaged with Sir Thomas More in a long-drawn-out vernacular religious
controversy, and so, while absent abroad, was recognised as the protagonist of Protestantism in this country.

A personal word or two as to the when, and the wherefore of
this book may not seem intrusive. The first notion of it came to me in
the December of 1896, when Cardinal, then Abbot, Gasquet preached a
sermon at Downside in honour of the newly beatified Benedictine
Abbots of Colchester, Glastonbury and Reading–Reading having
been my own school and, in pre-Reformation times, the school of
Reading Abbey. One of the points made in that sermon was that no
better service could be rendered to religion and sound learning than by
editing for publication available evidence for the study of the Reformation period in England. Moved by this suggestion, I began to read
what I could find about Sir Thomas More, who seemed to me to be a
typical Englishman, and, at the same time, a no less typical Catholic.

A second impression, and I think the more vivid of the two, was
made upon me somewhat later, when, going one day into the room of

Dom Leander Ramsay, then Headmaster of Downside School, with a copy of that small Scott Library edition of Roper's *Life of Sir Thomas More* in my hand, I happened to mention that I had just been reading in it Roper's account of More's trial. In his quick, eager way, he almost snatched the book from me, and taking it in his own left hand, while raising his right in emphasis, he read aloud to me, as only he could read, the words addressed by More to Rich, Henry VIII's Solicitor-General, who, on oath, had just borne false witness against him: "And if," said More, "this oath of yours, Master Rich, be true, then pray I that I never see God in the face, which I would not say, were it otherwise, to win the whole world."[1]

Not long afterwards, as a remote preparation, I went through the *Letters and Papers of the Reign of Henry VIII*, edited in the Rolls Series, first by Mr. J. S. Brewer, with their remarkable prefaces, and later by Dr. James Gairdner, who together must have known as much about that period as any historians who have written upon it.[2] This provided me with a chronological backbone for the whole epoch which has proved continuously useful.

On January 12th, 1911–a red-letter, or rather I should say a black-letter day for me–I became the fortunate possessor of the *English Works* of Sir Thomas More, published in 1557. It is a stout volume, bound in brown leather, of 1433 numbered pages, and printed in double-columned black-letter type, together with some thirty unnumbered pages, including the rare leaf, but lacking the title-page and also those from 831 to 834. The missing leaves were photographed from the complete copy in the British Museum, and added as obvious insertions to the precious volume.

Here, then, I had as my own, and permanently neighboured among my other books, the *materia prima* of much future happiness; and although I do not count myself *homo unius libri*, yet, in the literary rather than in the literal sense, such I became. More's *English Works* henceforward gave their own *forma substantialis* to most of my thought and writing. But perhaps I ought to say that I also devoted to the *Works* of Dean Colet, Erasmus and William Tyndale as much attention as to those of Sir Thomas More. What each of these had written, and not so much what others had written about them, although of interest and importance, became the first consideration.

[1] Roper, *Life of Sir Thomas More*, p. 51.
[2] Second Edition, revised and greatly enlarged by R. H. Brodie, 1920.

Owing to the accidents and vicissitudes of the war period, the prospect of completing my larger volumes of More's *Works* seemed doubtful. I therefore thought it prudent to begin this book, hoping therein to sum up the result of a good many years of study. And this I have now done.

Something perhaps may be said of its plan and pattern. I owe it to a very favourite book of mine, Mr. Frederic Seebohm's *Oxford Reformers*,[1] published so long ago as 1867. In his Preface the author told us he had "endeavoured to trace the *joint*-history of Dean Colet, Erasmus and Sir Thomas More". And so well did he do it, that his book has become an English historical classic. But it ended at Colet's death in 1519, while More lived on for another sixteen years, and Erasmus until the year following. My book, then, while covering in part the same period as his, will carry on, though from a rather different standpoint, the life-stories of More and Erasmus to their end; and to these that of Tyndale will be added. Tyndale, who is so well known as "the founder of the English version of the Bible", is probably much less so as More's opponent in a long-drawn-out controversy upon the very fundamentals of the Christian faith. At first sight, a considered study of such a controversy may seem to some a rather gratuitous revival of "battles long ago". But in this connection a conversation reported by James Anthony Froude in his *Life of Thomas Carlyle* may be recalled, perhaps not inappropriately :

In his earlier years Carlyle had spoken contemptuously of the Athanasian controversy, of the Christian world torn in pieces over a diphthong, and he would ring the changes in broad Annandale on the Hom*o*ousion and the Hom*oi*ousion. He told me now that he perceived Christianity itself to have been at stake. If the Arians had won, it would have dwindled away into legend.[2]

But these words from the lips of Carlyle reflect some light, too, upon the purpose and significance of the great theological duel between Tyndale and Sir Thomas More, one indeed which a contributor to the *Dictionary of National Biography* has described as "the classical controversy of the Reformation". "No other discussion", he writes, "was carried on between men of such pre-eminent ability and with so clear an apprehension of the points at issue. To More's assertion of the paramount authority of the Church, Tyndale replied by appealing to the

[1] Seebohm's *Oxford Reformers* may now be got in the Everyman series (Dent, 3s. 6d.).
[2] *Carlyle's Life in London*, vol. ii, p. 494.

Scripture, with an ultimate resort to individual judgment."[1] This controversy of theirs was indeed a crowning effort of dialectical skill and it had a determining effect, perhaps not quite immediately, but certainly in the long run, not only upon English life and religion, but also upon the development of our national literature.

"More's position, as a writer of English prose," says Professor R.W. Chambers, "is specially important. It was not till long after his day that anyone could rival his mastery of so many different types of English dramatic dialogue and rhetorical monologue, narrative and argument combined in a style at once scholarly and colloquial."[2]

And further, the opinion of the late W. P. Ker, another English scholar of unchallenged authority, may be added on Tyndale, in whose writings "there may be traced very easily a kinship to earlier and (Catholic) reformers, who were more tolerant than he. He translated the *Enchiridion* of Erasmus, and appreciated the Praise of Folly (*Encomium Moriae*), at least so far as to conclude from it that Sir Thomas More had been more liberal in his youth[3] than he showed himself in his later years. . . . As an original author (Tyndale) is distinguished for the humble yet not too ordinary virtues of clearness and directness. He had a complete command of language for the purposes of theological argument and controversy. His meaning is always plain, and if his treatises are not now popular, that comes from the loss of general interest in the matter, and not from any deterrent or wearisome qualities in his style."[4] This opinion applies in particular to his controversial style, which of its very nature one would expect to be plain, argumentative and, in Tudor times, not uncontentious. But the same critic, speaking of Tyndale's translations of the Bible, re-echoes the general opinion that "he is entitled to rank among the greatest of prose writers".[5]

In the sixteenth century, self-expression, whether on politics or religion, was not without mortal risk; and so it proved in Tyndale's case as in that of More. In the final issue each died for what he believed to be supremely true.

And now we come to the consideration at greater length of the life of Erasmus—Erasmus the championed friend of St. Thomas More; Erasmus the Catholic humanist, who, as Lord Acton said, "diverted the current of ancient learning from profane to Christian channels";[6]

[1] *D.N.B.*, art. "Tyndale", vol. lvii, p. 427.   [2] *Man's Unconquerable Mind*, p. 189.
[3] More was 38 when he wrote the *Utopia*. The *Praise of Folly* was published in 1511.
[4] *English Prose Selections*, ed. Sir Henry Craik, vol. i, pp. 181-2. (Macmillan, 1928.)
[5] *Ib.*, p. 181.   [6] *The Study of History*, p. 8.

IOANNES COLETVS

Cum colis Aonias exculte COLET & sorores
Te doctos inter posthuma fama refert.

AB

John Colet, Dean of St. Paul's
From the Engraving in Holland's *Heroologia*, 1620

Erasmus the prince of letter-writers, the pioneer of sounder and quite orthodox biblical criticism; Erasmus the first great editor of the Fathers of the Church who were the traditional authoritative interpreters of Holy Scripture; Erasmus, who, quick to realise that, after the invention of printing, books, good as well as bad, would be circulated far and wide, wrote one of the first books of simple Catholic devotion, then so much needed by ordinary lay folk; Erasmus, that courageous man, who, like St. Thomas More, when faced with untrue and malicious criticism, was so diffident about his own courage that many writers have taken him at his word; Erasmus, a great man, and, indeed, the greatest of the Renaissance Scholars who blazed the trail for still greater ones to come, as he himself would have been the first to acknowledge had he lived to know them.

. But any account of the lives of Erasmus and More and of their "fellow-work" must needs include some notice of John Colet, Dean of St. Paul's from 1505 to the year of his death in 1519, who was More's spiritual and Erasmus's intellectual counsellor. Born in the same year as Erasmus, and some twelve years older than More, he had a powerful and determining influence upon both their lives. Considered, too, in and by himself, he was a great ecclesiastic, of sterling probity, powerful in mind and spirit, and of deep and steadfast Catholic convictions. He is generally remembered, of course, as the founder of St. Paul's School, and of all that its foundation has since meant to public-school life in this country.

But, even so, he is all too little known or, shall we say, known as he really was. As Mr. Lupton, his biographer and late sur-master of St. Paul's School, tells us, so far as he knew, Colet was not once mentioned in the histories of Hume and Lingard, while in Green's *Short History of the English People* "an importance altogether unique is assigned to the part he played". But after reading what Mr. Green has there written, we feel constrained to say that "the part assigned to Colet" was not quite or altogether the part that in fact he did play.

Or, again, in Mr. Frederic Seebohm's delightfully written *Oxford Reformers*, Colet is unmistakably the author's hero–but hardly a Catholic hero at that, although Colet lived and died a Catholic. As a non-Catholic exactly states it, "The glory of Colet, Erasmus and More is that they maintained undimmed throughout their careers their ideal of the Church of Christ as a Catholic society, and that no possible combination of self-interest with the hopes of success for

B

their schemes could have availed to detach them from that Catholic unity."[1]

But while writing the last few lines a memory came to one's mind that may serve as a pointer in the right direction. On the last day of July 1547, in the first year of the reign of Edward VI, a royal injunction went forth that the interiors of all the churches in the country should be whitewashed–the intention being to banish from sight and memory the beautiful designs and colours that for centuries had done so much to foster religious devotion: "And so all images pulled down, with the commandments written on the walls."[2]

Following this analogy, may it not be said that just as so many of our pre-Reformation churches and cathedrals are, at long last, being un-whitewashed and revealed to us once more in their old and true colours, so, too, are the biographical portraits of certain undoubtedly Catholic men of the pre-Reformation period–as in Father Bridgett's standard *Life of Sir Thomas More*? And, much in the same way, the late Dr. P. S. Allen, with massive and unprejudiced learning, has "restored" the portrait of Erasmus, as we find it in his great edition of *Erasmi Epistolae*, now happily completed by the publication of the last and eleventh volume.

> "Erasmus, that great injured name,
> The glory of the priesthood and the shame."[3]

Mr. F. M. Nichols has also given us in English a three-volume translation of the *Epistles of Erasmus* down to 1518, making them even more attractive by his own criticism and comment.

But to return to Dean Colet. His father, Sir Henry Colet, was a well-to-do City magnate, twice Lord Mayor of London, and in favour at the Court of Henry VII. John Colet was educated at one of the City schools, and went up to Oxford about 1483. At the University he excelled in mathematics, mastered the philosophy of the Schools, was familiar with Cicero and had a particular bent towards Plato which he further gratified on his post-graduate tour through France and Italy between 1493 and 1497.

But he has left us all too little positive evidence of that continental

---

[1] G. V. Jourdan, *The Movement of Catholic Reform in the Early Sixteenth Century*, Introd., p. xxx.

[2] James Gairdner, *A History of the English Church in the Sixteenth Century*, pp. 246-8. Also *Chronicle of the Grey Friars of London* (Camden Society), p. 54.

[3] Pope, *Essay on Criticism* (1709), *Works*, vol. i, pp. 224-5. Pope, it will be remembered, was a Catholic poet. Croker interprets the second line as follows: "The glory, from his own greatness, the shame, from the rancour with which some of his brother priests assailed him".

wandejahre of his. We know that he stayed at Orleans, and at Paris both on his outward and homeward journey.

We may not unfairly conclude [writes Mr. Lupton] that Colet would visit Bologna and Florence on his way to Rome. . . . The objects which a young student from Western Europe would have in travelling in Italy are not far to seek. The universities north of the Alps were, in Colet's time, far behind those of the Peninsula. Not to speak of the munificent patrons of literature found in the Medici family, it was in Italy that the exiles from Constantinople had met with an asylum, and there the Greek learning they brought with them struck root and flourished again. . . . The great universities were not so self-complete as now. In most cases each had a special reputation, Paris for theology, Bologna for law, Salerno for medicine, and the like. Learned men, moreover, were tempted to a migratory life as professors, by the various inducements held out to attract them. . . . Whether Colet was one of the Englishmen attending the lectures of Beroaldus (at Bologna) cannot now be discovered . . . (but) his familiarity with canon law, shown in his Convocation sermon and elsewhere, would have made it probable; while his acquaintance with the writings of Pico della Mirandola and of Marsiglio Ficino forms a connecting link with Florence.[1]

At that moment of time Florence was at the height of its intellectual, artistic and social fame.

What an array of illustrious names were to be found there:

> "And when I think that Michael Angelo
> Hath leaned on me, I glory in myself,"

is the utterance ascribed by the poet to the Ponte Vecchio in Florence . . . Leonardo da Vinci was there; so was Fra Bartolommeo, whose pencil was even then adorning the walls of San Marco; so was Brunelleschi, who fifty years before had crowned the Cathedral with the famous dome that made it tower over St. Peter's. Bramante might often have been seen there, Machiavelli was in Florence, and Colet may often have passed the man, slightly his own junior.[2]

In this period, too, though somewhat earlier, other young Englishmen, who afterwards became famous, visited Italy—Grocyn and Linacre, for instance, who are sometimes said to be the first to do so, and to be the earliest pioneers of the Renaissance in their own country. But even before them, William Selling and his companion, William Hadley, two Benedictine monks of Christchurch, Canterbury, made their

---

[1] *Life of Dean Colet*, pp. 47-50 seriatim.   [2] *Ib.*, p. 51.

journey to Italy, and brought back to England the better rather than the
bitter fruits of the Italian Renaissance.[1]

Colet, in fact, presuming that he visited Florence, was seemingly
indifferent to its aesthetic and classical attractiveness, not being, it
would appear, over-susceptible to the "pure beauty of form" then so
much sought after under high Medicean patronage. By some he may
have been thought of the unnoticing sort; but others more discerning
may have recognised him as a contemplative, "a man of removed and
secluded excellence", given to going apart into quiet churches where
undisturbed he could "remain in cessation and silence before God". We
thus understand his preference for the writings of Ficino and of Pico
della Mirandola, a liking that later he communicated to the youthful
More. Perhaps, too, we may infer that he was impressed, and deeply
impressed, by that great and prophetic figure, Savonarola,[5] a man after
his own heart, and not unlike him in disposition, in character and in his
personal reactions to wickedness in high places and in low. Erasmus
mentions that Colet had told him that "among the Italians he had discovered some monks of true wisdom and piety". This, it may be, was a
reference to the Dominican community of San Marco, of which
Savonarola was then prior.

Savonarola [writes Father Ryder, the Oratorian] is not safe-
guarded by the sanction of authority as are the canonised saints; still there
is something, one would think, due to the type, apart from individual
registration. . . . I suppose one main ground for regarding Savonarola as a
saint, that is a conscientious persistent soldier of Christ, ever combating
for the right as it appears to him, and on the highest of motives, the
love of God, is this, that besides his actual fighting for the cause of
God, he has given clear evidence of a deep spiritual life which he not
only lived himself, but from which he nourished numberless children of
grace who could say, "In thy light we shall see light". From his earliest
days with his novices at San Marco, to the last days in the dungeons of
the Signory, when, with a frame broken by torture and his reputation
shattered, he converted his jailer by the energy of prayer–Burlamacchi
says that the man found him raised from the ground in ecstasy–he
was able to supply his neighbours' lamps with an oil that never failed. . . .
His memory was accepted as saintly by St. Philip Neri, who had his
picture over his prie-dieu with the inscription, "B. Hieron. Savonarola,
Martyr"; St. Catherine of Ricci had recourse to him as her special inter-
cessor with God; and there is a copy of his works now in the Vallicella

[1] Dom William Selling afterwards became prior of Christchurch, and Linacre was his
most celebrated pupil in the monastic school. He was also sent on an embassy to Rome as
Latin orator, to inform Innocent VIII of Henry VII's accession.

Library "which was given by the Blessed Giovenale Ancina to St. Philip, a saint to a saint".[1]

As with Florence, so with Rome, we cannot be sure that Colet ever went there; but it seems that he had an intention of doing so. Or perhaps what Baptist Mantuanus had written about it, truthful in this case, had reached him:

> Vivere qui cupitis, discedite Roma:
> Omnia cum liceant, non licet bonum,

and so dissuaded him from making the journey? As Mr. Lupton says, "Of one thing, at any rate, he could not but have ample evidence wherever his steps were directed in Italy between 1494 and 1497, that was the mischief done to true religion by the conduct of the occupant of the papal chair," Alexander VI.[2]

Erasmus tells us that Colet, while in France and Italy, "like a merchant seeking goodly wares", devoted himself to the study of the sacred writers, having previously roamed through literature of every kind with great zest. He found much pleasure in the earlier Fathers, Origen, Cyprian, Ambrose and Jerome, but even more, it would appear, in Dionysius, the so-called Areopagite, whose treatises on the spiritual life could not have been written earlier than, say, between 480 and 520, as Erasmus well knew.

Colet's keen interest in the Dionysian treatises is an indication of the contemplative nature of his own spiritual life, and, indirectly, of what he communicated to More, whose intimate friend and religious guide he was to become until his own death. It is enough to mention very briefly a number of these treatises which Colet put into English in order to appreciate the quality of the man to whom the young More owed his own piety. There is the *Heavenly Hierarchy*, the *Ecclesiastical Hierarchy*, the *De Sacramentis Ecclesiae*, and that tract *On the Divine Names*, so often quoted in the *Summa* of St. Thomas Aquinas—not at all, one would think, the sort of spiritual literature to be translated by a man who sometimes has been considered the herald of a new and Protestant dawn.

Dionysius has rightly been held *the* mediæval authority upon the contemplative life, "Starting from the Absolute, he passes through the succession of its descending manifestations, rising (again) in a final ascent to the Absolute in the ecstasy of a mystical union with God."[3]

[1] Rev. H. I. D. Ryder, *Essays*, pp. 58, 59, 74.

[2] A recent biography of Alexander VI notwithstanding.

[3] B. F. Westcott, *Contemporary Review*, art. "Dionysius the Areopagite", May 1867. The same writer points out that the works of Dionysius the Areopagite are pseudonymous, but that they are not spurious.

But, as St. Thomas Aquinas himself teaches, the complete Catholic life is both active and passive—passive in the highest that can be received direct from God, and active in what should be duly given back from man to man. There are four key-words which may give us, perhaps, a clue to the teaching of Dionysius. The first is *hierarchy*, which expresses the divine law of subordination and mutual dependence of the different ranks of created beings, angelical and human. Then there is the word *unity*, with its particular reference to the union of the soul with God. The third word is *fellowship*, a unity here on earth of men "of all nations, and tribes, and peoples and tongues" that together make up the great common society of Christendom—Christendom that is as Colet knew it as yet undisturbed by the Reformation—a unity in thought, in prayer, and in *fellow-work*—work which, rightly understood and carried into practice, would provide for all the common necessities of life, bodily and spiritual, and would distribute them always and everywhere to meet the common need, a truly Christian traffic carried on in justice and charity:

> "The traffic of Jacob's ladder
> Pitched between heaven and Charing Cross."[1]

Counted in the heavenly calculus, it may be, that after his return from Italy, Colet's most important achievement was his influence upon the youthful More then about twenty, Colet's age being thirty-one. Whether it was at Oxford or later that the two first met, it was not long before Colet, a man not given to exaggeration, could pronounce More, as we are told by Erasmus, to be the one genius he had found among his English friends. There must have been something very attractive and very impressive about Colet, certainly an outward dignity and reserve, concealing, as is often the case with Englishmen, a banked-up fire of deep personal affection. As Mr. Lupton so happily expressed it, "Colet succeeded in drawing out the *aurea bonitas* of both their natures."[2]

And there is no doubt that More returned Colet's affection, as witness a letter written by him to Colet in 1504, while away from London in the year before his marriage.

I was walking up and down the Law Courts when your servant met me. But when I learnt not only that you had not returned, but were not to return for a considerable time, I was dejected. What can be more dis-

[1] Francis Thompson, *Selected Poems*, "In No Strange Land", p. 131.
[2] Lupton, *Life of Dean Colet*, p. 99.

tressing to me than to be deprived of your most dear society, after being guided by your wise counsels, cheered by your charming familiarity, assured by your earnest sermons, and helped forward by your example, so that I used to obey your very look and nod? With these helps I felt myself strengthened, but without them I seem to languish. . . . What is there in the City to incite to virtue? On the contrary, when one wishes to live well, the life of a city drags one down. . . .

Come back, then, my dear Colet, even for the sake of your [own parish of] Stepney. . . . Come back for the sake of London, your native place which merits your care no less than do your parents. Lastly, though this is but a feeble motive, let your regard for me move you, since I have given myself entirely to you, and am awaiting your return full of solicitude.

Meanwhile I shall pass my time with Grocyn, Linacre and our friend Lily: the first of whom is, as you know, the only director of my life in your absence; the second, the master of my studies; the third, my most dear companion. Farewell, and continue to love me as you do.–From London, the 10th November.[1]

But Colet was now on the threshold of high preferment, having for six or seven years lectured at Oxford on the Epistles of St. Paul.[2] Here he made the acquaintance of Erasmus, since, as Erasmus tells us, "some kind providence brought me at that time to the same spot". He also tells us that Colet,

Although he had neither obtained nor sought any degree in divinity or law, no abbot or other dignitary but came to hear him, and often made notes on what he heard. . . . From these sacred occupations he was called back to London, in order to rule over the Cathedral of the apostle to whose epistles he was so devoted. And now, as Dean, feeling himself called to a great and serious work rather than to an empty honour, Colet restored the decayed discipline of the Cathedral body, and began to preach himself at every great feast in his own pulpit–and that not merely on isolated texts, but he would begin some connected subject and go through with it to the end in succeeding sermons, as for instance St. Matthew's Gospel, or the Creed, or the Lord's Prayer. His preaching became very popular, attracting as listeners most of the prominent people both of the City and of the Court.[3]

Colet delighted in good talk, but much less in the too-bountiful hospitality previously dispensed at the Deanery. He therefore cut down

[1] Bridgett, *Sir Thomas More*, pp. 46–8. Original in Latin.
[2] See J. W. H. Atkins, *English Literary Criticism—The Renascence*, pp. 37, 54–62. A remarkable recent appreciation of Colet's sermons on St. Paul's *Epistles* at Oxford, breaking new ground in biblical exposition by supplying the historical and local background and setting an example which Erasmus was to follow in his *Novum Instrumentum*.
[3] *Erasmus on Dean Colet*, trans. J. G. Nichols, pp. 147–8.

the food allowance, and with it apparently the quantity of his guests, but not without an improvement in their quality. His dress, his appearance and the general habit of his life betokened asceticism. Spending very little on himself, he left his income to his steward to be laid out economically; and his own private fortune–a very large one after his father's death–was spent on the new school which he built in St. Paul's Churchyard, although there had previously been one within the Cathedral precincts. The new St. Paul's School was a handsome building, with two masters of outstanding ability to look after it. The number of admissions was limited, and the boys were chosen according to their character and ability. Colet seems to have thought of everything that would help his great educational scheme. Over the high-master's chair there was a finely wrought figure of the Child Jesus, seated in the attitude of teaching, and above it a representation of God the Father, with a scroll issuing from the mouth which bore the words, Hear ye Him, "an inscription", adds Erasmus, "added at my uggestion."

Colet, in his *School Statutes,* which serve as a preface to his "Accidence", prefixes a religious instruction, called the *Cathechizon* containing *The Articles of the Faith*, followed in his "Rudiments" by *The Seven Sacraments, Our Duty to God and our Duty to our Neighbour,* and two of *The Precepts of Living*: "Believe and trust in Christ Jesu" and "Worship Him and His mother Mary". The *Cathechizon* ends with a prayer to our Lord, "Et tu quoque, Jesu benignissime, age cum patre tuo, et patre nostro, ut gratia sui spiritus nos suos filiolos faciat, sic te, Jesu, discere et imitari in hoc saeculo ut una tecum feliciter regnemus in futuro. Amen."

And also with a prayer to our Lady: "Sancta Maria, virgo et mater Jesu, age cum filio tuo, ut haec schola quotidie proficiat in ipso, utque omnes pueri in eadem discant ipsum, et erudiantur in ipso, tandem ut Perfecti filii Dei fiant per ipsum."

It may be noticed that while Colet would have his boys taught "good literature, both laten and greke", he found a place for Christian as well as classical authors, such as Lactantius and Prudentius, Juvencus, and Baptist Mantuanus. Indeed, he expresses himself very strongly on the point:

All barbary, all corruption, all laten adulterate, which ignorant blynde folis brought into this worlde, and with the same that distayned and poysenyd the old laten speche and the varay Romayne tong which

in the time of Tully and Salust and Virgill and Terence was usid; whiche
also seint Jerome and seint Ambrose and seint Austen and many hooly
doctors lernyd in theyr tymes,–I say that fylthynesse and all such abus-
ion which the later blynde worlde brought in, which more rathyr
may be callid blotterature thenne litterature, I utterly abbanysh and
exclude out of this scole.[1]

Dean Colet, however, had other and even greater cares than those
of the founder of a new school. He was a great preacher, and perhaps
his most famous sermon was the one he delivered at the meeting of
Convocation on February 6th, 1511–12.

The neglect of religion and the increase of heresy at this time gave
cause for great anxiety to the rulers of the Church; and so serious were
these heretical opinions deemed to be, that Henry VIII ordered the
Archbishop of Canterbury to summon a Convocation to meet at St.
Paul's in the February of 1511-12 to consider, among other things, how
best they could be dealt with. Archbishop Warham asked the Dean of
St. Paul's to preach at the opening, and, as Cardinal Gasquet wrote,
"Colet's sermon, delivered on that occasion, is perhaps the most valuable contemporary account of the state of the Church in England".[2]
The Cardinal's own summary of it will help us to realise how signi-
ficant an utterance it was

Taking for his text the words of St. Paul to the Romans–"Be not
conformed to this world, but be ye transformed by the renewing of
your mind, that ye may prove what is that good, and acceptable, and
perfect will of God."–the learned and uncompromising Dean proceeded
to speak boldly against "the fashion of secular and wordly living in
clerks and priests".

To this secularity of priests' lives Dean Colet attributed all the evils
which had befallen the Church, and he earnestly begged the English
clergy to turn their minds to the reformation of abuses if they would
desire to escape the dangers to religion which could be so plainly foreseen. *There was no need for new laws, but those which existed should be put
in force.* Ordination should be given only to such as had led pure and
holy lives, and the laws against clerics and monks occupying themselves
in secular business should be put in force. Also "let the laws be rehearsed",
begged the preacher, "that command the personal residence of curates
(*rectors*) in their churches. For of this many evils grow, because all things
nowadays are done by *vicars* and parish priests; yea, and those foolish,
also, and unmeet and oftentimes wicked, that seek none other thing in

[1] Lupton, *Life of Dean Colet,* p. 169. See also an interesting reference to the cruel and
barbarous sports indulged in by boys in the pre-Coletian period, pp. 173-5.
[2] *Henry VIII and the English Monasteries,* First Edition, vol. i, pp. 25-6.

the people than foul lucre, whereof cometh occasion of evil heresies and ill Christianity in the people."

So too, in this respect, *bishops should first look to themselves*. They should diligently look after the souls of those committed to them, *and reside in their dioceses*. Their revenues should not be spent on "feasting and banqueting", nor upon "sumptuous apparel and pomps", but in things profitable and necessary to the Church. For when St. Augustine, some-time bishop of England, did ask pope Gregory how that bishops and prelates of England should spend their goods that were the offerings of faithful people, the said pope answered that the goods of the bishops ought to be divided into four parts, whereof one part ought to be to the bishop and his household, another to his diocese, the third to repair and uphold his tenements, the fourth to the poor people.[1]

Dean Colet, especially in these last years, had a great longing to end his days in or near a monastic house. His foundation of St. Paul's School was now completed, and he had suffered a good deal at the hands of Fitz-James, the Bishop of London, who seemed to be envious of him. And so it was that he sought a place of rest and spiritual privilege near the Carthusian monastery at Shene, where, for the remainder of his life, he might have some experience of the contemplative life of which he had written in his *Hierarchies* of Dionysius as the summit of human perfection in this world. He writes to Erasmus on October 20th, 1514: "I am daily thinking of my retirement, and of my retreat with the Carthusians. My nest (the house he had built for himself near the monastery) is almost finished. So far as I can conjecture, you will find me there on your return, dead to the world." "And there (writes Erasmus) he was minded, as an oblate, to take a share in the liturgical services of the community, and, at the same time, to hold intercourse with two or three old and chosen friends, of whom I was one."

But though he had built his nest, he did not live to occupy it for long; for he went there only to die, at the age of fifty-three, on September 16th, 1519. *Sic vos non vobis nidificatis.*[2]

We may now go back to the very beginning and follow the earlier life of Erasmus, the eldest of our three who were to take so prominent and such inter-related parts in the religious history of their own times.

---

[1] *Henry VIII and the English Monasteries*, First Edition, pp. 25–6. Mr. Lupton writes: "With great candour, as well as mastery of his subject, Father Gasquet reviews in detail most of the evils on which Colet dwells. In fact, no better commentary on the sermon could be desired than the examples he quotes in illustration of it." *The Influence of Dean Colet upon the Reformation in the English Church*, p. 33.

[2] See also A. F. Pollard, *Wolsey*, p. 272.

Erasmus

ERASMUS WAS born on the Eve of the Feast of Saints Simon and
Jude in 1466, and, it would seem certain, without the inestimable
rights and privileges of honourable parentage. This, if true, would
of itself be sufficient to account for his sensitiveness throughout life,
although genius of itself is apt to be unduly sensitive. A good deal of
romance has been woven about the story of Erasmus's birth by Charles
Reade in that great novel *The Cloister and the Hearth*. One fact, however,
is certain, and that is "that his father was a priest", and, it is said, the
parish priest of Gouda, the little town where he was born. But whether
his father was a priest before Erasmus's birth we do not know. At
Gouda, under a master who became his guardian after the death of both
his parents, he was first taught his Latin Grammar. Then he went to the
choir school at Deventer, where at the end of his time he may have
been influenced by the great scholar Hegius. A little later Deventer was
to become the most celebrated school in the Netherlands, if not indeed
in all Europe, numbering at its height more than two thousand boys,
some of them afterwards to become widely famous. But of Erasmus's
life there we know nothing remarkable; for when he was eighteen he
left, being then still two classes from the top of the school. His opinion
of it, written much later, he summed up in one word, "barbarous", an
epithet often used before and since by many a sensitive lad who afterwards became famous, of the school to which he owed so much, or so
little.

In 1483 his mother, then living at Deventer, died of plague, and his
father removed him from school and himself died soon afterwards.
Being left to the care of guardians, he was sent with his brother to
another school at Hertogenbosch, kept by the Brethren of the Common
Life, a *Domus Pauperum* or House Preparatory for the monastic life.
Here he stayed for two years, and then begged to go to a university.
But no money seemed to be forthcoming for so laudable a purpose,

27

and instead, under the double pressure of his guardian and a friend ot his own age, who longed to have him as his companion in the monastic life, he consented to enter the novitiate of the Augustinian canons at Steyn. At the end of his novitiate in 1488 he was professed, and for seven years continued in this house of his probably mistaken choice. While here he led no idle life, but devoted himself most diligently to the study of the Fathers. Writing to a friend at a later date, he recommended him to read St. Jerome's *Letters*. "I have not only read them long ago, but have copied every one of them out with my own fingers." He also mentions his favourite classical authors: "My authorities in poetry are Maro (Virgil), Horace, Naso, Juvenal, Statius, Martial, Quintilian, Sallust, Terence." But when he had exploited to the full the classical treasures of Steyn, he began to feel the restraints of the religious enclosure too much for him; and his monastic superior, being wise, understood this, and made it easy for him, now a priest and in his twenty-seventh year, to become Latin secretary to Henry of Bergen, the stately Bishop of Cambrai, who wished for his services and company on a projected visit to Rome. It was said that his new patron was going to Rome in the hope of getting for himself a Cardinal's "hat". But some-things went wrong: the journey did not come off; nor did the "hat" come on.

After spending a little time with his Bishop amid the courtly surroundings of Brussels, Erasmus grew tired of it. So, with the episcopal blessing and some small monetary assistance, he set out for Paris, the America of his desires, where, with all its intellectual possibilities, he hoped to live a fuller, freer and, for him, a better life. Though still an Augustinian canon, he was now free to come and go at will, and must have greatly rejoiced in the prospect of embracing, at last, his true and learned "vocation".

He reached Paris in the autumn of 1495, and in order to obtain a Doctor's degree in theology, he entered the College of Montaigu, lately revived in reputation by its stern and zealous principal, John Standonck. But Erasmus, always delicate in health and fastidious in diet, found the fare too rough and meagre; indeed, it made him so ill that in the following summer he had to go home to his friends in Holland in order to recover his health. Returning soon afterwards, his life in Paris took on a more sociable colour, as he says of himself, "*vixit verius quam studuit*". He now lived at a rather sumptuous boarding-house in the Latin Quarter, much frequented by well-to-do young

Englishmen. Here he made the acquaintance of Lord Mountjoy, who introduced him to his own friends, William Blount, Thomas Grey and Robert Fisher, a cousin of St. John Fisher, the Bishop of Rochester. Living under pleasant conditions was an expensive matter, and so he was obliged to take pupils. He seems to have been treated with marked respect at his boarding-house, and dates a letter to his prior at Steyn, *E mea bibliotheca*, as if the whole household were his own. In the same letter he dilates upon his devotion to purely theological studies, as if wishing to impress his superior with the correctness of his daily life. It appears that some unfriendly gossip about him had reached Holland; but, as he said, a man so frail and delicate as himself was not in the least inclined to any serious irregularity. But he may have been thought self-indulgent by a few who had no idea of the devoted intensity of his intellectual labours and only saw him occasionally convivial and at ease among his friends. It may be, too, that some reported ill of him who had had painful experience of his caustic wit. Erasmus was never one to suffer fools gladly.

Meanwhile he stayed in Paris, supporting himself rather precariously by private teaching, particularly after help from the Bishop of Cambrai was no longer available. But assistance was soon forthcoming from another quarter–a friend of his, James Batt, a graduate of Paris, who had returned to his own country and had become tutor to the son of Anne of Borsselen, widow of an Admiral of Flanders and hereditary Lady of Veer. Such were his kindly offices on Erasmus's behalf, that he was invited to pay her a visit, and became from that time a recipient of her generous help. This greatly eased his poverty and, what is more, gave him time and opportunity to get on with the work that he most wished to do.

It is not surprising that such a relationship of dependency between a a poor but great scholar and a rich widow lady may have been a subject for criticism, and even for satire, from some who perhaps had never themselves known what it was to be both scholarly and poor. In fairness to Erasmus it should be remembered that time and again he refused ecclesiastical preferment, even when his friend and fellow-countryman, Pope Adrian VI, and later Leo X, wished to make him a Cardinal, knowing that whatever he gave to high office would be lost to sound learning–the cause he had most at heart. On the other hand, he often accepted monetary gifts without scruple, provided only they were given to him without any binding or tiresome conditions. It has been well said that "the scandal was not so much that Erasmus begged as that he was forced to beg".[1]

The same discerning writer has also put his finger upon what we may perhaps call Erasmus's besetting virtue—his *moderation*, nay his passion for moderation.

It is apt to strike the modern man as a strange or even impossible emotion. And whenever civilisation breaks down into barbarism it is only by a passion for moderation that it can be rescued and restored. . . . That, at least, was the Greek view, the very definition of barbarism being, for the Greeks, the man who goes to extremes. They thought him a weakling, and they proved they were right by beating him and then making a man of him. The whole ancient morality is based on the conviction that moderation is strength–but moderation at white heat.[2]

Now, is not this exactly what we find in Erasmus?

Meanwhile (1499) he was much more comfortably settled in Paris, better off, in better health than he had been under the rules and severities of Montaigu, and rapidly making influential friends. But, for all that, he had a strong aversion to the theological lectures, or rather to the theological lecturers he was obliged to listen to in order to get his degree in divinity. He writes about them, in a mood of superfluous naughtiness, to a friend of his:

I would not have you put any wrong interpretation on what I am going to say as against theology, for which, as you know, I have always entertained the greatest respect. I wish only to have a joke at the expense of certain theologists of the present generation, whose brains are rotten, their language barbarous, their apprehension dull, their learning thorny, their manners rude, their life mere hypocrisy, and their hearts as black as hell.[3]

Erasmus Visits England for the First Time

At this dark and midnight hour of his spirit an invitation came from Lord Mountjoy, his favourite pupil, to go home with him to England for a holiday. We can picture the delight with which it was accepted, the "barbarous theologists" now well forgotten. And so it was in the summer of 1499 that Erasmus was carried off on his first visit to this country. It is probable that he was taken, soon after landing, to Lord Mountjoy's house at Bedwell in Hertfordshire, and there he made the

[1] *Social and Political Ideas of the Renaissance and Reformation*, art. by J. A. K. Thomson, p. 154.
[2] *Ib.*, p. 156. Cf. "Ad litteras tantum rapiebatur animus," P. S. Allen, *Erasmic Epistolae*, tom. i, Ep. 296, p. 565.
[3] Cf. "Erasmus never flouted at religion nor even at theology as such, but only at blind and intemperate theologians." Mark Pattison, *Encycl. Brit.*, vol. 9, p. 731a, XI. edn.

acquaintance of some very delightful people. He writes, now, to another friend:

The Erasmus you once knew is now become almost a sportsman, no bad rider, a courtier of some practice, who bows with politeness and smiles with grace, all this in spite of himself. If you were wise you would fly over here.... To take one attraction out of many, the English girls are divinely pretty and as pleasant, gentle and charming as the Muses. They have one custom which cannot be too much admired. When you go anywhere on a visit the girls all kiss you. They kiss you when you arrive. They kiss you when you go away; and they kiss you when you return. In fact you are never without kisses. Did you once come here you would never wish to go away again.

But this, though pleasant gossip, was no serious matter. That was to follow. For it was in England, and at Oxford, that Erasmus was to have the great purpose of his life made clear to him. Let us follow him, then, "as he rides over Shotover and across Milham Ford, alone, into Oxford".

As an Austin Canon, he had a claim for hospitality on St. Mary's, a College which had been founded in 1435 by the Augustinians in order to enable their more promising younger subjects to profit by University studies. Here he stayed for two or three months, meeting learned people and listening to Colet's lectures on the Epistles of St. Paul—for him, as for others, a new and momentous experience. His own wide learning, ready wit and good talk made him popular wherever he went, not least in College Halls and Common Rooms where he was to meet Colet himself and engage both his interest and lasting friendship. But, as perhaps the most important result of it all, there came home to him, more and more insistently, his own need of a working knowledge of Greek. Colet might urge him to follow on the same lines as himself; but Erasmus was convinced, even more perhaps than Colet, that without Greek no adequate service could be rendered to Sacred Letters. And sufficient Greek was not to be had in Oxford, where as yet it was hardly tolerated by the unco' guid or encouraged by anybody else. The coming of good things is often slow, and the story of how Greek came to England more than a quarter of a century before the time of Erasmus's visit, and very, very gradually established itself in the great universities, principally through his own influence and that of St. John Fisher and St. Thomas More, will be told later.[1] It is enough to say here that Oxford, always slow to welcome

[1] But see also Introduction, p. 14.

novelties, was particularly so at the beginning of the sixteenth century in welcoming so ancient a novelty as Greek. It is true that in 1311, at the Council of Vienne, the Church itself had recommended that lectures in Greek should be established in the universities of Paris, Bologna, Oxford and Salamanca. But the decree had not been carried out, as many influential churchmen still regarded Greek as the language of the unorthodox, as indeed it often had been. As Dr. P. S. Allen wrote: "It needs no eyes (now) to see where they were wrong: where they were right–and they were right often enough–can only be seen by taking trouble."[1]

So Erasmus left Oxford with two valuable gifts–the friendship of Colet and the knowledge, at least, of what he did not know.[2]

He then went on to London, where he found something as precious to him as Greek itself–the friendship of men who understood and appreciated his rare qualities, and chief among them Thomas More.

At this time (1499) London was far more the centre of new intellectual life than either Oxford or Cambridge; and to Erasmus it brought new hopes, new stimulus, new friends. Writing several years later, he thus speaks of his first visit. "There are in London five or six men who are accurate scholars both in Latin and Greek, such as I think Italy itself does not at present possess." And in the following year to Colet he writes: "No place in the world has given me such friends as your City of London." And yet again, to Robert Fisher, he speaks of his first English visit in terms of sincere enthusiasm:

I never liked anything so much before. I find the [English] climate both pleasant and wholesome; and I have met with such kindness, and so much learning, not hackneyed and trivial, but deep, accurate, ancient Latin and Greek, that but for the curiosity of seeing it, I do not now much care for Italy. When I hear Colet I seem to be listening to Plato himself. In Grocyn who does not marvel at such a perfect round of learning? What can be more acute, profound and delicate than the judgment of Linacre? What has nature ever created more gentle, more sweet, more happy than the genius of Thomas More?[3]

There is a story of the first meeting of More and Erasmus which at any rate is *ben trovato*. While still unacquainted they were both guests at the table of the Lord Mayor, and were equally impressed by each other's

---

[1] P. S. Allen, *The Age of Erasmus*, pp. 118–19.

[2] In September 1500 he writes that he cannot read a copy of Homer he just then had in his possession, but that he is consoled by the mere look of it. He was then 34. Allen, *Erasmi Epistolae*, 131, p. 305.

[3] Allen, *Erasmi Epistolae*, 5 Dec., 1499, vol. i, No. 118.

Old St. Paul's as it was in Dean Colet's time and before the spire fell
Reconstructed from old drawings

conversation. Suddenly it dawned upon Erasmus that the brilliant talk he was listening to came from More. "You must be More or no one," he exclaimed; and received as the instant and happy reply, "Then you are Erasmus or the devil."[1]

But Erasmus himself tells another story of their first meeting which has a more genuine ring about it.

Thomas More [he writes], who had visited me when I was staying in Mountjoy's country house, had taken me out for a walk as far as the next village of Eltham; for there all the royal children were being educated, Arthur, the eldest, alone excepted. When we came to the Hall, all the retinue were assembled. . . . In the midst stood Henry [afterwards Henry VIII], aged nine, already with a certain royal demeanour; I mean a dignity of mind combined with a remarkable courtesy. . . . Meantime I was a bit annoyed because More had given me no warning, especially because the boy, during dinner, sent me a note inviting me to write something.[2]

But a little later a poem was forthcoming in praise of Henry VII, his children and his kingdom.

Erasmus could have seen but little of More upon this occasion, for almost at once he went to Oxford as the guest of Prior Charnock; but they corresponded, as an only surviving letter shows, and after his Oxford visit he stayed either in London or at Greenwich with Lord Mountjoy for a month previous to his departure for Paris on January 27th, 1500. At Dover he was deprived at the Custom-house of all but £2 out of the £20 he had with him: it was never recovered, and the loss remained as a bitter remembrance of the end of his first visit to England. From Dover he crossed to Boulogne, visited his friend Batt for two nights at Tournehem, and reached Paris on February 2nd.

Erasmus was now thirty-five, and for the next five or six years closely applied himself to the study of Greek. As Dr. Allen writes, "In quest of Greek, in quest of the proper equipment for his life-work, he went back to the old precarious existence, pupils and starvation, the dependence and flattery that he loathed."[3] This, indeed, was the self-imposed novitiate of a brave man to the true vocation he had now found to Sacred Letters. And, at this stage, it was not without additional hardship. He writes to his friend Batt, who urges him to write to the Lady of Veer thanking her for her generous patronage. "Letters, it's always

---

[1] R.W. Chambers, *Thomas More*, p. 70.
[2] Allen, *Erasmi Epistolae*, vol. i, No. 1, p. 6.
[3] P. S. Allen, *The Age of Erasmus*, p. 130.

letters. You seem to think I am made of adamant. . . . There is nothing I detest more than these sycophantic epistles."[1] He writes again to Batt from Paris in March 1500: "My Greek studies are almost too much for my courage; while I have not the means of purchasing books, or the help of a teacher. And while I am in all this trouble, I have scarcely the wherewithal to sustain life; so much is our learning worth to us."[2] And again to the same:

A little money must be scraped together from somewhere, with which I may get clothes, buy the whole works of Jerome (upon whom I am preparing commentaries), as well as Plato, procure Greek books and hire the services of a Greek teacher. How much all these things are necessary to my glory, and even to the security of my position, I think you are aware; at any rate I beg you to believe it when I affirm it of my own knowledge. It is incredible, how my heart burns to bring all my poor lucubrations to completion, and at the same time to attain some moderate capacity in Greek. *I shall then devote myself entirely to the study of Sacred Literature, as for some time I have longed to do.*[3]

So then and thus he turned from Pagan to Sacred Letters.

In the summer an outbreak of plague drove him to Orleans, where he continued his Attic drudgery. But a growing sense of mastery over Greek, the indispensable instrument of all his future labours, must now and again have broken in upon him like sunshine amid his toil.

In 1502 a new and great inspiration came to him when one day, walking to the Abbey of the White Carmelites at Parc, outside Louvain, he found in their library a manuscript of the Annotations of Laurentius Valla on the New Testament. He then determined to make a thorough study of the Bible, by comparing it with the Greek versions, from which he hoped to establish a critical text, the only foundation for sound work in theological research. Having first trained himself by translating Plutarch's treatises, he prepared Valla's manuscript for the press in 1504, and carrying with him the subject of his future life-work, he hastened to Paris to have it printed. He was now thirty-eight, and upon the threshold of long-desired achievement.

During this period, in 1503, he had written his *Enchiridion Militis Christiani*, or the *Manual of the Christian Knight*, a work of solid piety well suited to laymen, now, since the coming of the printed word, much more easily within reach of religious instruction. The *Enchiridion*

[1] P. S. Allen, *The Age of Erasmus*, p. 131.
[2] Nichols, *The Epistles of Erasmus*, vol. i, p. 233.
[3] *Ib.*, p. 283.

was considered by Froude to be the finest of his minor compositions. Whether it achieved its immediate purpose of converting a military man of doubtful morals we do not know. In a closing passage he sums up his advice to his military friend:

Shun bad company, and make the prophets, Christ, and the apostles your friends. Above all choose Paul. For long I have been labouring over a commentary upon him. A bold task this seems; but I follow Origen, Ambrose, Augustine, and many later theologians, and with God's help I trust that I do not labour in vain . . . . *It has long been my cherished wish to cleanse the Lord's temple of barbarous ignorance, and to adorn it with treasures brought from afar, such as may kindle in generous hearts a warm love for the Scriptures.*

An unkind friend said there was more holiness in the book than in the author; and St. Ignatius, who like Erasmus had been at the College Montaigu, thought it calculated to quench, little by little, the fervour of its readers. But Erasmus was writing for laymen, and possibly knew something of their ordinary spiritual needs. Nevertheless, by degrees, it achieved great popularity, being first published in 1503 and again in 1515, 1518, 1520, 1525 and 1540. As compared with previous books of devotion it emphasised the intellectual side of religion. Prayer and almsdeeds, he taught, had always been the staple weapons of the spiritual life, but in the new age of printed matter there was a third *knowledge*-which he deemed of great importance. "Whoever", he writes, "will take upon him to fight against the whole host of vices, of which seven be counted as chief captains, must provide him with two special weapons, *prayer and knowledge, otherwise called learning.* Prayer verily is the more excellent, as she that cometh and talketh familiarly with God. Yet for all this doctrine is no less necessary." In another place he compares prayer and knowledge to Aaron and Moses, who led the Israelites out of Egypt.

I cannot tell whether that thou, fled from Egypt, mightest without great jeopardy commit thyself to so long a journey, so hard and so full of difficulty, without the captains Aaron and Moses. Aaron which was charged with things dedicate to the service of God's temple, betokeneth prayer. By Moses is figured the knowledge of the law of God.

And again he writes:

The surest thing of all is to be occupied in deeds of piety. . . . Yet lest thou shouldst despise the help of knowledge, consider one thing. The Israelites were never so bold as to provoke the Amalachytes until they had been refreshed with manna from heaven and water running out of the hard rock. . . . And what thing, I pray thee, could more properly have signified the knowledge of the secret law of God than did manna? For first in that it sprang not out of the earth, but rained down from heaven. By this property thou perceivest the difference between the doctrine of God and the doctrine of man. For all holy Scripture came by divine inspiration from God, the author. In that it is small or little in quantity is signified the humility, lowliness or home-liness of the style, under rude words including great mystery. That it is white, by this property is signified the purity and cleanness of God's law. For there is no doctrine of man which is not defiled with some black spot or error, only the doctrine of Christ is everywhere bright, pure and clean.

In the same way the water running out of the hard rock is used to signify the knowledge of the law of God, (for) what signifieth water hid in the veins of the earth but mystery covered or hid in the literal sense? What meaneth the same conveyed abroad but mystery open and expounded? Wherefore if thou dedicate thyself wholly to the study of Scripture, and exercise thy mind night and day in the law of God, no fear shall trouble thee, but thou shalt against all assaults of thine enemies be armed and exercised also.[1]

Erasmus defends the study of profane authors as a help to the study of Sacred Scripture itself. "It shall be no rebuke to thee", he quaintly argues, "if after the example of Solomon thou nourish up at home in thy house sixty queens, eighty sovereign ladies, and damsels innumer-able of secular wisdom; so that the wisdom of God be above all other thy best beloved, thy dove, thy sweetheart, which only seemeth beautiful."[2]

As for the interpreters of Scripture, he advises his penitent "to choose, above all, them that go farthest from the letter, which chiefly after Paul be Origen, Ambrose, Jerome and Augustine".[3] He attributes the lack of fervour so much to be observed among professedly religious men to be due to a mistaken clinging to the literal sense rather than to the spiritual sense of Scipture.

It is of interest to notice that Erasmus favoured allegorical as well as literal interpretation.

---

[1] P. 61. Cf. Aquinas, *Summa*: "Sensus spiritualis vel mysticus quem res habent, et est triplex, allegoricus, tropologicus, et analogicus" (1.1.10.0 and (1-2, 102, 2.c.). Also "Sensus spiritualis vel mysticus fundatur super literalem, et eum praesupponit" (1.1.10.c.1).
[2] *Enchiridion*, translated in all probability by William Tyndale, p. 64.
[3] P. 66.

In another place he writes, "Bread is not so natural to the body as the word of God is meat to the soul. If it seem bitter, if thy mind rise against it, why doubtest thou yet but that the mouth of thy soul is out of taste and infected with some disease?" And he adds, "Thou must ever remember that Sacred Scripture may not be touched but with clean and washen hands, that is with high pureness of mind, lest that which of itself is a preservative or treacle, by thine own fault, turn into a poison. ... (Thou wilt remember) that Oza, which feared not to set his profane and unclean hands to the ark of God (inclining on one side), was punished with sudden death for his lewd service."[1]

Finally, Erasmus impresses upon the reader the dignity of his Christian calling, almost in the very words of St. Leo, "Agnosce, O Christiane, dignitatem tuam".[2]

Shall we not reckon and account with our mind of how noble a Craftsman we were made, in how excellent estate we are set, with how exceeding great price we are bought, unto how great felicity we are called, and that man is that gentle and noble creature for whose sake God hath forged the marvellous building of the world; that he is of the company of angels, the son of God, the heir of immortality, a member of Christ, a member of the Church, that our bodies are temples of the Holy Ghost, our minds the images and also the secret habitations of the Deity.[3]

Surely Erasmus had a shrewd spiritual sense as to what the ordinary layman, amid the business and distractions of daily life, most needed?

Know thyself and pass not the bounds [he wrote], keep thee within thy lists. It is better to have less knowledge and more love, than to have more knowledge and less love. So only shall thy soul depart happily from her body at the last end, if aforesaid she have diligently through true knowledge recorded and practised death, and have also long time before, by the despising of things corporeal and by the contemplation and loving of things spiritual, used herself to be, as it were, in a manner absent from the body.[4]

He warns his penitents of human frailty, but encourages them to valiant perseverance. "When thou hast grounded thyself upon a sure purpose, set upon it and go to it lustily: man's mind never proposed anything fervently that he was not able to bring to pass. It is a great part of the Christian life to desire with full purpose and with all his

heart to be a Christian man."[1] "Though it fortune not to all men to
attain to perfect imitation or following of the Head, yet all must enforce
with feet and hands to come thereto. He hath a great part of a Christian
man's living, which with all his heart, with a sure and steadfast purpose,
hath determined to be a Christian man."[2]

Erasmus also understood that the coming of the printed word
involved many new dangers to the faith of simple as well as of learned
folk.

As a recent writer put it:

Before the invention of printing, men were free to criticise the
Church in Latin and the ecclesiastical authorities were only occasionally disturbed. Such criticisms circulated among scholars and were
duly answered according to the rules of logic. An ambitious young
man offered to maintain some daring thesis or attack some scholar
with an established reputation. A controversy ensued and the language
was violent, but it only provided intellectual excitement for a leisured
class. The printing press changed all this. The men who were in earnest
soon learnt to write for the people, and the men who were half in
earnest were apt to be taken too seriously. The battledore and shuttle-
cock of mediaeval disputations ceased, and the controversies of the
Reformation were more like the exchange of cannon shot. The cul-
tured Leo X thought the multiplication of books would be for the
advantage of mankind. . . . He was thinking of the books he had read
with Politian in his youth and not of the theses propounded by Martin
Luther. 'Another monkish quarrel', was his contemptuous comment
when he heard of them; but because of the printing press the quarrel
divided Europe into two hostile camps.[3]

Erasmus not only realised the danger; but also was among the first to
provide the remedy. I think we may say that, to him, the Reformers
seemed like the Philistines of old who carried off the Ark–the ark in this
case being the New Testament; and, having carried it off, they then
glossed it with new and unorthodox interpretations. And so it was that
he was anxious not only to provide a sounder text for the New Testament itself, but also to spend the rest of his long life in editing "the old
holy fathers" who had been its traditional and authoritative interpreters.

And so, too, before others had thought much about it, he wrote his
Enchiridion, a manual of simple devotion for lay folk who had little

[1] *Lectio v. de Nativ. Dni*, p. 94.
[2] Pp. 121–2.
[3] H. Maynard-Smith, *Pre-Reformation England*, pp. 425–6. But it should not be forgotten
that Leo X laid before the fifth Lateran Council a decree forbidding the printing of any
book without ecclesiastical approbation, Pastor, *Hist. of the Popes*, trans., vol. viii, p. 398.

time or taste for the more recondite spiritual literature. The Church of the present as well as of the future will, I am sure, increasingly award him the credit for this needed service.

St. Ignatius, who, like Erasmus, had been a student at the College Montaigu in Paris, though some thirty years later, compared the *Enchiridion* with the *Imitation*,[1] much to the advantage of the latter. But the two books were written for such different kinds of people, and at such different levels of spirituality, that a comparison between them seems hardly fair. It should not, however, be forgotten that both books owed their origin to the *Brethren of the Common Life*, who educated Erasmus at Deventer and did so much to renew the Catholic piety of northern Europe in the fifteenth century, and from whom such men as Gerard Groot, Florentius Radewin and Thomas à Kempis derived their spiritual quality. Should we be far wrong in presuming that both St. Ignatius and Erasmus were raised up by God to render valuable but very different services to the Church?

[1] Dom E. C. Butler, when Abbot of Downside, writing in the *Encyclopædia Britannica*, vol. 14, on *The Imitation* claims that its author was undoubtedly Thomas à Kempis, and describes it in a few words so admirably that we may be permitted to quote his opinion. "The *Imitation* stands apart, unique, as the principal and most representative utterance of a special phase of religious thought, reflecting faithfully the spirit of the movement initiated by Gerhard Groot, and carried forward by the circles (of the *Brethren of the Common Life*) in which Thomas à Kempis lived. In contrast with more mystical writings it is of limped clearness, every sentence being early understandable by all whose spiritual sense is in any degree awakened. No doubt it owes its universal power to this simplicity, to its freedom from intellectualism, and its direct appeal to the religious sense and to the extraordinary genius of its author. Professor Harnack counts the *Imitation* as one of the chief spiritual forces of Catholicism: 'it kindles independent religious life, and a fire which burns with a flame of its own'." No better book on *The Origin of the Jesuits* and its sequel, *The Progress of the Jesuits*, by Father James Brodrick, S. J., could be read in connection with the life and work of St. Ignatius (Longmans, 1940 and 1946).

3

Erasmus's Second Visit to England

AT THE end of 1505, or at the beginning of 1506, Erasmus paid his second visit to England, and spent the greater part of it in London. "No place in the world", he writes to Colet in the following year, "has given me so many friends as your City of London, so true, so learned, so generous, so distinguished, so unselfish, so numerous." It was in London, and not at either of the Universities, that he found the most genuine enthusiasm for learning. For some months he was the guest of Lord Mountjoy, then twenty-six years of age, who had been chosen as an elder companion to the young Prince Henry, now fifteen, and heir to the throne. So it was that Erasmus found himself very pleasantly included within the royal circle and on easy terms with the distinguished men who were responsible for the government of the country. Thus he came to know William Warham, Archbishop of Canterbury, and for some time Chancellor of the realm, who was to remain his generous patron and steadfast friend for many years to come. Staying in London after the departure of the Court, he sought the companionship of Thomas More, recently married to his young wife, Jane Colt, and living in Bucklersbury. More at that time was suffering from the displeasure of Henry VII on account of his opposition to a certain money grant demanded by the King from Parliament. As a consequence he might have been less engrossed in professional business and only too ready to enjoy Erasmus's stimulating company. They seem to have spent a good deal of time together and, among other things, each made translations from Lucian's witty dialogues, and one, indeed, of the *Tyrannicida*–a reminder, perhaps, that More was still smarting under the royal displeasure. There is a letter of More's to Thomas Ruthall, the King's Secretary, written in the early summer of 1506, showing what he and Erasmus were thinking about. It was originally attributed to Erasmus, but can now be definitely assigned to More. As Mr. F. M. Nichols says, "The candour and honesty of the opinions expressed in it are characteristic of More, while the freedom with which established errors are exploded might well excuse its attribution to Erasmus."[1]

[1] F. M. Nichols, *The Epistles of Erasmus*, vol. i, p. 403.

Thomas More to Dr. Thomas Ruthall.

... The *Necyomantia*, attacks in wittiest fashion the impositions of conjurors, the empty fictions of poets, and the uncertain sparring of philosophers on every possible subject. There remains the *Philopseudes*, a dialogue as profitable as it is witty, which exposes and ridicules with Socratic irony the common appetite for lying; wherein it does not much disturb me to find that the author was not sure of his own immortality; sharing in this respect the error of Democritus, Lucretius, Pliny and many others. Why indeed should I care for the opinion of a pagan upon matters which are among the chief mysteries of the Christian faith? The dialogue at any rate teaches us, on the one hand, not to put faith in the illusions of magic, and on the other, to keep our minds clear of the superstition which creeps in under the guise of religion. We shall lead a happier life, when we are less terrified by those dismal and super-stitious lies, which are so often repeated with so much confidence and authority. . . . No wonder then, if ruder minds are affected by the fic-tions of those who think they have done a lasting service to Christ, when they have invented a fable about some saint, or a frightening story of hell, which either melts an old woman to tears, or makes her blood run cold. There is scarcely a life of a martyr or virgin in which some falsehood of this kind has not been inserted; an act of piety no doubt, considering the risk that Truth would be insufficient, unless propped up by lies! They have failed to see, that such fables are so far from aiding religion, that nothing can be more injurious to it. It is obvious, as Augustine himself has observed, that where there is any scent of a lie the authority of truth is immediately weakened and destroyed. . . .[1]

Erasmus himself then writes to Richard Whitford a letter which gives his own opinion of More in the early days of their friendship:

I do not think, unless the vehemence of my love leads me astray, that Nature ever formed a mind more present, ready, sharp-sighted and subtle, or in a word more absolutely furnished with every kind of faculty than his. Add to this a power of expression equal to his intellect, a singular cheerfulness of character and an abundance of wit, but only of the candid sort; and you miss nothing that should be found in a perfect advocate.[2]

At this time Erasmus made his first acquaintance with St. John Fisher, who was Bishop of Rochester, President of Queens' College, Cambridge, and Chancellor of the University. He asked Erasmus to accompany him there on one rather important occasion, when Henry

---

[1] F. M. Nichols, *The Epistles of Erasmus*, vol. i, pp. 403–5.
[2] *Ib.*, pp. 406–7.

VII visited Christ's College in order to see its new buildings, just nearing completion. It was a new foundation, made at Fisher's suggestion by the Lady Margaret Tudor, the mother of King Henry VII. Fisher, no doubt, talked much about it to Erasmus and how best it could be made a welcome home for true learning. Erasmus, too, had a good deal to do with drawing up the statutes.

And now, suddenly, there came to him a golden opportunity, the chance of going to Italy–Italy, his long-promised land of desire. He was to take charge of the two young sons of Dr. Boerio, the King's physician, and make the journey with them and their tutor.

> Per varios casus, per tot discrimina rerum,
> Tendimus in Latium.[1]

He left London at the beginning of June 1506, and, after reaching Calais, went on to Paris, visiting Lord Mountjoy at Hammes on the way. He stayed at Paris sufficiently long to make arrangements for the publication of his translations from Euripides and later of his own and More's translations from Lucian. In August they travelled to Orleans, touched at Lyons, and passed through Savoy over Mont Cenis to Turin, where on September 4th he received his long-coveted doctorate of theology. On their way to Bologna they seem to have visited that architectural wonder, the Certosa at Pavia. Arrived at Bologna, they intended to settle there in order that the two boys might study at the University. But the coming of the army of Julius II compelled them to leave for Florence, where they remained for about six weeks. The resistance of Bologna to Julius II being overcome, they returned in time to see the triumphal entry of the Pope into that city on November 11th, in lovely summer-like weather, the roses being still in bloom. The triumphal procession to San Petronio, the Cathedral of Bologna, was a perfect specimen of the festive art of the Renaissance.

Thirteen triumphal arches were erected bearing the inscription in large letters, "Julius II, our Liberator and most beneficent Father". A hundred young noblemen formed a cordon to keep the people back. First came a number of horsemen as outriders to clear the way, the light cavalry, the infantry in glistening armour, the baggage of the Pope and the Cardinals, and finally the bands of the regiments. These were followed by sixteen Bolognese and four papal standard-bearers with their banners, the ten white palfreys of the Pope with golden bridles and lastly the officials of the Court. Next there came the envoys, Duke

---

[1] Virgil, *Aeneid*, I, ll. 204–5.

Guido of Urbino, the Marquess Francesco Gonzaga, Francesco Maria, the Prefect of Rome, Constantino Arentini, the Duke of Achaia and Macedonia, fourteen lictors with silver staves to keep the crowd back, and two Masters of Ceremonies, the first of whom, Paris de Grassis, was the organiser of the whole pageant. The Papal Cross was carried by Carlo Rotario; he was closely followed by forty of the clergy with lighted candles and the Papal choir accompanying the Sacred Host. The Cardinals walked immediately in front of Julius II, who was carried in the *Sedia Gestatoria*; his purple cope, shot with gold thread and fastened across the breast with the *formale pretiosum* set with emeralds and sapphires, was a splendid work of art. On his head he wore an unusually large mitre glistening with pearls and jewels. He was accompanied by two private chamberlains, his secretary Sigismondo de Conti, and his physicians, the Roman Mariano dei Dossi, and the Sienese Arcangelo dei Tuti. He was followed by the patriarchs, the Archbishops and Bishops, the Protonotary, the ecclesiastical Envoys, the Abbots and Generals of religious orders, the Penitentiaries and the Referendaries. The whole procession was closed by a body of the Papal Guard. It moved slowly, owing to the immense concourse of spectators, all decked with holiday garb, who had come in from the country round to receive the Pope's blessing. Gold and silver coins, struck for the occasion, were scattered among them. At the Cathedral the Pope first made his act of thanksgiving and then he solemnly blessed the people. It was dusk before he got back to the palace, now attended by the magistrates of the city, who joined the procession after it left the Cathedral.[1]

Erasmus was a man of peace, and seems to have been troubled by the warlike atmosphere that surrounded him. "On St. Martin's day", he writes, "Pope Julius entered Bologna, and the next Sunday celebrated mass in the Cathedral." And to another friend, "In Italy at present studies are singularly chilled, while wars are warm. Pope Julius fights, conquers, triumphs, and in fact plays the part of Julius to perfection." And once again, in reference to the same events, "*Spectabam, ut ingenue dicam, non sine tacito gemitu*".

When the University of Bologna reassembled in the autumn of 1506, Erasmus settled there with the two boys and their English tutor. As he had only to supervise their studies in a general way, he found plenty of time for his own work. But the tutor was unpleasant, and gave him so much trouble that at the end of the agreed year he got rid of him, to the delight of the boys as well as of himself! He was then able to make

[1] Sigismondo de Conti, vol. ii, pp. 358–62, quoted from Pastor, *History of the Popes*, vol. vi, pp. 281–3.

friends with Paul Bombasio, Professor of Latin and Greek in the University, of whom he speaks as a delightful companion. He also got to know Scipio Fortiguerra, with whom, two years later, he was to spend some very pleasant days in Rome.

His chief preoccupation throughout the year 1507 was the preparation of the new edition of his *Adagia*. He first published it in 1500 as a collection of some 800 Latin sayings with brief explanations of his own. But now he had sufficient Greek to add to the collection both from Greek and Latin, and his commentary, too, was proportionately enlarged, so that finally his collection made a fine folio volume. Its publication in Italy, where it could be properly appreciated, was of high importance, bringing him widespread fame. It became, too, a well of classics undefiled from which future generations could draw at will. Finally, and not least of all, it brought him the friendship of Aldus Manutius, the founder at Venice in 1494 of the famous Aldine Press. It was fortunate that these two great men should meet; for in addition to an equal taste for the classics, they had also in common a great enthusiasm for the publication of an edition of the New Testament as worthy in scholarship as it was in type. Erasmus first approaches Aldus Manutius by letter.

Erasmus to Aldus Manutius.

There is a wish, most learned Manutius, which has many times occurred to my mind. As not only by your skill and the unrivalled beauty of your typography, but also by intelligence and learning of no common order, you have thrown a vast light upon the literature of Greece and Rome, I should be glad if those merits had brought you in return an adequate profit; for as to fame the name of Aldus Manutius will pass from mouth to mouth among all that are initiated in the religion of letters. Your memory, then, as your character, now, will deserve not only admiration but love, because you devote yourself to the restoration and publication of good authors with the greatest solicitude, but, as I hear, with no proportionate gain. Like Hercules you are employed on labours of the noblest kind, which are of more advantage to others than to yourself. . . . I wonder what has so long prevented you from publishing the New Testament,[1] a work, which if I guess aright will be exceedingly welcome. . . . I send you two tragedies [the *Hecuba* and *Iphigenia in Aulis*], which I have translated boldly enough, but whether with corresponding success you will judge for yourself.

[1] In 1499, Aldus had thought of publishing an edition of the Bible; but it did not come out until 1518.

Thomas Linacre, William Grocyn, William Latimer, and Cuthbert Tunstall, friends of yours as well as of mine, approved them highly. You know these men are too learned to be mistaken in their judgment, and too honest to be flatterers, unless indeed they are a little blinded by their partiality for me. Those Italians also to whom I have shown my attempt, do not condemn it. Bade has printed the plays, and I hear from him, has no reason to regret it, for he has already succeeded in selling all his impressions. But my reputation has been somewhat compromised, the pages being full of misprints. He offers himself to print a new edition to correct the former one, but I am afraid, to use the phrase of Sophocles, that he will mend one mischief with another. I should think my lucubrations secure of immortality, if they came out printed in your type, especially that miniscule type which is the most elegant of all. In that case the volume will be very small, and the matter may be carried out at a trifling cost. If you find it convenient to undertake the business, I propose to supply the corrected copy sent by bearer without any charge, except that you will be so good as to send me a few volumes for presentation to friends. . . .

Farewell, most learned Aldus, and pray rank Erasmus among those who heartily wish you well. . . . If, on the whole, you are not inclined to print the Tragedies, please return the copy to the bearer, to be brought back to me.[1]

Bologna, 28 Oct. [1507].

This letter brought back a favourable reply. For some time, however, the Aldine printing-machines had been silent; for Aldus himself had been thrown into prison in the struggles between the warlike Julius II and the Venetian Republic. But he was now free, and Erasmus, too, was free from the burden of his two young pupils and their tiresome tutor, and so was able to leave Bologna before the close of the year.

Not long after, he presented himself to the great printer at Venice. Aldus Manutius was then living in the house of his father-in-law at San Paterniano, near the Rialto Bridge; and here Erasmus remained for ten months, working at various projects, the most important of all being the second edition of his *Adagia*, which had already won him fame. The first edition consisted of some 800 Latin sayings, but in the second he added more quotations from the Latin and from the Greek as well, so he was persuaded to remain in Venice to superintend its publication. In a still later edition he tells us some interesting things about Aldus Manutius and his Aldine Press, and also about that other

---

[1] F. M. Nichols, *The Epistles of Erasmus*, vol. i, pp. 428-30.

great printer and, as we should now say, publisher, John Froben of Basle, to whose generous friendship he owed the publication of most of the works of his later years.

Who was there among the learned [he writes] that did not uphold the efforts of Aldus? [And] what Aldus attempted in Italy, John Froben is now attempting on this side of the Alps with no less zeal than Aldus, with considerable success, though it must be owned with less profit. . . . There is not the same liberality among us (of the north) as among the Italians, so far at any rate as concerns literature. . . . Aldus had nothing in his treasures which he did not place at my service. . . . I brought nothing with me to Venice but the confused and undigested material of future work, and that compiled only from authors already published. With great temerity on my part we began together, I to write, and Aldus to print.[1]

Erasmus seems to have worked harder perhaps than ever before; and the book was completed in nine months. He speaks of the generosity of scholars and others possessing rare classical manuscripts which so far had never been printed.

Among these were the works of Plato, Plutarch's *Lives*, his *Moralia*, the printing of which was begun about the time my book ended, the *Deipnosophistae* of Athenaeus, Aphthonius, Hermogenes with commentaries, Aristotle's *Rhetoric* with the scholia of Gregory Nazianzen, all Aristides with scholia, the commentaries on Hesiod and Theocritus, Eustathius upon the whole of Homer, Pausanias, Pindar with some accurate commentaries, the collection of proverbs with the title of Plutarch, and another with that of Apostolius. The last was lent me by Jerome Aleander. There were other materials of smaller importance, which I have either forgotten, or need not mention. And of all these none had yet been printed. . . .[2]

And so in the September of 1508 this great edition of the *Adagia* was brought to its completion. It had been perhaps the hardest and most rapid piece of work as yet accomplished by Erasmus.

He tells us that the compositors printed as he wrote, and that he had hard work to keep pace with them. Some of his rough manuscripts–written rapidly in his smooth hand and flowing sentences–survive still to help us to picture the scene. It is remarkable how little correction there is. Here and there a whole page is drawn straight through, to be rewritten, or a passage is inserted in the margin; but there is little botching, little mending of words or transposing of phrases, such as make the work of other humanists difficult reading. As he wished the sentences to

[1] F. M. Nichols, *The Epistles of Erasmus*, vol. i, pp. 437–8.   [2] *Ib.*, pp. 438–9.

run, so they flowed on his pages, and so they actually were printed. The importance of Erasmus's time in Italy [concludes Dr. Allen] is that he completed, or at any rate published, the enlarged *Adagia*, his first considerable book which carried his name far and wide through Europe, and won him fame amongst all who had pretensions to scholarship.[1]

We are all familiar with the press-mark of Aldus Manutius, an anchor with a dolphin, while John Froben's was an upright staff, upheld by two hands with two serpents intertwined and surmounted by a dove. These two designs might worthily be commemorated in stained glass in the main window of every important library, for they sum up in themselves the life-work of two of the first, and two of the greatest printers, and may we not say publishers? that the world has known.

After paying such honourable attention to the classics by so many months of incessant labour, Erasmus remained at Venice until towards the end of 1508, doing some work for Aldus Manutius on Plautus and Terence and on the tragedies of Seneca. Being now released from his strenuous tasks, he had more time, no doubt, to appreciate his host's good talk, his great hospitality, and his good wine as well; but here, alas! there was a penalty to be paid; for at Venice he had his first attack of stone, that painful complaint that was to trouble him for the remainder of his days.

He left Venice for Padua, meaning to winter there; and was asked to give lessons in rhetoric to Alexander Stewart, a natural son of James IV of Scotland, who was pursuing his studies in that city. This attractive young man was about eighteen and already Archbishop of St. Andrews. In his company Erasmus found his stay at Padua very agreeable. Here, too, he made the acquaintance of Marcus Musurus, Raphael Reggio and other learned people. But the threat of approaching hostilities warned him to withdraw from that part of Italy, and so, with the young Archbishop in his suite, he set out for Siena about the middle of December 1508. They stayed for a few days at Ferrara, where he was glad to renew his acquaintance with Richard Pace, who was on a diplomatic mission, also at Bologna, where he found his friend Bombasio, and he reached Siena, that most beautiful and most mediæval of Tuscan cities, sometime towards the close of the year.

During the first two months of his stay Erasmus seems to have spent his time in looking after his young pupil and in recruiting his own

[1] P. S. Allen, *The Age of Erasmus*, p. 136.

health. Commenting later upon one of his *Adagia*,[1] he gives a sketch
of his royal and most reverend young Scottish prelate, who was tall,
handsome and of good intellectual capacity. Besides his work with
Erasmus, he was devoted to the study of Latin, Greek and Canon Law.
We gather, too, that his suite was not a small one which he ruled
both with strictness and urbanity as if it had been a monastic community. During meals, passages were read aloud from St. Jerome and
St. Ambrose, and afterwards discussed. Then came the siesta, and after
that, by way of recreation, music and singing. But, as Erasmus says,
everything was managed with prudence and good temper. But alas!
this pupil to whom Erasmus was so greatly attached, did not live to
realise the great promise of his youth, for in 1513, four years later, he
and his father James IV were slain at Flodden Field.

Probably during the Carnival week of 1509, Erasmus took leave of
his pupil for a while and made his first visit to Rome; but his stay was
short. All we know of it is that he renewed his acquaintance with Scipio
Fortiguerra, whom he had first met at Bologna; also, that he was introduced to Tomasso Inghirami, the librarian of the Vatican, and probably
through him to Cardinal Riario, who was to befriend him in many ways.

It has been said that no one who visits Rome for the first time leaves
it the same man as entered it; for better or worse he becomes a
different man. So it was with Luther; and so, in a far different way, was
it with Erasmus himself. "Before I can forget Rome," he writes in later
years, "I must plunge into the river of Lethe." And each time he recalls
his sojourn there this cold and sometimes satirical scholar is seized with
a longing to return to a place which offered much more to him
than the mere monuments of antiquity. "What precious freedom,"
he writes again, "what treasures in the way of books, what depths of
knowledge among the learned, what beneficial social intercourse!
Where else could one find such literary society or such versatility of
talent in one and the same place?"[2]

Erasmus was also presented to Cardinal Guiliano Medici, afterwards
Pope Leo X, and was graciously received at his house. He returned to
Siena, this time accompanied by his pupil, and they were there on
Good Friday, April 6th. Naples may also have been visited, but they
were back in Rome by April 30th, and Erasmus said his sad good-

[1] *Adagia*, first published in 1500, was followed by successive editions in 1506, 1508,
1515, 1518, 1520, 1523, 1526, 1528, 1533, 1536, eleven in all to the year of Erasmus's
death.
[2] P. de Nolhac, *Erasme in Italie*, p. 65.

Saint John Fisher
From the bust by Torrigiano

bye to the young Archbishop, who was suddenly called back to Scotland. On April 22nd, 1509, Henry VII of England died, and in the second week of May Erasmus received a letter from Lord Mountjoy bidding him hasten to England, now suddenly become, by the accession of Henry VIII, a land of literary promise and reward.

But there were reasons for hesitation. Erasmus had made friends in Rome who were in high position and anxious to keep him there for the rest of his life and to use his great knowledge and wide experience in meeting the difficulties that now began to crowd upon the Roman Curia from the countries north of the Alps, and especially from Germany. The Cardinal who had seen most of him was Raffaelo Riario, Cardinal of San Giorgio-in-Velabro, and the nephew of Julius II, who lived in that admirable building of Bramante's now known as the Cancelleria. This great prelate had a spirit open to all that was beautiful, and was a friend to Letters and to antiquity as well. He it was who asked Erasmus to write a dialogue on the subject of war, first on one side and then on the other. Again, there was Cardinal de Medici, who, when he became Pope in 1513, begged Erasmus to return to Rome. And there was Domenico Grimani, Cardinal of St. Mark, who occupied the splendid Palazzo di Venezia built by Paul II, and of whom Erasmus wrote in affectionate memory so many years later, in 1531.

Erasmus to Augustinus Eugubinus.

When I was in Rome, and after I had been invited to visit him more than once, so much did I dislike paying court to the great, at last I went to his palace, rather from shame than from inclination. It was in the afternoon, and there was no one to be seen either in the court or in the vestibule. So I gave my horse to my servant, and mounting the stairs by myself, went into the first reception room. Again I saw no one; so I went on to the second and third with no better success. No door was closed and I marvelled at the solitude. Coming to the last room I found someone keeping watch at an open door. He had the tonsure, and was, I think, a Greek physician. I asked for the Cardinal; and he said that he was engaged with several gentlemen within. I did not reply to this, and he asked me what I wanted. "I want to pay my respect to him," I answered, "if convenient, but if he is not at leisure, I will call again." As I turned to go I lingered at the window to look at the view; and the Greek came to me again, to inquire whether I wished any message to be taken to the Cardinal. "There is no need," said I, "to interrupt his conversation, but I will come back shortly." And then he asked my name, which I gave him. As soon as he heard it, he hastily

D

went in without my noticing it, and coming out directly, bade me not to go. Without further delay I was taken in, and the Cardinal received me not as a Cardinal, and such a Cardinal, might receive a person of humble rank, but as he might a colleague. A chair being placed for me, we talked together for more than two hours, and all that time I was not allowed to remove my hat, a marvellous act of courtesy from a man of such rank. In the midst of much learned discourse about literary studies, in which he sufficiently showed that he already intended what I now hear he has done about his library, he began to advise me not to leave Rome, the nursing mother of intellect. He invited me to share his house and all his fortunes, adding that the climate of Rome being damp and warm would agree with my constitution, especially that part of the city where he had his palace, which had been built by one of the Popes, who had chosen it as the most healthy situation that could be found. After much talk on the one side and the other, he sent for his nephew, already an Archbishop, and a young man of noble character. As I offered to rise, he stopped me, saying that a disciple should stand before his master. At last he showed me his library, rich in many languages. If I had happened to have become acquainted with this personage earlier, I should never have left the city, where I found more favour than I deserved. But I had already made up my mind to go, and things had gone so far that it was scarcely open for me to stay. When I told him I had been sent for by the King of England, he ceased to press me. Still he begged me over and over again, not to think that his promises were merely conventional, or to judge his character by the ordinary manners of a court. It was with difficulty that I had leave to depart, but when he found that I wished to go, he consented to detain me no longer, stipulating with his last words, that I should pay him one more visit before leaving Rome. Unfortunately I did not go, fearing that I might be overcome by his eloquence and change my mind. I never made a more unlucky choice. But what can you do, when driven by destiny? . . .[1]

What, then, was the effect upon Erasmus of his stay of three years in Italy, culminating as it did in his last visit to Rome?

It has been variously assessed. Dr. Allen gives a little more than two pages to it, concluding with the remark that "it need not detain us long". Another authority, the author of *Erasme en Italie*, perhaps better informed on this period of Erasmus's life, considers "that it was there that his talent as a writer came to its maturity enabling it to stir the ideas of a whole generation and that the most brilliant of the century. It was there too he was filled with the new spirit which he, in turn, infused into the northern countries. By this double title, the sojourn [of Eras-

[1] F. M. Nichols, *The Epistles of Erasmus*. To Augustinus Eugubinus, pp. 461-3 (Freiburg, March 27th, 1531).

mus in Italy] may be considered as one of the most important facts of the Renaissance."[1]

Mr. F. M. Nichols tells us on Erasmus's own authority that

Italy had three attractions for him, the Sacred Places, the Libraries, and the society of learned men. He had fairly completed his programme. He had made the acquaintance of the most eminent scholars of the country, and his own position as a man of letters had been established and recognised. He had published his enlarged *Adagia*, by the completion of which his rank in literature was permanently assured; and he was now free to apply himself to the important theological works which he was ambitious of editing. It was open to him to use his great reputation as a scholar for the purpose of pushing his fortune at the Papal Court where he appears to have been given to understand that the office of a Penitentiary was open to him, a profitable place and a stepping-stone to higher dignities. But if there was one motive by which Erasmus was consistently influenced through life, it was his anxiety to avoid any position in which his liberty could be curtailed. Office, or even residence, in Rome necessarily involved a sacrifice of independence; and the character of the reigning pontiff [the warlike Julius II] was especially repugnant to him. If he was hesitating as to the acceptance of Roman preferment, the news that arrived in May 1509, after the accession of Henry VIII, made him less inclined to yield to the temptation.[2]

But perhaps the most discriminating sentence upon Erasmus's Italian visit comes from Professor H. de Vocht of Louvain, his own fellow-countryman, and a high authority upon Erasmian matters.

That journey [he writes] had an influence on his formation which we can hardly gauge: nowadays even the rarest documents can be placed at our disposal wherever we like: whereas, in those times, a scholar had to go about to look for the books he wanted, and to avail himself of them wherever they were found. To be accurate, the works of the great authors of antiquity were then printing in magnificent editions, but even these editions were drugs on the market. Fortunate were the scholars who lived or resided in Italy, for there manuscripts of the old writers were collected by generous patrons, studied carefully by the erudite, copied and reproduced in print with such zeal that, with few exceptions, all the *editiones principes* up to 1505 were published in that country. . . . It was as the guest of Aldus Manutius that Erasmus garnered the astoundingly rich harvest of knowledge, which made him a wonder to his own and all subsequent generations.[3]

[1] P. de Nolhac, *Erasme en Italie*, pp. 94–5.
[2] F. M. Nichols, *The Epistles of Erasmus*, vol. i, p. 456.
[3] *The Clergy Review*, July 1936, pp. 13–28.

4

Erasmus's Third Visit to England

AT THE end of September 1509 Erasmus left Rome, travelling over the Splugen to Chur, Constance, Strasburg, and down the Rhine to Antwerp, and after a visit to Louvain he crossed to England for the third time. From then until his journey to Paris in 1511, two years later, "his movements", writes Dr. Allen, "can only be a matter of conjecture".[1] For a part of the time he probably stayed with Lord Mountjoy; and before this visit he seemed to have spent his time in London, living with Ammonius in More's house, the last in Bucklersbury at the end farthest from St. Paul's, Ammonius at that time being a papal agent in England, and one of the More circle.

During the leisure of his first weeks in England, lengthened by the non-arrival of his books, Erasmus seems to have put the finishing touches to his *Encomium Moriae* or *Praise of Folly,* and, as its title indicates, he dedicated it to More, with whom he was staying at the time. Like More's own *Utopia,* it is difficult to tell while reading it which part of it was written in fun and which in earnest.

Much of it, however, is an undoubtedly serious criticism of the Church as he had seen it in Italy under Julius II (1503–1513).

Now, as to the popes [he writes], if they claim to be the successors of the Apostles they should consider that the same things are required of them as were practised by their predecessors. So if they, being Vicars of Christ, endeavour to emulate his life, his labours, his teachings, his Cross, his contempt of this world, if they thought only of their name of Pope, that is Father, and their title, Most Holy, what more afflicted beings would there be on earth? Who in that case would purchase the post with all his fortune, and when purchased, keep it with the sword, with poison and with violence? If Wisdom once stepped in, what abasement would indeed be theirs! Wisdom, did I say? Nay, [If they had] one grain of that salt of which Christ speaks, their wealth, their honours, their victories and their pleasures would all be gone, and in

---

[1] P. S. Allen, *Erasmi Epistolae,* tom. i, p. 455 note. There can be no doubt that at some time during this period Erasmus was in England and communicated with Abbot Bere either in London or at Glastonbury itself, see P. S. Allen, *Erasmi Epistolae,* tom. v, ep. 1490. To Richard Bere, p. 539 *n.*

their place would be studies, sermons, prayers, tears, vigils, fastings, and a thousand penitential labours of the same kind.

Neither should we forget what would follow: a whole host of clerks, notaries, advocates, and secretaries, of muleteers, grooms and serving-men (I might add other words which would shock modest ears) would be reduced to famine. This would be a cruel result; but it would be still more shocking to see the very Head of the Church, reduced to scrip and staff! As things are now, if there is any labour, it is left to Peter and Paul, who have the leisure to attend to it; if there is any splendour or pleasure, it is taken for themselves. And so, thanks to My influence [says Folly], there is scarcely any kind of people who live more at ease than do these successors of the Apostles, thinking that Christ is quite satisfied with their great state and magnificence, with the cere-monies of instalments, with the titles of reverence and holiness, and with the exercising of their episcopal function only in blessing and cursing.

The working of miracles is old and out of date; to teach the people is too laborious; to interpret the scripture is to invade the prerogative of the schoolmen; to pray is too idle; to shed tears is cowardly and un-manly; to fast is too mean and sordid; to be easy and familiar is beneath the grandeur of him who unless he be sued and entreated, will scarce give princes the honour of kissing his toe; finally to die for religion is too self-denying; and to be crucified, as their Lord of life was, is base and ignominious.

Their only weapons ought to be those of the spirit; and of these, indeed, they are liberal enough, with their suspensions, their denuncia-tions, their aggravations, their greater and lesser excommunications, and their roaring bulls that frighten whomsoever they are thundered against. . . .

Further, when the Church has been first planted, then confirmed, and since established by the blood of her martyrs . . . they invert the order, and now propagate religion by arms and violence. And though war is so unchristian that it is contrary to the express commands of the gospel, yet in spite of all this they must engage in the boisterousness of war. And among the popes who carry it on, some are so old that they can scarce creep, yea, they will spare themselves no pains or cost or incon-venience in order that they may involve laws, religion, peace and all other concerns in unappeasable tumult and distraction.

One has only to read the history of the papacy under Julius II[1] to understand what violence the peace-loving mind of Erasmus must have suffered while staying in Italy during that pontificate. It must also be remembered that all this frank criticism was written from within the household of the faith by one of its most learned, most moderate and most loyal children—if only those in high authority could have been

[1] Pastor, *The History of the Popes*, Eng. trans., vol. iv, pp. 185–319 *passim*.

forewarned by it, and so have averted the threatened catastrophe of the Reformation before it was too late!

And as it was a warning to the Head of the Church, so, too, was it to her members whether kings, clergy, laity or monks.

Every king, within his own territories, is placed for a shining example as it were in the firmament of his wide-spread dominions, to prove either a glorious star of benign influence, if his behaviour be just and innocent, or a threatening comet, if his power be pestilent and hurtful. Kings are tried with so many temptations and opportunities to vice and immorality . . . that they must stand perpetually on their guard. . . . But, by the assistance of Folly, they leave all this to the care of the gods and only mind their own ease and pleasure. They think they have sufficiently acquitted themselves in the duty of governing if they do but ride constantly a-hunting, breed up good race-horses, sell places and offices to those of their courtiers that will give most for them, and find out new ways of invading other people's property, and hooking in a larger revenue for their own exchequer. . . .

Let us feign now a person ignorant of the laws . . . an enemy to the public good, studious only for his own private interest, addicted wholly to pleasures and delights, a hater of learning, a professed enemy of liberty and truth, careless and unmindful of the common concerns, taking all the measures of justice and honesty from the false scales of self-interest and advantage, and after this hang about his neck a gold chain, as an intimation that he ought to have all virtues linked together. Then set a crown of gold and jewels upon his head, for a token that he ought to excel and outshine others in all commendable qualities; next put into his hand a royal sceptre for a symbol of justice and integrity; lastly clothe him with purple, for an hieroglyphic of a tender love and affection for the commonwealth. Surely if a prince should look upon such a portrait as this, and then draw a comparison between it and himself, would he not be ashamed of such ensigns of majesty, and be afraid of being laughed out of his own Court?

Lesser folk are sketched out with inimitable lightness of touch, but never without an underlying seriousness of purpose. As Erasmus said in his dedication to More, "Nothing is more amusing than to treat trifles in such a way as to show yourself anything but a trifler. Woman, it goes without saying, owes all her triumphs to Folly; for is not the end of her existence to please men, and how could she do it without the help of Folly?" Or again, with what delicious absurdity does he describe the end of a day's hunting, surely learned from his own experience in England? "The poor stag is slaughtered at last, but none but a gentleman may administer the *coup de grâce* of the whole business. Armed, therefore, with a special kind of knife provided for just that purpose, he gravely approaches the kill and cuts from it certain slices, the company standing around in perfect silence with looks of wonder and awe."

And so this all-too-human procession passes before our eyes, showing for our entertainment every variety and posture of folly, merchants made foolish by their love of money, grammarians, poets, scholars, lawyers, philosophers, monks and theologians.

When the *Encomium Moriae* was finished, Erasmus read it to More and to other friends as well. It was received with rapturous amusement; and so, on their recommendation, and overcoming some scruples of his own, he decided to publish it, thinking perhaps that, as it was written in Latin, it might amuse and peradventure help to reform the few, but would not give scandal to the many. It was first printed in Paris, probably in 1511, and at once became an entertainment to kings, cardinals, archbishops and bishops, and, perhaps most entertaining of all, to Pope Leo X himself, who read it from beginning to end. But it made enemies for Erasmus, as well as friends, and some undoubtedly of the unforgiving sort. The *Praise of Folly* was too strong a medicine for those who could never admit–no, not even to themselves–that they also were subject to folly. But its popularity went beyond the limits Erasmus had intended for it. In 1514 Froben printed an edition in Basle with a commentary that attempted to soften somewhat its more pungent satire. Aldus printed a neat edition in 1515, illustrated by Holbein, and in the end it was translated into most European languages. And, indeed, it became, what Erasmus must have deplored, a pattern to others who wrote with malice and far greater bitterness and severity. "Wit is the fruit of contrast" and to people of ill-will no contrast is so agreeable at that between holy professions and far from holy practice. Compared with the sort of things that were being written in Florence and Rome at the same time, the *EncomiumMoriae* or *Praise of Folly* was mere badinage, and nothing more. There calumny became universal with Filelfo, Poggio, and Lorenzo Valla leading the way. "Italy had in fact become a school for scandal, the like of which the world cannot show, not even in France at the time of Voltaire. In the course of time calumny became universal, and the strictest virtue was the most certain of all to challenge the attacks of malice."[1] Adrian VI, the school-fellow of Erasmus, was held up to scorn as "the comical Dutch barbarian".[2]

---

[1] Burckhardt, *The Civilisation of the Renaissance in Italy*, pp. 160–4 *passim*.
[2] Cf. Pastor, *The History of the Popes*, trans., vol. ix, pp. 222–3.

And all this malicious folly went on and increased right up to the Sack of Rome in 1527. After that terrible event, which was looked upon as a judgment of God, "slander visibly declined", and along with it, "the unrestrained wickedness of private life".[1]

Having finished his *Encomium Moriae*, Erasmus left London with Lord Mountjoy in the April of 1511, visiting Archbishop Warham at his Palace in Canterbury before crossing the Channel on his way to Paris. We hear of him there on April 27th, where he stayed with an Englishman, named Eden, in the Street of St. John, and was there visited by Stephen Gardiner, then but a lad, who won his heart by preparing for him a lettuce, cooked with butter and sour wine–a dish very pleasing to his delicate palate. He returned to London about the middle of May, and stayed with Grocyn, the eldest and most affluent member of the More circle, "the patron and preceptor of them all", a learned physician who in 1501 had lectured on the *Ecclesiastical Hierarchy* of Dionysius, the supposed Areopagite. He also became intimate with Andreas Ammonius, soon to become Latin Secretary to Henry VIII, and to whom he wrote many of his most charming letters.

It was now August 1511, and for more than two years Erasmus had been in touch with the English Court, "waiting for something to turn up". While still waiting, he was persuaded by Bishop Fisher, now Chancellor of Cambridge University, to go there and give some lectures on Greek Grammar. In the ample correspondence of the next few months we get an entertaining picture of his experiences.

Sir Richard Jebb has given us a delightful description of him in his new university quarters. "At this point", he writes, "we may attempt, aided by Holbein and tradition, some idea of his personal appearance."[2]

He was rather a small man, slight but well-built; he had, as became a Teuton, blue eyes, yellowish or light brown hair, and a fair complexion. The face is rather a remarkable one. It has two chief characteristics–quiet, watchful sagacity–and humour, half-playful, half sarcastic. The eyes are calm, critical, steadily observant, with a half-latent twinkle in them; the nose is straight, rather long and pointed; the rippling curves of the large mouth indicate a certain vivacity of temperament and tenacity of purpose; while the pose of the head suggests vigilant caution, almost timidity. As we continue to study the

---

[1] See More's description of the Sack of Rome, *English Works, The Dialogue Concerning Tyndale*, bk. iv, c. vii.
[2] See frontispiece.

features, they speak more and more clearly of insight and refinement; of a worldly yet very gentle shrewdness; of cheerful self-mastery; and of a mind that has its weapons ready at every instant. But there is no suggestion of enthusiasm–unless it be the literary enthusiasm of the student. It is difficult to imagine those cool eyes kindled by any glow of passion, or that genial serenity broken by a spiritual struggle. This man, we feel, would be an intellectual champion of truth and reason; his wit might be a spear of Ithuriel, and his satire as the sword of Gideon; but he has not the face of a hero or a martyr.[1]

Bishop Fisher arranged that rooms were assigned to him at Queens', the College of which he himself had been President a few years before.

In that beautiful old cloister at Queens', where the spirit of the fifteenth century seems to linger, an entrance at the south-east corner gives access to a small court which is known as the court of Erasmus. His lodgings were in a square turret of red brick at the south-east angle of the court. His study was probably a good-sized room which is now used as a lecture-room; on the floor above this was his bedroom, with an adjoining attic for his servant. From the south windows of these rooms–looking on the modern Silver Street–he had a wide view over what was then open country, interspersed with cornfields; the windings of the river could be seen as far as the Trumpington woods. The walk on the west side of the Cam, which is called the walk of Erasmus, was not laid out till 1864: in his time it was open ground, with probably no trees on it. . . .

It is interesting to think of him–now a man of forty-four, but prematurely old in appearance–moving about the narrow streets or quiet courts of mediæval Cambridge. . . . Eleven of our Colleges existed. Peterhouse was in the third century of its life; others also were of venerable age. Erasmus would have heard the rumour that a house of his own order, the Hospital of the Brethren of St. John, was about to be merged into a new and splendid foundation, the College of St. John the Evangelist. Where Trinity College now stands, he would have seen the separate institutions which, after another generation were to be united by Henry VIII; he would have seen a hostel of the Benedictines where Magdalene College was soon to arise; the Franciscans on the site of Sidney Sussex, and the Dominicans on the site of Emmanuel. North of Queens' College, he would have found the convent of the Carmelites; and then rising in lonely majesty–with no other College buildings as yet on its south side–the chapel of King's, completed as to the walls but not yet roofed.[2]

To a casual observer Erasmus's work at Cambridge may have seemed a failure; but it was not so. Was he not poor and neglected, a foreigner

[1] *Essays and Addresses*, p. 326 (C.U.P., 1907).   [2] *Ib.*, pp. 337–8.

unable to speak the language of his pupils, wasting his own time, and probably theirs, in trying to teach them the beggarly elements of Greek? For all they wanted from him was a small addition to their own pitiful stores of marketable knowledge. From the letters he wrote to his friend Ammonius during his three years' stay at the University one might think him to have been an altogether dissatisfied man--dissatisfied with the work he had to do, with the people he had to live with, with the food he had to eat, and with the wine he had to drink. The truth is that never had he worked harder at what most mattered and with more permanent and rich results. Within the walls of this beautiful old College he began and carried on some of the best work of his lifetime--his *Novum Instrumentum*, or *Novum Testamentum*, as later it was called, and, perhaps the most scholarly undertaking of all, the great edition of St. Jerome,[1] not to mention the text of Seneca, some Latin manuals for St. Paul's School, and other things as well. "My mind is in a glow over Jerome," he writes, "that I could fancy myself actually inspired."

Not only this, but his official work at Cambridge was important, for it was part of a great plan conceived by St. John Fisher as Bishop, and Chancellor of the University, to bring about, not merely a revival of letters, but a renewal of the faith throughout the country.

Mr. Froude speaks of Fisher as "weak, superstitious, pedantical";[2] but Mr. Mullinger, the historian of Cambridge University, wrote rather differently about him:

Very soon after Erasmus had taken up his residence at Queens' College, we find him intimating in a letter to Colet, that he was beginning to be aware of the presence in the university of a certain class of men respecting whom his friend had warned him. They were probably men of the same intolerant character as those who a few years later, at one of the colleges, prohibited the introduction of his edition of the New Testament. That their opposition was not more demonstrative during his stay, is perhaps to be attributed to the influence of Fisher. The latter indeed was at this time almost omnipotent at Cambridge; he had been regularly re-elected chancellor, at the expiration of each term of office, ever since his first election; and it would have been perhaps impossible to find, in an equal degree, in any one of his contemporaries, at once that moderation, integrity of life, and disinterestedness of purpose, which left the bigot no fault to find, and that liberality of sentiment and earnest desire for reform, which conciliated far bolder

---

[1] Cf. J. B. Mullinger, *The University of Cambridge*, p. 494.
[2] *History of England*, vol. i, p. 301.

and more advanced thinkers. Over Erasmus . . . a character so saintly and yet so sympathising exercised a kind of spell. Of all the men whom he ever knew, Fisher seems to have most inspired his reverence and regard.[1]

The same writer continues a little later:

On the other hand, it is equally evident that Fisher was not less influenced, though in a different manner, by Erasmus. Of the moderation which Erasmus so much admired in his patron, he was himself a conspicuous example. The good bishop took to heart his advocacy of the new learning, when he found the foremost scholar of the age not less ready to denounce the profanity of the Italian sceptics than the degeneracy of the mendicant orders and able both to discuss with masterly discrimination the merits of classical authors and to recognise the real value of the writings of St. Thomas and St. Jerome. The various evidence indeed which we find of their interchange of opinion on such subjects, would seem to indicate that Erasmus's influence over Fisher, and through Fisher over Cambridge at large, was far greater and more enduring than their respective biographers would lead us to suppose. In their views with respect to the necessity for a thorough reform in the prevailing style of preaching, they were so far at unison, that Fisher, as we have already noted, could think of no one better qualified than Erasmus to prepare a manual of the preacher's art.[2]

Preaching, then, and religious instruction at the universities, had reached a very low ebb, and, as a direct consequence, almost everywhere else in England. As Father Bridgett says, *"Neglect of preaching was perhaps the greatest evil of the fifteenth century, and the source of every other."*[3] Edward Lee, Archbishop of York, complains, at a later date, that he does not know twelve secular priests in his diocese who can preach. "Only a few friars can preach, and none of any other religious order."[4] The sermon was an exception rather than the rule, because a timid policy brought about by the active preaching of the Lollards had encouraged its decline. The clergy in general were directed to preach once a quarter to their congregations; and Latimer relates that sermons might be omitted twenty Sundays together without fear of complaint. Rare as was the sermon, a simple exposition of the Scripture was rarer still. In their zeal to prevent the growth of tares, the husbandmen had forgotten to sow the wheat. The Lady Margaret preachership was Fisher's eminently practical design to meet this long neglect. He

[1] J. B. Mullinger, *The University of Cambridge*, pp. 495–6.   [2] *Ib.*, p. 497.
[3] T. E. Bridgett, *St. John Fisher*, p. 105.   [4] *Ib.*, p. 327.

also wanted to make such preaching as there was more simple, and to this end he encouraged Erasmus to write his treatise *De Ratione Concionandi*. By the regulations now given in connexion with the new foundation (of the Lady Margaret), the preacher was required to deliver six sermons annually–that is to say in the course of every two years at each of the following places: on some Sunday at St. Paul's Cross . . . and once, on some feast day, in each of the following churches of Ware and Cheshunt in Hertfordshire; Bassingbourne, Orwell and Babraham in Cambridgeshire; Maney, St. James Deeping, St. John Deeping, Bourne, Boston, and Swineshead in Lincolnshire. . . . On the whole, looking to the scope of these several designs of the Countess (the Lady Margaret) and her adviser–the provision of gratuitous instruction in the university, the direct application of the learning thus acquired in sermons to the laity–and the introduction of a more simple and evangelical method of scriptural exposition–we can scarcely deny Fisher's claim to rank with the theological reformers (within the Church) of his own and the preceding age, with Gerson, Hegius, Rudolph Lange, and Rudolphus Agricola.[1]

Nor was Erasmus's influence at Cambridge confined to that which he exercised through its Chancellor. The one of whom, next to Fisher, he speaks in the most emphatic praise is perhaps Henry Bullock, a Fellow of Queens' College, mathematical lecturer, and afterwards Vice-Chancellor. In him Erasmus found an enthusiastic pupil during his residence, and a valued correspondent when far away. Bullock it was who, along with one or two others, sustained the tradition of Greek learning, in the perilous interval between their preceptor's departure and the advent of Richard Croke; and somewhat later we find his talents and attainments earning for him the notice of Wolsey, by whom he was induced to enter the lists against the Lutheran party, and was rewarded by a chaplaincy in the Cardinal's household. Another student for whom Erasmus entertained real regard was William Gunnell, sometime of Wolsey's household, and later a tutor in the family of Sir Thomas More. There was also a Fellow of King's, whom he styles *doctissimus* and *carissimus*, John Bryan, a public reader upon Aristotle in the schools. Another Fellow on the same foundation was Robert Aldrich, the *"juvenis blandae cujusdam eloquentiae"* who accompanied Erasmus to Walsingham and "who lived to become Bishop of Carlisle . . . and a

[1] J. B. Mullinger, *The University of Cambridge*, pp. 440–1. The places mentioned were in Fisher's diocese.

commissioner against heretics in Queen Mary's reign".[1] There was also Dr. Fawne, his successor in the Lady Margaret Professorship, and Richard Whitford, More's familiar friend, who used to call Erasmus and More "the twins". He was chaplain to Bishop Fox of Winchester, and afterwards joined the Brigettine community of Sion.

From all this we can gather that Fisher was greatly influenced by Erasmus in his sound scheme for the betterment of English Catholic life, and that the several brilliant young men he taught at Cambridge remained true to the faith to the end of their days. It is sufficient to mention that while at Cambridge Erasmus had no personal connection with Tyndale, or others like him, who a few years later were to make that University so influentially Protestant.[2] *Post Erasmum* does not necessarily mean *propter Erasmum*. Erasmus's influence was in quite another direction. The work that Fisher had given him to do at Cambridge was to teach Greek; and this he did; for seven years later he could write: "In both universities Greek letters are taught, but at Cambridge peacefully."[3] Through him the study of Greek had quietly become a part of the University curriculum. But to foster incipient Protestantism was not to Erasmus's taste or inclination, either then or at any other time.

In September of 1513 the plague broke out in Cambridge, and Erasmus took refuge with his friends the Gunnells at Landbeach, not far away. By the beginning of November he was back again; but by January 1514 he had made up his mind to leave England, return to the Continent and settle down at Basle, and there superintend the publication of his *Novum Instrumentum*. From his letters to Ammonius we gather that his departure from Cambridge was due to a sudden impulse of discontent for which there was no real foundation. Had he bided his time he might, almost immediately, have enjoyed in Cambridge the rewards of substantial success. As it was he left the University too soon for the consolidation of what he had done by way of influence and example. But, alas! as he was not there, his name and work were left to the mercy of an alien generation. On the other hand, his *Novum Instrumentum*—certainly the most widely influential of all his works—was, almost, completed there and, being published in the following year (1516) at Basle, met with the approval of such high authorities as Bishop Fox of Winchester, Tunstall of London, St. John Fisher,

---

[1] J. B. Mullinger, *The University of Cambridge*, pp. 498–500.
[2] See E. G. Rupp, *The English Protestant Tradition* (O.U.P., 1947).
[3] P. S. Allen, *Erasmi Epistolae*, tom. iii, p. 546.

William Warham, Archbishop of Canterbury and of Pope Leo X himself.

But all this was done before the storm of the Reformation had come to disturb and divide the balance of scholarly opinion. After Luther had published his German translation of the New Testament in 1522, and Tyndale his English one in 1526, vernacular translations, and indeed any translations whatever, became suspect. Is it not, then, to the credit of both Erasmus and of that great worker in the same field, Cardinal Ximenes, that each independently of the other had foreseen the necessity of providing the Church with newer weapons wherewith to encounter the onset of heresy–the two most important being the *Novum Instrumentum* of the one and the *Complutensian Polyglot* of the other?

The *Complutensian Polyglot*, although completed by 1514, was not published until 1522, thus giving Erasmus an honourable priority in publication. The often-repeated story that he hurried on his own work in order to forestall that of Cardinal Ximenes is without foundation.[1] In 1508 Ximenes had founded the University of Alcala, which became the centre of exegetical theology, as Salamanca was that of dogmatic. He planned the *Polyglot*, most of the work being done by Greek and Jewish converts, and under his auspices was produced the first edition of the Bible complete in the original tongues; for it contained the Hebrew side by side with the Septuagint and the Vulgate, and, for the Pentateuch, a Syriac paraphrase. His New Testament was finished by 1514, and the whole Bible by 1517, shortly before he died.

Erasmus tells us that Cardinal Ximenes being well pleased with his *Novum Instrumentum*, Stunica, a Spanish theologian, expressed his surprise, since, as he said, it had so many errors. But he may have been still more surprised when the Cardinal replied: "Would that all were such prophets! Go you and do better, if you can; but do not disparage another man's labour." Nor was it until after the Cardinal's death that Stunica ventured to publish his attack upon Erasmus.[2]

The second piece of learned work begun by Erasmus during the Cambridge period was his edition of the works of St. Jerome. Of all the Fathers of the Church, St. Jerome was the one for whom he had a first preference. In his youthful days he had copied out with his own hand St. Jerome's *Letters*. Such was the affinity between these two minds

---

[1] P. S. Allen, *Proceedings of the British Academy*, vol. xi, p. 359.
[2] Drummond, *Erasmus*, vol. i, p. 337.

that it has been said that "Erasmus would have been a Jerome had he lived in the fourth century; and St. Jerome an Erasmus had he lived in the sixteenth." "Jerome", he exclaimed, "is a river of gold; and he who possesses his works needs no other library."

But the task he had set before himself was no easy one.

There were manuscripts, moth-eaten and mutilated, and covered with filth, to be deciphered. The very letters in which they were written were strange Gothic characters, which had to be learned like a new alphabet. There was a text, corrupted partly by carelessness or ignorance, partly by the wilful dishonesty of transcribers. Finally there were spurious works to be separated from the genuine. . . . In such a miserable state indeed had these precious remains been suffered to fall, that if Jerome had returned to life he would have been unable either to recognise or read his own works.[1]

But Erasmus bravely shouldered his task, and he furnished a text which met with the commendation of the later Benedictine editors. He also added, as was his wont, brief critical and explanatory notes, in which all the resources of his own learning were drawn upon. For this, too, he composed a life of St. Jerome, perhaps the best that has ever been written, though said to contain mistakes; but we could readily have forgiven him one more had he only left us the delightful story of St. Jerome and his lion.

Just then he was faced with a grave difficulty which, had it found no reasonable solution, might have prevented him from going to Basle, as he hoped to do, in order to see his works through the press. Servatius Rogerus, the close friend of his early religious life, had become the prior of the Augustinian House at Steyn, where some twenty-five years previously they had both taken their monastic vows. And now, as Erasmus's religious superior, he wrote to remind him of the fact and recall him to his monastery, where it was hoped he would end his days. Erasmus's reply was necessarily one of a very delicate and confidential kind, meant for no other eye than that of his prior, and never published by himself. It will be remembered that a former prior had given him a full permission of absence in order to follow, as we said before, his true calling.

[1] Drummond, *Erasmus*, vol. i, p. 347.

Erasmus to Servatius Rogerus.[1]

MOST GRACIOUS FATHER,

Your letter has reached me and has indeed given me the greatest pleasure inasmuch as it still breathes your old affection for me. . . .

I will address myself to the main questions about which you write. . . .

I am disposed to follow whatever course is best; God is my witness. Age and experience have corrected my youthful follies. I left my monastery not because I had any fault to find with it but in order to avoid disedification. You know yourself that I was forced into it by the insistence of my guardians and, by the importunate exhortation of others, I was driven rather than persuaded to that kind of life. Different persons have different aptitudes. I found fasting difficult and suffered from sleeplessness. I had a passion for literature. I knew that I could be happy and useful as a man of letters. But to break my vow was held to be a crime, and I tried to bear my unhappiness. You will say that there was a year of probation, and that I might have known my own mind. What can a boy of seventeen brought up on books know of his own mind? I was released. I was left to my own will to choose such a kind of life as would suit me; and I think it is that which I have followed. I have lived among discreet people, and in literary pursuits which have turned my thoughts from evil; and I have been able to spend my time among men of a Christian spirit whose influence has been all for good.

I say nothing of my writings. You perhaps despise them; though there are those who think them to be not without merit. The love of money has never touched me, nor have I at all deliberately sought for fame. Pleasures have tempted me, but I have not been a slave to them; and grossness of any kind I have always abhorred.

What should I regain by coming back to you? I should only be a topic for gossip; nor could I put up with the kind of conversation I should have to endure, a whole system of life, in fact, in which I, personally, could find no spiritual savour, intellectual interest or moral betterment. I should die of it. Whenever I have thought of coming back to you, I have thought, at the same time, of the envy of many of the community towards me and of the secret contempt of them all, of their conversation so cold, stupid and devoid of Christian sentiment, and of their convivial recreations certainly not less so—their whole system of life, in fact, if you except the ceremonial part of it, having nothing in it, that to me at any rate seems at all desirable.

He then speaks of his delicate health and his painful bodily infirmity; add to this the unsuitable climate, and it will be seen that nothing could result from his return but trouble to his brethren and the not improb-

[1] P. S. Allen, *Erasmi Epistolae*, vol. i, pp. 564–73; F. M. Nichols, *The Epistles of Erasmus*, vol. ii, pp. 141–51.

John Froben
From the portrait by Holbein

able hastening of his own death. He goes out of his way to stress with exaggerated severity the unseverity of their own conventual life, and "nothing", he loftily adds, "is worse than relaxed religion, the greatest bane of Christian piety". For him, it would seem, all the world is a monastery, in which the sacrament of baptism constitutes a religious order, the order of most good men.

Permanent residence is for people who are getting old; but Erasmus, like St. Paul, would be a wanderer to his life's end, as his hero St. Jerome was, who, though a monk, is now found in Rome, now in Africa, now in Syria, or elsewhere, and even in old age, devoted to sacred letters. "I am not to be compared with him, I admit, but I have never changed my place, unless either forced by the plague, or for the sake of study or of health; and wherever I have lived (perhaps I am speaking too arrogantly of myself, but I will say the truth), I have been approved by those most approved and praised by those most praised. There is no country, whether Spain, or Italy, or England, or Scotland which has not offered me its hospitality." He relates at considerable length all the good things that have happened to him on his travels, and the kindness he has received at the hands of good and distinguished people. But all this is adduced to prove one thing, the fact that one would have thought, in Erasmus's case, needed no proof, his incapacity for the "religious" life. "Your own predecessor," he concludes, "Nicholas Werner, of happy memory, was wont to dissuade me from returning to it, advising me rather to attach myself to some bishop, and adding that he knew both my own disposition and the character of his poor brethren."

Then follow particulars about his change from monastic to clerical dress; and, drawing this *Apologia* to an end, he says that he has explained the whole scheme of his life, and what his ideas are, and that he is quite ready to change even this mode of life if he sees anything better. "But I do not see what I can do in Holland."

I should like to talk to you about these matters in person; for one cannot do so by letter either in comfort or safety. Yours, though sent by the surest of messengers, has so far gone astray, that unless I had happened to come to this castle, I should never have seen it, and I received it after it had already been read by many others. Please therefore do not write any secret matter unless you know where I am and have a very sure messenger. I am now on my way to Germany, that is to Basle, for the purpose of publishing my lucubrations, and in the

E

winter I may perhaps go to Rome. On my way back I will arrange
for our having an interview somewhere; but now the summer is almost
gone, and the journey before me is long.

Farewell, once my dearest companion and now my religious superior.
July 8th, 1514.

Fearing that this long epistle of his might be followed by a peremp-
tory recall to his monastery "under obedience", Erasmus at once
applied to Rome for the renewal of a dispensation granted to him by
Julius II, but now invalidated by the death of that Pope the year before.
This renewal, after careful formalities, was conceded by Leo X in the
March of 1517, so that from that time he was relieved from further
apprehension in the matter.

Erasmus, then, had determined to proceed to Basle in direct disobedience to his own prior. And yet, considering the man himself and
his subsequent achievements for the ultimate good of the Church, we
hardly need hesitate to say, "*O felix culpa!*"

5

Erasmus at Basle – Earlier Period

O<small>N HIS</small> way to Basle, Erasmus left Hammes and continued his journey by way of St. Omer, Ghent, Antwerp, Bergen, Louvain, Liége and Mainz, where he met Ulrich von Hutten, a young German of dissipated life, but with learning of a sort and very witty–a stormy petrel, if ever there was one, and the principal contributor to the notorious *EpistolaeObscurorum Virorum*; an acquaintance, indeed, that in later years Erasmus was glad to drop. At Strasburg he was given a great welcome by a number of scholars, among them Sebastian Brandt author of the *Ship of Fools*. At Schlettstadt, his next stopping-place, the magistrates of the town presented him with three jars of the choicest wine, and on August 16th, 1514, he arrived at Basle, "the haven where he would be", and where, remaining for many years, he was to produce his *Novum Instrumentum,* and with immense and unceasing labour to inspire the first great effort at scholarly editions of the Fathers of the Church.

Just then Basle was a city that suited him well.

The Rhine dashing against the piers of the bridge which joined the great and little towns, brought fresh air and coolness and health. The University, founded in 1460, was active and liberally minded. The town had recently (1501) thrown in its lot with the confederacy of Swiss cantons, thereby strengthening the political immunity which it enjoyed. Between the citizens and the religious orders complete concord prevailed; and finally except Paris there was no town north of the Alps which could vie with Basle in the splendour and number of the books it produced. "Truly Basle was a βασίλεια, a queen of cities."[1]

But other and practical reasons made Basle a suitable place of residence for Erasmus: its central and independent position, the society of learned men who shared his tastes and enthusiasm, and, most practical of all, immediate contact with the printing firm of Amorbach and Froben, comparable only in reputation, wide sympathy and generous understanding with that other firm across the Alps, the

[1] P. S. Allen, *The Age of Erasmus*, p. 146.

Aldine Press. The year before Erasmus's arrival the head of it was
John Amorbach, a man who had first graduated at Paris before
learning his business at Nuremberg. About 1475 he set up at Basle,
and devoted himself to the printing of books that would further the
cause of sound learning. One of his ambitions was to publish editions,
worthy in text and format, of the four doctors of the Church. St.
Ambrose came out in 1492, St. Augustine in 1506, and St. Jerome was
now under consideration. He had already persuaded several scholars to
help him: Reuchlin was with him in 1510 in order to supervise Greek and
Hebrew texts, and was succeeded by Pellican, a Franciscan, and John
Cono, a Dominican who had just come back from Italy with copies of
Greek manuscripts. Others who helped were Conrad Leontorius, Sapidus
and Gregory Reisch, the learned prior of the Carthusians at Freiburg and
who shared with Erasmus a special interest in the Letters of St. Jerome.

But on Christmas Day, 1513, John Amorbach died, leaving his work
to his three sons, Bruno, Basil and Boniface. Bruno was the eldest, and
with Basil had matriculated at Basle University in 1500, and then went
on to Paris where they had taken their degrees. The youngest son,
Boniface, had been kept at home, although he, too, had learned some
Greek from John Cono not long before.

The other partner in the firm was John Froben, now a man of fifty-
three, not a scholar himself, but undoubtedly the executive brain of the
business—a plain man, whose well-marked features still live for us in his
portrait by Holbein, and with a smile lurking about the corners of his
mouth that must have recommended him to Erasmus when first he
called upon him *incognito*, on the day after the Assumption, 1514.
He introduced himself as "sent from Erasmus with whom he was on
terms of closest intimacy". Froben pierced the disguise, welcomed him
cordially, had his bill at the Inn settled, and received him as a guest at
his own house.[1] In this case, as in that of his first meeting with Aldus
Manutius at Venice, he evidently made a good impression, and a
lasting one, as a letter from Froben to Erasmus himself written a couple of
years later sufficiently testifies: "We are all hoping for your return, and
prepared to show you every attention. (My son-in-law) Lachner sends
his greetings, as does his wife Gertrude and all our family. Farewell,
dear gossip."[2] Erasmus, too, was the godfather of Froben's son, Erasmius.

In later years, after Amorbach's death, the marked advance in the output of the firm as regards type and paper and title-pages and designs

[1] F. M. Nichols, *The Epistles of Erasmus*, vol. ii, p. 160.   [2] *Ib.*, p. 280.

may be attributed to Froben, who also realised the importance of getting good men to serve him—Erasmus to edit books, Gerbell and Œcolampadius to correct proofs, Graf and Holbein to provide the ornaments. For thirteen years he was Erasmus's printer-in-chief, and produced edition after edition of his works, both small and great. . . . It is pleasant to find that the harmony of this long co-operation was never disturbed. Erasmus occasionally lets fall a word of disapproval; but what friends have ever seen eye to eye in all matters of business? When Froben died in October 1527, Erasmus wrote with most heartfelt sorrow in eulogy of his friend:

He was the soul of honesty himself, and slow to think evil of others; so that he was often taken in. Of envy and jealousy he knew as little as the blind do of colour. He was swift to forgive and to forget even serious injuries. To me he was most generous, ever seeking excuses to make me presents. If I ordered my servants to buy anything, such as a piece of cloth for a new coat, he would get hold of the bill and pay it off; and he would accept nothing himself, so that it was only by similar artifices that I could make him any return. He was enthusiastic for good learning, and felt his work to be its own reward. It was delightful to see him with the first pages of some new book in his hands, some author of whom he approved. His face was radiant with pleasure, and you might suppose that he had already received a huge sum in profit. The excellence of his work will compare with that of the best printers of Venice and Rome.[1]

And now that he was at Basle, Erasmus soon settled down to work. In a letter written about a month after his arrival he apologises to Zasius, an elderly professor of law at Freiburg-im-Bresigau, for delay in answering a letter of his, on the plea of hard work.

I am so fixed and bound to this treadmill that I have scarcely time for my meals. My book of *Adages* is being so enriched that it may be thought to be another work. Jerome is in hand, and is soon to be printed without annotations. The New Testament is being prepared, corrected and explained with our scholia. A revised edition of the *Copia* is being brought out, and a book on *Similes* is also being published. My translations from Plutarch are already printed; and I am preparing with great pains an amended edition of Seneca Annaeus. When you consider that any one of these tasks is enough to require a whole man, and that not Erasmus but a man of adamant, you may guess how completely I am without a vacant moment.[2]

[1] P. S. Allen, *The Age of Erasmus*, pp. 151-3. See also p. 232, *infra*.
[2] F. M. Nichols, *The Epistles of Erasmus*, vol. ii, pp. 161-2.

Incidentally, the professor's acknowledgment of this letter shows with what enthusiastic admiration Erasmus was being received by the learned men of the Rhine country.

In the spring of 1515, after a heavy spell of work, he felt himself in need of rest and change; so he left Basle about the middle of March in company with a party of book-dealers who were going to the annual fair at Frankfort, where he had a second meeting with Ulrich von Hutten. He then went on to Antwerp, probably stayed there with that fascinating personality Peter Gillis, and saw for the first time the Epistle which Martin Dorpius had addressed to him. At Ghent he was the guest of the Chancellor of Burgundy, and at Tournai of Lord Mountjoy, now governor of the town. At St. Omer he saw the Abbot of St. Bertin, and, crossing to England, reached London during the first week of May.

During this short visit we have little record of personal intercourse with his English friends. More and Tunstall were just setting out on an embassy to the Netherlands, and Erasmus was able, after his arrival in London, to write a letter of introduction to Peter Gillis for "these two most learned men of all England: both my warmest friends".

Before leaving this country, and in view of the approaching publication of his *Novum Instrumentum*, Erasmus thought it well to ensure as far as possible beforehand the favour of his highly-placed friends in Rome. He writes to Cardinals Grimani and Riario, and a month later to Leo X himself. The replies, though all of them did not reach him, were genuinely favourable, and went far to sustain his position when later he was criticised by certain people of the narrower sort.

Meanwhile, refreshed no doubt by his holiday, he returned to Basle by easy stages, getting a glimpse of More at Bruges, and reaching Strasburg on June 1st, made some stay there, so that his journey was prolonged until July.

A very interesting correspondence took place at this time between Martin Dorpius, Erasmus and More. Erasmus had met Dorpius at Louvain, and, becoming intimate with him, had talked over all his plans for the publication of his New Testament. Dorpius was some twenty years younger than Erasmus, and a canon and professor of theology at Louvain. He was evidently an enthusiastic admirer of his, but, thinking matters over after his departure and talking them over with his theological friends, became greatly apprehensive on his account. He then writes with all the courtesy of a true disciple to beg Erasmus to consider whether he is doing the right thing in publishing his New Testament.

In the earlier part of the letter he speaks about the *Encomium Moriae* and the forthcoming edition of St. Jerome, and then goes on:

I also understand that you have corrected the New Testament, and written notes on more than a thousand passages, not without profit to theologians. There is another matter upon which in all friendship I have longed to convey a warning to a friend. You are proposing to correct Latin copies by the Greek. But if I prove to you that there is no error or falsity in the Latin translation, will you not admit that their labour is superfluous who try to mend it? I insist, then, on the correctness and integrity of the Vulgate. For is it likely that the whole Catholic Church would have erred for so many centuries, seeing that she has always used and sanctioned this translation? Is it probable that so many holy fathers, so many consummate scholars would have been mistaken; who have relied on the authority of the Vulgate for their decisions in Councils, their defence and explanation of the faith, and the framing of those canons to which all rulers have submitted? . . .

You have here a prolix and foolish epistle, but one which cannot be unwelcome to you, as coming from a person that loves you. . . . Farewell, most learned and most dear Erasmus.[1]

Louvain [c. September 1514].

Erasmus's reply is interesting, but less so perhaps than a letter written by St. Thomas More in defence of his friend and of the great work that he was doing; for it puts the case for Erasmus, as against his critics, even better than he was able to do himself. More, having seen Dorpius's letter, had hoped to meet him, but, being unable to do so, writes to him forthwith. "Erasmus", he says, "is not as you seem to suppose a mere grammarian but a theologian too, and he is only at pains to criticise those who give themselves up to scholastic subtleties—men as far removed from true theology as they are from common sense."

I was dining [he writes] with an Italian merchant [probably his friend Bonvisi] as learned as he is rich. There was present at the table a monk who was a theologian and a notable disputant just come to England to increase his fame by further disputation. . . . Now, at that dinner, nothing was said by any one that this man, before it was well uttered, did not try to refute with a syllogism, though the matter belonged neither to theology nor philosophy and was altogether outside his own profession. I am wrong. His profession was to dispute. . . .

[1] F. M. Nichols, *The Epistles of Erasmus*, vol. ii, pp. 168–70.

By degrees our host turned the conversation to theological topics. . . . But no matter what was said the theologian at once took the opposite view. Then, the merchant, perceiving that his guest was not so well up in his Bible as he was ready with his syllogisms, began to draw his arguments rather from biblical authorities. He even went so far as to invent certain quotations, on the spur of the moment, in favour of his own side of the question, taking one from a supposed Epistle of St. Paul, another from St. Peter, a third from the Gospel, and affecting to do this with the greatest exactness. . . . The theologian had no notion that the passages quoted were spurious. He could not refuse the (supposed) authority of Scripture; but as, on the other hand, it would be a base thing to own himself beaten, he had his answer ready at once. "Yes, Sir," he said, "your quotation is good, but I understand the text in this way," and then made a distinction of senses, one of which might be in favour of his adversary, the other of himself; and when the merchant insisted that his was the only possible sense, the theologian swore till you would almost believe him, that the sense which he had selected was that given by Nicolas of Lyra. How [concludes More] can any one help laughing at theologians like this? And such are the only men ridiculed by Erasmus. . . .

More's letter is too long for full quotation, but we may notice that he counsels Dorpius not to underrate the difficulties of scriptural study in order to exalt scholastic theology.

But let us suppose that Scripture is easy [he continues] and your questions difficult, yet the knowledge of the former may be far more fruitful than the guessing at the latter. To dance or to bend double like an acrobat is more difficult than to walk, and it is easier to eat bread than to grind potsherds between the teeth, but who would not prefer the ordinary processes of nature to such empty feats? Which, then, of these disciplines is the easier I will not ask, but I cannot hear it said that these minute questionings are more useful than the knowledge of the sacred writings to the flock for which Christ died. If you merely contend that these things are worth study, I will not deny it; but if you put them on level with the discourses of the ancient Fathers, I cannot listen to you. . . .
I do not think you will question that whatever is necessary to salvation is communicated to us in the first place from the sacred Scriptures then from the ancient interpreters, and by traditional customs handed down through the ancient Fathers from hand to hand, and, finally, by the sacred definitions of the Church. If, in addition to all this, these acute disputants have curiously discovered anything, though I grant it may be convenient and useful, yet I think it belongs to the class of things without which it is possible to live. . . . The reason why the ancient inter-

preters are so much neglected is because certain unhappy geniuses have first persuaded themselves, and then led others to believe, that there is nowhere any honey to be found except in the hives of the Summists. . . .

And what purpose does this kind of apologetic serve? Does it help to confute or convert heretics? By no means. If these are unlearned you might just as well try to bring a Turk to the faith by a sermon in French. It becomes like a fight between two naked men among a sharp heap of stones; each of them has the means of injuring the other, and neither of them can defend himself.

More's criticism succeeded in persuading Dorpius to retract what he had written against Erasmus. More then writes a concluding letter to congratulate his friend upon his magnanimity.

It is well nigh impossible to extort a retractation even from the most modest. Almost all are so stupid with false shame that they would rather show themselves always to be foolish than to acknowledge that they were so on one particular occasion; while you . . . who have so much ability, learning and eloquence . . . caring more for truth than for appearances, prefer to tell all the world that you were once deceived, rather than go on deceiving yourself and others. Such an act will bring you eternal glory.[1]

More, *amicus certus in re incerta*, upon this as upon other difficult occasions, stood by his friend.

And now, having lived some eighteen months at Basle, Erasmus has reached the last stages of his two most important works—the *Novum Instrumentum* and St. Jerome. His task has been long and wearisome, but he has around him sympathetic collaborators who enjoy with him his learned as well as his leisure hours. He sends a present of his *Enchiridion* to the daughter of his friend Zasius at Freiburg, close by, on the occasion of her marriage; and he writes to Ammonius and tells him how well things have gone until the cold weather has brought with it the unendurable smell of German stoves.

At last, on March 7th, 1516, he is able to tell his friends that the *Novum Instrumentum* is out—a folio of over a thousand pages, consisting of the Latin Vulgate, his own Greek version of the New Testament and the *Annotations* which he has written upon it. It had taken sixteen long years to write, but it was printed in five or six months. Listen to its first and prefatory words:

I would have the weakest woman read the Gospels and the Epistles of St. Paul . . . I would have those words translated into all languages, so

[1] Bridgett, *Sir Thomas More*, pp. 90–4 *passim*, *Eras. Epp.*, vol. ii, Ep. 337, pp. 91–114.

that not only Scots and Irish, but Turks and Saracens too might read
them. I long for the plough-boy to sing them to himself as he follows
his plough, the weaver to hum them to the tune of his shuttle, the
traveller to beguile with them the dullness of his journey. . . . Other
studies we may regret to have undertaken, but happy is the man upon
whom death comes when he is engaged in these. These sacred words
give you the very image of Christ speaking, healing, dying, rising
again, and make him so present, that were he before your very eyes
you would not more truly see him.[1]

The day on which Erasmus brought out his *Novum Instrumentum*[2]
should be worthy of high remembrance in the history of the Church,
not mainly on account of its scholarship, for other and later works
were much more scholarly, not for the perfection of its style, nor again
for the worth of its commentary, based for the most part on St. Jerome,
but for all these things taken together, and above all as the expression of
the spiritual genius of a man who saw before others, and more clearly,
what the Church most needed at the moment—a newer and simpler
apologetic based on the New Testament, and that as interpreted through
the Christian centuries by Catholic tradition and the Fathers of the
Church. As Professor Henry de Vocht writes:

When, in 1516, the *Novum Instrumentum* came out, there was general
surprise at the bold, and yet successful undertaking. It was the first
critical, scientific edition of part of the Bible, aiming at establishing,
elucidating and illustrating its text by all that human erudition and
judgment could offer, preparatory to the authoritative interpretation of
the Church. Whatever helps us to understand the obvious meaning of
the Holy Books is an inestimable advantage to man; it is a direct preparation of the intelligence for the acceptance of the message of God
through the Church. The book was the more valuable since it brought
from its very sources the means of studying exegetic and theological
science at a time when the *Liber Sententiarum* and the *Summae* were held
in such esteem that it almost seemed a heresy to consider them as insufficient for an adequate knowledge. Since this edition was, moreover,
intended to be an example for all other critical editions of literary and
scientific documents, its importance in the history of civilisation is, at
least, quite as great as that of the printing of the first book by Gutenberg.[3]

[1] Trans. R. W. Chambers, *Thomas More*, p. 122
[2] It seems likely that the title *Novum Instrumentum* was suggested to Erasmus from his
thorough knowledge of the *Letters* of St. Jerome, in which the term is often used. Cf.
Epp. lxxi, cviii, cxxi; also *Comm. on Jeremiah*, vol. iv, p. 61, *Ep. ad Damasum*, pp. 1, 2.
I owe these references to Dom R. H. Connolly.
[3] "Erasmus," by Professor H. de Vocht of the University of Louvain, art. in *The Clergy
Review*, July 1936, pp. 18–19.

The *Novum Instrumentum* was well received when it first appeared. In a letter to More written in June 1516, Erasmus says: "The New Testament is approved even by those whom I thought likely to find fault; and the leading theologians like it very much."[1] But he was the first to acknowledge its mistakes and shortcomings; and in the four editions that followed in 1519, 1522, 1527 and 1535, the year before his death, he did his best to improve it. The *Novum Instrumentum*, it has been said, was the starting-point for all modern biblical criticism. "Erasmus did nothing to solve the problem, but to him belongs the honour of having first propounded it."

Dean Colet acknowledges the receipt of a copy of it in terms of genuine praise.

I understand what you say about the New Testament. Your new edition is bought with avidity, and read everywhere here. There are many that approve and admire your studies, others that disapprove and find fault. . . . For my part I am so devoted to your studies and so charmed with your new edition, that it produces in me a variety of emotions. At one moment I am full of sorrow that I have not learned Greek; at another I rejoice in that light which is emitted by the rays of your genius. Indeed, Erasmus, I am surprised at the fertility of your mind, which conceives so many projects, and brings such important works to birth, day after day in such perfection, especially when you have no fixed abode, and are not assisted by any great or certain emoluments. We are expecting your Jerome. . . . My lord of Canterbury, when I was with him a few days ago, spoke of you a great deal, and wished very much that you were here. . . . Love me as you do, and if you return to us, you will find me devoted to you.[2]

Archbishop Warham writes to Erasmus at about the same time:

I have communicated your publication of the New Testament to several of my brother bishops and doctors of Theology, who agree in declaring that you have executed a work well worth doing. Adhering to their judgment I exalt it with every praise. I received by the bearer of this letter the volumes of Jerome, for which I return you endless thanks—I mean for the labour you have spent on them.[3]

Bearing upon all this, and may we not say confirming Erasmus's sound judgment in matters concerning the Vulgate, the Council of Trent in 1546, thirty years after the appearance of the *Novum Instrumentum*, published a Decree on "the editing and use of the Sacred

[1] There were seventy editions before Erasmus's death. F. M. Nichols, *The Epistles of Erasmus*, vol. iii, p. 415. Froude says that 100,000 copies were sold in France alone. *Life and Letters of Erasmus*, p. 134.
[2] F. M. Nichols, *The Epistles of Erasmus*, vol. ii, pp. 286–7.   [3] *Ib.*, p. 290.

Books". In this-"it was declared in the first place that the ancient Latin
version, preserved for us for so many centuries by the usage of the
Church under the name of '*Vulgata*', was in public recitals, disputations,
sermons and expositions to be held authentic. . . . This, as had been set
forth in the preceding discussions (of the Council), did not assert that
the language and form of the Vulgate was incapable of improvement,
but only that in matters of faith and morals it contained no errors." [1]

And this "improvement" goes on; for a Vulgate Commission is still
at work within the Vatican itself upon a revision of the Vulgate.

Finally, in this connection, a few sentences may be quoted from St.
Thomas More's *Dialogue Concerning Tyndale*, written with regard to
authorised translations of the Scripture but, *a fortiori*, even more
applicable to Erasmus's Greek version.

[The] fear [which some of the clergy have of an authorised translation of the Scripture] nothing feareth me; but whosoever would of
their malice and folly take harm of that thing that is of itself ordained
to do all men good, I would never, for the avoiding of their harm,
take from other the profit they might take, and nothing deserve to lose.
For else, if the abuse of a good thing should cause the taking away
thereof from another that would use it well, Christ should himself have
never been born.[2]

But the year 1516 was to see the publication of another work in
which Erasmus played the leading part. He had long wished to supplement his labours on the New Testament with commentaries upon it by
the Fathers of the Church. And of these St. Jerome had always been his
favourite. The same thought had been in the mind of John Amorbach,
the printer at Basle, who had died on the previous Christmas Day,
and had left it as a spiritual legacy to his partner John Froben, now the
head of the firm. So in the autumn Froben published his edition of St.
Jerome in nine volumes, four of them the work of Erasmus; and
dedicated to the Archbishop of Canterbury, whose acknowledgment
we have quoted above.

It is not surprising that 1516 has been called "the wonderful year of
Erasmian reform" by Professor R. W. Chambers; for, as he says:

In February Erasmus dedicated his Greek Testament, the great work
of his life, to Pope Leo X. In March he dedicated the *Institute of the
Christian Prince* to the sixteen year old King Charles of Castile and the
Netherlands (afterwards the Emperor Charles V). The book is a

[1] Pastor, *The History of the Popes*, vol. xii, p. 260.
[2] More, *E.W.* (1557), p. 241 D.

passionate plea for peace, arbitration, mercy to the poor, the fostering of learning–but, above all, for peace. In April Erasmus had the first part of the great edition of Jerome ready; he had been at work at it intermittently for sixteen years. . . . Finally on the first of November of this year of wonders, we have [More's] *Utopia*.

The triumph of the humanists was to be short. Just one year later, the first of November 1517, Luther was to nail his theses to the church door of Wittenberg, and the Erasmian reformers were to be rapidly thrust out of the way by figures more passionate and violent. Some would say, greater? It will be easier to estimate that a hundred years from now.[1]

But even during the period that followed this "wonderful year" Erasmus went on quietly producing volume after volume of the Fathers of the Church, which found their way into every monastery and learned house throughout Europe. And there they were to remain as the sources of patristic learning until, with dutiful acknowledgment, they were superseded by the work of the Maurist Benedictines at the end of the 17th and during the 18th centuries.

With the publication of his New Testament and of St. Jerome, Erasmus entered upon the major part of his life-work. So, too, St. Thomas More. And perhaps nothing will give us a better idea of their united literary accomplishment than a simple record in parallel columns of their notable publications. And in More's case this will become even clearer if we add in a third column the writings of William Tyndale, St. Thomas More's opponent in their great vernacular controversy.

	ERASMUS (1466-1536)	MORE (1478-1535)	TYNDALE (1494-1536)
1500	*Adagia*		
1503	*Enchiridion*		
1506	*Adagia* (2nd edn.)		
1508	*Adagia* (3rd edn.)		
1510		*Pico della Mirandola*	
1511	*Moriae Encomium*		
1514		*Richard III*	
1516	*Novum Instrumentum*	*Utopia*	
	St. Jerome	*Letter to Dorpius*	
1517	St. Athanasius		
	Querela Pacis		

[1] *Thomas More*, pp. 121-2. But while in agreement with Professor Chambers as to "Erasmian reformers", we should judge that Erasmus himself, although a genius, had not the deep spirituality, nor had he the executive power and wisdom of a great ecclesiastical statesman.

	ERASMUS [1] (1466–1536)	MORE (1478–1535)	TYNDALE (1494–1536)
1518	St. Basil Colloquies	Epigrams	
1519	Novum Testamentum (2nd edn. with Introd.)		
1520	St. Cyprian		
1522	Arnobius	Four Last Things	
1523	St. Hilary	Answer to Luther	
1524	Prudentius Treatise on Free-will St. Jerome (revised)		
1525	St. John Chrysostom (incomplete) St. Cyprian (3rd edn.)		
1526	Irenaeus (4 folio vols.) Trans. of SS. Cyprian and Athanasius		New Testament
1527	St. Ambrose (4 vols.) N.T. (3rd edn.) Origen		Parable of the Wicked Mammon
1528	St. Augustine (part)		Obedience of the Christian Man
1529	St. Augustine (10 vols.)	Dialogue Concerning Tyndale Supplication of Souls	The Pentateuch
1530	Froben's St. Chrysostom		Practice of Prelates
1531	St. Gregory Nazienzen Aristotle (4 vols.)	Dialogue (2nd edn.)	Answer to More
1532		Confutation (1st part) Answer to Frith	
1533	Haymo	Confutation (2nd part) Apology Debellacion of Salem and Bizance	Exposition of Matthew
1534		Dialogue of Comfort Treatise on the Passion Meditations	
1535	New Testament (4th edn.) "Ecclesiastes" on Preach- ing	Prayers Death (July 6th)	
1536	Death at Basle (July 12)		Death (early October)

[1] An index of Erasmus's Writings will be found in P. S. Allen, *Erasmi Epistolae*, tom. xi, pp. 399–400 (Oxford, Clarendon Press, 1947).

6

More's Utopia

THE PUBLICATION of More's *Utopia* in 1516 has been mentioned
already, and something about its author and of the book itself
seems necessary at this point. So much has so recently been
written about St. Thomas More that one dare not lightly add anything
to that holy acreage of print. But Erasmus has done what is needed so
well in a letter written to Ulrich von Hutten in 1519, and gives us so
accurate, and so unexaggerated a contemporary picture of More that
with some abbreviation it will serve to revive our recollections of one
whom Dean Swift, no easy creditor of our frail human nature,
described as the person "of the greatest virtue this kingdom ever
produced". [1]

Erasmus to Ulrich von Hutten. [2]

As to your asking me to paint you a full-length portrait of More, I
only wish my power of satisfying your request were equal to your
earnestness in pressing for it. For me too, it will be no unpleasant task to
linger awhile in the contemplation of a friend who is the most delightful character in the world. . . . But if some diplomatic employment
should ever bring you and More together, you will find out how poor
an artist you have chosen for this commission; and I am afraid you will
think me guilty of envy or wilful blindness in taking note of so few
out of so many good points of his character.

. . . In shape and stature More is not a tall man. . . . His complexion
is fair, his face being rather blond than pale, but with no approach to
high colour except a very delicate flush which lights up the whole. His
hair is auburn inclining to black . . . his eyes bluish grey with some sort
of tinting upon them. . . . His countenance answers to his character,
having an expression of kind and friendly cheerfulness with a little
air of raillery. . . . His right shoulder seems a little higher than his left,
especially when he is walking. In the rest of his body there is nothing
displeasing—only his hands are a little coarse, or appear so, as compared

---

[1] *Works*, vol. iii, p. 301.
[2] The English translation of the original letter in Latin is that of the late Mr. F. M.
Nichols, used by the kind permission of Mr. P. B. B. Nichols and of Messrs. Longmans,
Green & Co.

with the rest of his figure. What a charm there was in his looks when young, may even now be inferred. . . . His health is sound rather than robust.

I have never seen a person less fastidious in his choice of food. As a young man, he was by preference a water-drinker, a practice he derived from his father. But not to give annoyance to others, he used at table to conceal this habit from his guests by drinking out of a pewter vessel, either small beer almost as weak as water, or plain water itself. For his eating he has been accustomed to prefer beef and salt meats and household bread, thoroughly fermented, to those articles of diet which are commonly regarded as delicacies.

His voice is neither loud nor excessively low, but of a penetrating tone. He does not seem to have a natural talent for singing, though he takes pleasure in music of every kind. His articulation is wonderfully distinct, being free from hurry and from hesitation.

He likes to be dressed simply, and does not wear silk, or purple, or gold chains, except when it is not allowable to dispense with them. . . . He cares marvellously little for those formalities which with ordinary people are the test of politeness; and as he does not exact these ceremonies from others, so he is not scrupulous in observing them himself.

He was formerly rather disinclined to a Court life and to any intimacy with princes, having always a special hatred of tyranny and a great fancy for equality. . . . He could not even be tempted to Henry VIII's Court without great trouble, although nothing could be desired more courteous or less exacting than this Prince.[1] He is naturally fond of liberty and leisure; but as he enjoys a holiday when he has it, so whenever business requires it, no one is more vigilant or more patient.

He seems to be born and made for friendship. . . . If anyone requires a perfect example of true friendship, it is in More that he will find it.

In company his extraordinary kindness and sweetness of temper are such as to cheer the dullest spirit, and alleviate the annoyance of the most trying circumstances. From boyhood he was always pleased with a joke; but with all that never had any inclination towards bitterness. If a thing were said facetiously, even though aimed at himself, he was charmed with it, so much did he enjoy any witticism that had a flavour of subtlety or genius. This led him as a young man to amuse himself with epigrams and to take a great delight in *Lucian*. Indeed it was he that suggested my writing the *Moria*, or *Praise of Folly*. . . .

One of his amusements is in observing the forms, characters and instincts of different animals. Accordingly there is scarcely any kind of bird that he does not keep about his house and the same of other animals not quite so common, as monkeys, foxes, ferrets, weasels and the like.

When young he was not a stranger to the emotions of love, but

[1] Date 1517, Henry VIII was then 26.

Tho: Moor L'Chancelour

Thomas More

Thomas More
From the drawing by Holbein at Windsor Castle

without loss of character, and being more attracted by a mutual liking than by any licentious object.

From his earliest years he was a student of good letters; when a young man he applied himself to Greek and to philosophy; but his father, so far from encouraging him in these pursuits, withdrew his allowance and almost disowned him, because they withdrew him from the study of the Law. It was natural, indeed, that in his younger days he should have an aversion for this study; nevertheless, after he had had a taste of the learning of the schools (of law), he became so conversant with it, that there was no one more eagerly consulted by suitors; and the income he made by it was not surpassed by any of those who spent all their time at it; such was the power and quickness of his intellect.

He also expended considerable labour in perusing the volumes of the orthodox Fathers; and when scarcely more than a youth, he lectured publicly on the *De Civitate Dei* of Augustine before a numerous audience, old men and priests not being ashamed to take a lesson in divinity from a young layman. Meantime he applied his whole mind to religion, having some thought of taking orders, for which he prepared himself by watchings and fastings and prayers and suchlike exercises. But he could not shake off a desire for marriage which never left him; so he chose for his wife a very young girl of good birth, with her character still unformed–so that he was all the better able to fashion her character according to his own hopes. Under his guidance she was instructed in learning and in every kind of music, and had almost completely become just the companion he would have wished for the length of his life, when she died. She had however given him several children, of whom three were girls, Margaret, Alice and Cecily, and one a boy, John, still living.

More, however, did not long remain single, but contrary to his friends' advice, he married, a few months[1] after his first wife's death, a widow, no great beauty, nor yet young, *nec bella admodum nec puella*, as he sometimes laughingly says, but a shrewd and watchful housewife with whom, nevertheless, he lives on as sweet and pleasant terms as if she were both young and lovely. With similar kindness he rules his whole household, in which there are no tragic incidents and no quarrels. Indeed his house seemed to have a sort of heavenly felicity about it, for no one ever lived in it without being advanced to higher fortune or left it with a stain upon his character. . . .

More is entirely free from any touch of avarice. He has set aside out of his property what he thinks sufficient for his children, and spends the rest in generous fashion.

In the city of London, where he was born, he acted for some years as judge in civil causes (Under-Sheriff). This office, by no means

---

[1] His parish priest says "within a month", *q.v.* R. W. Chambers, *Thomas More*, p. 109.

F

burdensome, as the Court sits only on Thursdays, is considered highly honourable; and no judge ever disposed of more suits, or conducted himself with more perfect integrity. In most cases he remitted the fees which are due from the litigants, the practice being for the plaintiff to deposit three groats before the hearing, and the defendant a like sum, and no other exaction being allowed. By such conduct he made himself extremely popular in the City.

He had made up his mind to be contented with this position, which was sufficiently dignified without being exposed to serious dangers. He has been thrust more than once into an embassy, in the conduct of which he has shown great ability; and King Henry in consequence would never rest until he dragged him into the Court. "Dragged him," I say, and with reason; for no one was ever more ambitious of being admitted into a Court, than he was anxious to escape it. But as this excellent monarch was resolved to have his Court leavened with learned, serious, intelligent and honest men, he especially insisted upon having More among them; and he is on such terms of intimacy with him that he cannot bear to let him go. If serious affairs are in hand, no one gives wiser counsel; if it pleases the King to relax his mind with agreeable conversation, no man is better company. Difficult questions are often arising which require a grave and prudent judge; and these questions are resolved by More in such a way that both sides are satisfied. And yet no one has ever induced him to accept a present. What a blessing it would be for the world if magistrates like More were everywhere put into office by their sovereigns!

Meanwhile there is no assumption of authority. In the midst of so great a pressure of business he remembers his humbler friends; and from time to time he returns to his beloved studies. Whatever authority he derives from his rank, and whatever influence he enjoys by favour of a powerful sovereign, are employed in the service of the public, or in that of his friends. It has always been part of his character to be most obliging to everybody, and marvellously ready with his sympathy; and this disposition is more conspicuous than ever, now that his power of doing good is greater. Some he relieves with money, some he protects by his authority, some he promotes by his recommendation, while those whom he cannot otherwise assist have the free benefit of his advice. No one is sent away in distress, and you might call him the general patron of all poor people. He counts it a great gain to himself if he has relieved some oppressed person, made the path clear for one that was in difficulties, or brought back into favour one that was in disgrace. No man more readily confers a benefit, no man expects less in return. And successful as he is in so many ways–while success is generally accompanied by self-conceit–I have never seen any mortal being more free from this failing.

Erasmus then turns to the consideration of the studies that have brought them together in friendship.

In his youth his principal literary exercises were in verse.[1] He afterwards wrestled for a long time to make his prose more smooth; practicing his pen in every kind of writing in order to form that style, the character of which there is no occasion for me to recall, especially to you who have his books already in your hands. Hence, while still a youth, he attempted a dialogue in which he carried the defence of Plato's community even to the matter of wives! He wrote an answer to Lucian's *Tyrannicide*, in which argument it was his wish to have me for a rival, in order to test his own proficiency in this kind of writing.

He published his *Utopia* for the purpose of showing what are the things that occasion mischief in commonwealths; having the English constitution especially in view, which he so thoroughly knows and understands He had written the second book at his leisure, and afterwards when he found it was required, added the first off-hand. Hence there is some inequality in style.

It would be difficult to find any one more successful in speaking *ex tempore*, the happiest thoughts being attended by the happiest language; while a mind that catches and anticipates all that passes, and a ready memory, having everything as it were in stock, promptly supply whatever time, or the occasion, demands. In disputations nothing can be imagined more acute, so that the most eminent theologians often find their match, when he meets them on their own ground. Hence John Colet, a man of keen and exact judgment, is wont to say in familiar conversation, that England has only one genius, whereas that island abounds in intellects of distinction.

However averse he may be from all superstition, he is a steady adherent of true piety; having regular hours for his prayers, which are not uttered by rote, but from the heart. He talks with his friends about the future life in such a way as to make you feel that he believes what he says, and does not speak without the best hope. Such is More, even at Court. . . . If you had lived at this Court, you would, I am sure, give a new description of Court life . . . though you too live with such a prince, that you cannot wish for a better, and have some whose sympathies are on the right side. But what is their small number compared with such a society of distinguished men as Mountjoy, Linacre, Pace, Colet, Stokesley, Latimer, More, Tunstall, Clerk, and others like them?

You have now before you an ill-drawn portrait, by a poor artist, of an excellent original! But meantime I have made sure that you will not be able to charge me with neglecting your command nor will my

[1] Presumably Latin verse.

account, I am confident, seem prolix to you as you read it; our More's own sweetness will secure that. . . . Farewell.[1]

Antwerp, 23 July [1519].[2]

With this introduction from his friend Erasmus we may now pass on to More's *Utopia*, that much-discussed and much-misunderstood social classic.

In 1516, when the *Utopia* was first published in Latin,[3] the mediæval world was on the threshold of religious and social change. And in this brilliant essay we have contemporary reflections not only of More's opinions but of others very different from his own. It is a pity that it is generally read in a translation by another hand, and at a later date, made by Ralph Robynson in 1551, with a dedication to William Cecil, afterwards Lord Burleigh. As the late Dr. Alexander Nairne put it, "The classic mark of More's *De optimo reipublicae statu* is sincerity, nobility, and unaffected solemnity", whereas Ralph Robynson "made a 'fruteful and pleasant worke' with his English version, but the dignity had gone and the very act of translation contracts the inspired dream into a defined system. More himself quitely put off his friends' petitions for a popular version. Herein, as always, he declined utterance where conscience did not call him to speak out."[4]

I know no better *Introduction to Utopia* than Professor H. W. Donner's recent book, with that title, where we shall find an adequate account of the sources from which it was composed, such as the narratives of Vespucci and Peter Martyr, not forgetting Plato's *Republic* and *Laws* and the *Germania* of Tacitus. He also points out that More put into the mouth of Raphael Hythlodaye, his interlocutor in that dialogue, *the suggestion that English wool should be converted into cloth in our own country, instead of being sent as raw material to the Netherlands.*[5] As the same writer views it, the *Utopia* is a protest, first, against the new capitalist economics being then introduced, More himself being fully convinced that agriculture should be our staple industry; secondly, against the new Machiavellian method in politics used by Henry VIII and

[1] F. M. Nichols, *The Epistles of Erasmus* (Longmans, Green & Co., 1917), vol. iii, pp. 387–401.
[2] The translator, the late Mr. F. M. Nichols, dated this letter 1517; but the late Dr. P. S. Allen established, I think, 1519 as the correct date. *Erasmi Epistolae*, tom. iv, p. 13 note.
[3] More wrote it in Latin, not wishing it to be read by those who might read it amiss.
[4] *Downside Review*, May 1932, p. 198. One may suggest as a preferable alternative to Robynson's translation, *More's Utopia*, translated into modern English by G. C. Richards (Oxford: Basil Blackwell, 1923).
[5] This suggestion, in the opinion of some critics, makes More the founder of modern capitalism. In Russia, if patron saints are still permissible, More would be regarded as the patron saint of communism.

Thomas Cromwell; and, thirdly, against the spirit of cynicism and unbelief so rapidly spreading through Europe. Seebohm seems to have looked upon More's *Utopia* as an ultimate ideal; but that could hardly have been so, since the Utopians were without the supernatural revelation of Christianity. But, as Professor Chambers tells us, the more we read the *Utopia*, and particularly the section on religion, and compare it with More's treatises against heresy, "the more they reveal the same mind".[1] In Utopia people could think freely about religious and political matters; but they could not freely express their thoughts in public; for if they did, and in any subversive way, they became liable to punishment, and should they persist in so doing the final punishment was death.

More's background when he wrote the *Utopia* was nothing less than Catholic Christendom with its steadfast mountains and eternal hills, towards which he never failed to look for help. But in the foreground, with which the *Utopia* is mainly concerned, great changes–secular, spatial and spiritual–were going forward, changes soon to become of immense and tragic consequence to those then living, and hardly less so to us who live so many centuries later.

Twenty-five years before More was born, Constantinople had fallen to the Turks; and those who fled from it brought with them not only a great fear, but also the matter and spirit of a great and learned change. Almost within a year of More's birth Caxton had returned from the beautiful city of Bruges, bringing with him his first printing-press and a knowledge and enthusiasm for "good letters" which enabled him to put it to full use. And what he did in London, other printer-publishers, Aldus Manutius at Venice, John Froben at Basle and others in other cities of the Continent also did. Thus, by the invention of printing, and subsequently the much wider and more rapid distribution of the printed word, the records both of the old learning and the new were circulated throughout the then known civilised world.

Again, when More was a lad of fifteen, Columbus had brought to the Old World its first tidings of the New; and in the years that followed the famous seamen of the time made perilous voyages to new territories and opened up sea routes to the east and west for the merchant adventurers of England, of Portugal and of Spain.

Under such unwonted and inspiring circumstances it is not surprising that the *Utopia* begins as a record of the plans, ideas and adventures of

[1] R. W. Chambers, *Thomas More*, p. 256.

Raphael Hythlodaye, a supposedly sea-faring man, who, while discussing his experiences with Peter Gillis, is introduced to More himself,
then staying at Antwerp upon a diplomatic mission. And such is the
verisimilitude of More's delightful fantasy that not a few of its first
readers seriously applied to him for knowledge of the best way of
getting to Utopia, which, in plain English, means Nowhere. But, for
all this, the first book of the *Utopia* is about very real happenings both
in England and abroad; and the second, written before the first, is
in fact a criticism, and indeed a satire, upon the devastating wars so
lightly waged by European princes, and upon the miserable condition
of the English poor, brought into idleness and poverty as a consequence
of these wars and of the enclosures that accompanied them. Then there
are social theories that go back to Plato's *Republic*, but with the difference that *the institution of the family is taken as the unit of Utopian well-
being*. And although the pre-conditions of marriage are very modern
and scientific, they give no countenance whatever to birth prevention
in any artificial form.

The *Utopia* has been called by many a very disturbing book, and is
so, even in our day. But More himself tells us that he deliberately wrote
it in Latin, then the common language of the learned, in order that no
simple or unlearned folk should, through misunderstandings, take any
harm from it either to their faith or to their morals, or even to their
commonly held political opinions. Writing many years later in his
Confutation, he says:

I say therefore in these days in which men by their own default mis-
construe and take harm of the very scripture of God, until men better
amend, if any man would now translate *Utopia* into English, or some
works either that I have myself written ere this, albeit there be none
harm therein–folk yet being (as they be) given to take harm of that that
is good, I would, not only my darling's[1] books but mine own also,
help to burn them both with mine own hands, rather than folk should
(though through their own fault) take any harm of them, seeing that I
see them likely in these days so to do.[2]

Again, in his *Apology*[3] More writes in approval of John Gerson
because he published his criticisms of the clergy in Latin, and not in the
vulgar tongue, as Tyndale had done.

But in 1551, sixteen years after More's martyrdom, Ralph Robynson

---

[1] Tyndale in derision of More called Erasmus his "darling".
[2] *English Works* (1557), *The Confutation*, bk. ii, pp. 422–3.
[3] E.W., *The Apology*, p. 873 G.

published an English translation of the *Utopia*; and in this form it has
become an English classic, the best-known and the least understood of
all More's writings. It may therefore be well worth while to attempt to
interpret it in the sense in which More himself understood it.

One simple fact should be firmly grasped by every reader of the
Utopia from the very outset–namely, that it was written in the form
of a *dialogue*. For subsequent disregard of this fact has made fair
judgment upon the book itself, and also upon its author, almost
impossible.

It goes almost without saying that More was brought up on the old
scholastic form of discussion. When this was in a written form the disputant upon any particular thesis first of all enumerated fairly and at
their full strength the main objections to his own opinion. Then, having
given some general and formal reason for a contrary view, he goes on to
justify it as strongly but as concisely as may be. This done, he answers in
turn each of the objections at first raised against it, and so brings the
discussion to an end.[1]

The invention of printing about the middle of the fifteenth century
made discussion on paper, and printed discussion at that, much easier
and much lengthier than had ever been possible before. And thus the
older and briefer type of scholastic disputation was modified, and soon
passed into the *dialogue form* as previously used by Plato. But both it and
the dialogue form which followed it were very well suited to the
purposes of accurate thought and expression. In More's time, then,
whenever he or any of his thoughtful contemporaries wished to
examine with judicial care important opinions of a political, social or
religious kind, the dialogue was adopted as the most fitting vehicle not
only of their own opinions, but also of those to which they themselves
were most definitely opposed. And it had this further advantage, that it
enabled them, *under their own names*, to state their own opinions in
quite definite contradistinction to those of people from whom they
differed. Whence it was that among More's literary productions we have
first of all the *Utopia*, in which he uses the dialogue to discuss political,
social and religious matters; then the *Dialogue Concerning Tyndale* and
the *Confutation*, in which he controverts the opinions of the Protestant
reformers; and, finally, his *Dialogue of Comfort*, which was written when
he was imprisoned in the Tower, in order to fortify his reasonable soul

---

[1] William James, *The Will to Believe*, p. 13, speaks of "Scholastic orthodoxy to which
one must always go when one wishes to find perfectly clear statement".

against the miseries of close confinement and the final onset of death itself.

It need hardly be said that in every discussion there must always be a common ground of agreement as well as a ground of difference; and it is only when the differences grow to a crucial point that such very careful distinctions as More makes under his own name in the *Utopia* and in his other controversial writings are necessary. In order, then, to be quite fair to More's consistency of mind and character, one should regard these distinctions as carefully as he did; for only thus can he be understood exactly in his own sense. And this is as necessary in reading his *Utopia*, where he accurately, through the mouth of Hythlodaye, expresses the contentions of Communism, and as clearly differs from them in his own proper person, as it is is studying his *Dialogue Concerning Tyndale*, where he fairly states and fully answers the religious arguments of Tyndale and Luther.

The circumstances which occasioned the writing of the *Utopia*, the first book being written after the second, add to its interest. In May 1515, More, as Under-Sheriff of London, and in the full tide of professional work and success, was chosen by the City merchants to represent them in an embassy that was setting out for Flanders to treat of important business with the representatives of the Archduke Charles, who later became Charles V. This kept him away from England for more than six months and, as he says in a letter to Erasmus, very much against his will. However, there were consolations.

In my legation [he continues] some things greatly delight me. First, living so long and so continuously with Cuthbert Tunstall [afterwards Bishop of London, and later of Durham], a man who, while he is surpassed by none in culture and strictness of life, is also unequalled in the pleasantness of his demeanour. Next I have acquired the friendship of Busleiden, who received me with a magnificence proportionate to his great riches, and a cordiality in keeping with the goodness of his soul. He showed me his house so marvellously built and so splendidly furnished and with so many antiquities in which you know my curiosity and delight; and above all his library is so well filled and his mind more richly stocked than his library. . . . But in my travels nothing was more to my content than my intercourse with your host, Peter Gillis of Antwerp,[1] a man so learned, so witty, so modest, and so true a friend that I would willingly purchase my intimacy with him at the cost of a fortune.[2]

[1] Peter Gillis was Town-clerk of Antwerp.
[2] F. M. Nichols, *The Epistles of Erasmus*, vol. ii, p. 261.

Peter Gillis, or Peter Giles, as Ralph Robynson calls him, has been made familiar to us in Quentin Matsys' fascinating portrait, in company with Erasmus at the age of fifty, and beautifully reproduced for us by the late Dr. P. S. Allen.[1] It is to Peter Gillis that the *Utopia* is dedicated in More's introductory letter.

While I was at Antwerp among many that visited me there was one that was more acceptable to me than any other–Peter Gillis, born at Antwerp, a man of great honour and good rank in that town; for I do not know if there be anywhere to be found a more learned or better bred young man. . . . One day, as I was returning from Mass, I saw him by accident talking with a stranger that seemed past the flower of his age; his face was tanned, he had a long beard, and his cloak was hanging carelessly about him, so that by his looks and habit I concluded he was a seaman. As soon as Peter saw me he came and saluted me; and as I was returning his civility, he took me aside and pointing to him with whom he had been talking, said: "Do you see that man? I was just thinking of bringing him to you." I answered, "He should have been very welcome on your account." "Then," said I, "I did not guess amiss; for at first sight I took him for a seaman."

"Nay (quoth he) there ye were greatly deceived; for he hath sailed indeed, not as the seaman Palinure, but as the expert and prudent prince Ulysses: yea, rather as the ancient and sage philosopher Plato. For this same Raphael Hythlodaye (for this is his name) is very well learned in the Latin tongue: but profound and excellent in the Greek language, wherein he ever bestowed more study than in Latin, because he has given himself wholly to the study of philosophy. Whereof he knew that there is nothing extant in Latin, that is to say to any purpose, saving a few of Seneca's, and Cicero's doings."

Raphael Hythlodaye, who is to be More's interlocutor in this Utopian dialogue, is evidently a great traveller, both in time and space, his chief interest being to discover new peoples and civilisations, and then to compare them with those of his own or of classical times, not omitting to observe their religious customs as contrasted with the "one religion that is true", the supernatural revelation of Christianity.

More, Giles and Hythlodaye, being now on terms, engage in pleasant talk as they make their way to the house where More is staying in Antwerp, and, going out into the garden, they sit down upon a green bank and enter into a more serious discussion.

[1] *Erasmi Epistolae*, tom. ii, between pages 577 and 578. Both are taken from the Diptych painted in 1517 for presentation to More and now at Longford Castle, near Salisbury, in possession of the Earl of Radnor.

We may recollect that just at this time Henry VIII, about twenty-five, and most attractive in his youthful beauty and varied accomplishments, was doing his best to attract More within the circle of political and Court life. So it is not unlikely that More himself, while engaged upon his embassy at Antwerp, may have been preoccupied with the pros and cons of such a possibility–one, indeed, that in Tudor days was absorbing, difficult and not without danger. Could a man seriously bent upon practical reforms that would benefit his oppressed and less-well-off countrymen look for anything but sad disillusionment should he try to impress his views upon a headstrong young prince and his selfish courtiers and politicians? And thus we find him discussing these very possibilities within the framework of this charming fantasy. For does he not, in company with Peter Giles, try to persuade Hythlodaye to put his own varied and practical knowledge and experience at the disposal of some powerful prince? Hythlodaye, on his side, demurs to this, thinking it unreasonable that they should ask him to give up the philosophic and unhampered tenor of his life in this way. And to this More then makes answer:

I perceive, Raphael, that you desire neither wealth nor greatness; and indeed I value and admire such a man as yourself more than I do any of the great ones of the world. Yet I think that you would do a thing well becoming a generous and philosophic soul, such as yours is, if you would apply your time and thought to public affairs even though you may find it inconvenient to yourself: and this you can never do with so much advantage as by being taken into the council of some great prince and there setting him on to noble and worthy deeds . . . for the springs of both good and evil flow over a whole nation from its prince as from a perpetual fountain.

Hythlodaye insists that princes are generally more set on acquiring new kingdoms than on governing well those that they have already. Courtiers, too, take it ill if any man sets out to be wiser than they; and although willing to let go all the good things that have been done in former ages, yet if better things are proposed they cover themselves obstinately with the excuse of reverence for the past. Indeed, he himself has met with these proud, morose and absurd judgments of things in many places, particularly once in England. He then continues:

There are those who think it is to the prince's interest that there should be as little private property as possible left in the hands of ordinary people; and that they should have neither riches nor liberty;

since these things make them less submissive and subservient to a cruel and unjust government; whereas necessity and poverty blunts them, makes them patient, and bears them down and breaks their height of spirit, and takes away from them any disposition to rebel.[1]

Now what would happen [Hythlodaye asks] if I should assert that such counsels were both unbecoming to a king, and hurtful to him, and that not only his honour, but his safety, consisted more in his people's well-being than in his own . . . and that a prince, like a shepherd, is to take more care of his flock than of himself ?

It is also certain that they are much mistaken who think that the poverty of a nation is a means to public safety. Who quarrel more than beggars do? Who more earnestly longs for change than he who is in miserable circumstances? And who are readier to run to revolution than those who, having nothing to lose, hope to gain by it? . . . He that can find no other way for correcting the errors of his people but by taking from them the conveniences of daily life, shows that he knows not what it is to govern a free nation.

He adds some further sound advice to princes in general:

Let the prince live upon what belongs to himself, without wronging others, and let him accommodate his expense to his revenue. Let him punish crimes; but let him endeavour by wise conduct to prevent them rather than be severe on those who have been made criminal by his own bad government. Let him not rashly revive laws that have fallen into disuse and that have been long forgotten and never wanted.

And, having said all this, can we not see our seafaring philosopher turning to More with a smile and asking him what chance such a social reformer as himself would have of becoming at all acceptable as a counsellor to any prince then reigning in Europe? How deaf every one of them would be to his political advice!

"No doubt they would," replies More, "and no wonder. What you have said is all very well in a friendly discussion; but there is no place for it in the court of princes where great affairs are carried on by authority." More's meaning is clear, as if he said: "People do not talk as you have been talking when every word of theirs results in action, and action taken under a sobering sense of personal and moral responsibility for the good order and stability of the state."

"Then it is as I said," concludes Hythlodaye. "There *is* no room for philosophy in the courts of princes."

Yes, there is [answers More], but not for a speculative philosophy

---

[1] Cf. Aristotle, *Politics*, bk. v, p. 8

that makes everything to be alike fitting at all times. But there is
another philosophy that is more pliable, that knows its proper scene,
and accommodates itself to it; and that teaches a man to act that part
which has fallen to his share fitly and decently.

If [he continues], when one of Plautus's comedies is upon the stage,
and a company of servants are acting their parts, you should come out
in the garb of a philosopher and repeat out of *Octavia* a discourse of
Seneca's to Nero, had it not been better for you to have said nothing
than, by mixing things of different natures, to have made such an
impertinent tragi-comedy? For you spoil and corrupt the play in hand
when you mix with it things disagreeing to it, even though they were
better than it is; therefore go through with the play that is acting the
best you can; and do not confound it, because another that is pleasanter
comes into your thoughts. It is even so in a commonwealth, and in the
councils of princes. If ill opinions cannot be quite rooted out, and if you
cannot cure some received vices according to your wishes, you must
not therefore abandon the ship in a storm, because you cannot command the winds; nor ought you to assault people with discourses that
are out of their road, when you see their notions are such that you can
make no impression on them; but you ought to cast about, and as far
as you can to manage things dexterously, that so if you cannot make
matters go well they may be as little ill as is possible. For except all men
were good, all things cannot go well; which I do not hope to see in a
great while.

At this point More begins to define his differences from Hythlodaye;
and these will become clearer and much more explicit as the argument
proceeds. Hythlodaye, as we see him in the *Utopia*, is a theorist, presumptuous, inexperienced, impatient and unpractical, in spite of his
journey to Nowhere, and perhaps because of it. More, on the other
hand, after a life of severe self-discipline, had gone far along the path
of political common sense and of social virtue. Hythlodaye had only
dreamt of perfection, whether individual or social. He lacked humility,
the virtue "that tempers and restrains the mind, lest it tend to high
things immoderately":[1] he also lacked its balancing virtue, magnanimity, "that strengthens the mind against despair, and urges it on to
the pursuit of great things according to right reason".[2]

The crux of this high argument is now at hand, wherein Hythlodaye
develops his own great social remedy in contradistinction to that of
More. "*I cannot think*", he says, "*that a nation can be governed justly or
happily as long as there is any private property.*"

[1] Aquinas, *Summa*, II–II, Q. 161, art. 1.   [2] *Ib.*

"*On the contrary,*" replies More, "*it seems to me that one cannot live conveniently where all things are held in common.* How can there be plenty where everyone will excuse himself from labour? For since the hope of gain doth not excite a man, he will trust to other men to do for him what he is under no necessity to do for himself; and he will become lazy," and therefore unproductive.

And if people come to be pinched with want and yet cannot dispose of anything of their own, what can follow upon this but perpetual sedition and bloodshed, especially since reverence and authority due to magistrates fall to the ground? For I cannot imagine how reverence and authority can be kept up among those that are in all material things equal to one another.

It is of interest to notice that More attaches an almost capital importance to the maintenance of reverence and authority, a point, perhaps, somewhat neglected by modern sociologists.

In the second book of the *Utopia*, written, as we said, before the first, we are made to realise a ground of difference between Hythlodaye and More not quite the same as that just mentioned. More finds Hythlodaye's compulsory State Communism impracticable; but in its place he does defend another kind of Communism, neither compulsory nor enforced by the State in any way; but one that is voluntary, and so practical that it has been in practice for fifteen hundred years.

The early Christians, he tells us, as well as "the more serious sort of Christians ever since", voluntarily gave up their private property, and shared their goods among those of their brethren who were in need, under the divine and supernatural impulse which we call charity[1] or love. And this is just the contrary of State Communism, which compels its subjects to have no private property because, and precisely because, it has no effective belief that the divine impulse of charity can take possession of the human heart. Nor should we expect it to do so since, for the most part, State Communists have no effective belief in God Himself.

But More believed that *the Holy Spirit*, speaking, not only in the hearts of individual men and women, but also and always until the end

---

[1] One must be careful to distinguish "charity" as understood in pre-Reformation England and the word "charity" as it is commonly used in England to-day. To be charitable, then, meant to be generous to the limit for the love of one's neighbour; and in the supernatural sense of the word. "This is my commandment, that you love one another, as I have loved you. Greater love than this no man hath, that a man lay down his life for his friends." *John* xv. 12–13.

of the world *through the mouth of the Catholic Church, teaches us how to turn our naturally increasing desires for pleasure, for property and for power, into a supernaturally decreasing desire for these very same things, good though they be, but better when given than when received, and best of all when for-gone for the love and glory of God and the relief of man's estate.*

Here, then, we touch the *fons et origo* of Catholic Social Philosophy–a philosophy of human desires, disciplined, supernaturalised, re-directed and re-energised by the grace of God.

Let us reconsider it very briefly.

Concerning the natural religion of the Utopians, Hythlodaye says:

After the Utopians had heard from us an account of the doctrine, the course of life, and the miracles of Christ, and of the wonderful constancy of so many martyrs whose blood, that was so willingly offered by them, was the chief occasion of spreading their religion over a vast number of nations, it is not to be imagined how inclined they were to receive it. I shall not determine whether this proceeded from any secret inspiration of God, or whether it was because it seemed so favourable to the community of goods, which is an opinion so particular as well as so dear to them; since they perceived that Christ and his followers lived by that rule; and that it was still kept up among the sincerest sort of Christians.[1]

We may notice that in the paragraph just quoted from the *Utopia* two kinds of Communism are spoken of–the State Communism of the Utopians and the Religious Communism "still kept up in some communities among the sincerest sort of Christians".

And in this connection we may remember Lord Macaulay's saying that Catholicism, unlike so many other varieties of institutional Christianity, has ever found a place within its ordered system for every genuine manifestation of human religious enthusiasm, provided only that it will voluntarily submit itself to such mental and moral discipline as will fashion it to spiritual and social uses. And in proof of this he points to the Religious Orders of the Catholic Church, which are, of course, of a voluntary and communistic character, and have arisen and persisted within that Church now for nineteen hundred years.[2]

We learn from the *Acts of the Apostles* that Communism of a kind existed in the first days of the Church; for we are told that the early Christians "were persevering in the doctrine of the apostles, and in the communication of the breaking of bread and in prayers. . . . And they

---

[1] Burnet, *Utopia*, p. 172.
[2] Macaulay, *Critical and Historical Essays*, Essay on Ranke's *History of the Popes*.

that believed were together and had all things in common. Their possessions and goods they sold and divided them all according as each had need."[1]

But how did this kind of Communism arise? Let us go farther back to the Gospels themselves. Christ's work while on earth consisted partly in forming a special band of close followers who, after the Ascension and the Coming of the Holy Spirit, were to be the rulers of His Church, teachers of His doctrine, and examples of His life to the world. They were to be the spearhead of His Church Militant. This, for them, would be a difficult work; and it required a training and self-dedication of no ordinary kind–something that the rest of the Christian body would not be called upon to undergo. For these immediate and specially chosen followers were to be as He had been while on earth. He had given up His own will; He was poor; He led a single life. And so, to perpetuate His own living example in the world, they also were called to give up their own wills, to be poor, and to live unmarried–they were called to be what He had been, and to forgo what He had forgone. And from their example arose the monastic life which was a kind of Communism, and so recommended itself to the Utopians as being, at first sight, somewhat like their own.

But it was not like their own; for Utopian Communism was a kind compulsorily enforced by the secular power of the State, with an equal obligation upon all alike, while the kind practised "by the sincerest sort of Christians until now" was a special form of the supernatural life to which only a few are called by God Himself in each succeeding generation. Looking back over the long history of Christendom, how few of the innumerable souls now in heaven were called, while on earth, to lead this voluntary and supernatural life of religious communism in this or that religious order? And when we remember how difficult the religious vocation is, and recall our Lord's own words about it, we are not surprised. How few in any single generation can voluntarily give up even their small possessions in this world? Yet our Lord asked the rich young man to give up his, although they were great. How few can forgo the prospect of wedded happiness? Yet our Lord said of the unwedded life, "He that can take it, let him take it." And last, and perhaps most difficult of all, how few, for His sake, can bear to be until death at the beck and call of another's will not only in the ordinary, but also in the most intimate things of their private lives? Yet all this has

[1] *Acts* ii. 42–5.

been the voluntary sacrifice of the "few that are chosen" by God Him-self for lifelong self-sacrifice upon the altars of the "religious" life. These, indeed, are the "sincerest sort of Christians", are they not? And these are they who from the first days of Christianity until now, in spite of the betrayals of many a Judas, and the failure of many a Peter, have perpetuated, like a seal upon the wax, the impression of the fullness of the likeness of Christ upon the succeeding generations of mankind.

But let us not forget that while this threefold renunciation of human desires, good and natural in themselves, provides the foundation upon which the highest kind of our earthly Christian life has rested, yet, for all that, it is a renunciation of the "good life" ordained by God for the vast majority of Christian souls, a multitude no man can number. Wherefore it is that the Catholic Church has ever been the stoutest and most constant champion of the ordinary life of the normal man, a life, inspired, as it is, by the three strongest natural desires known to human nature—the desire for pleasure, the desire for property, and the desire for power.

To sum up, then, a man's desires are the dynamic of his very being, *trahit sua quemque voluptas:*[1] by the alteration of these desires for the better he can be made into a better man; and nothing short of such an alteration can do it. We are not surprised to find that an eminent non-Catholic writer has observed that "the problem which the Catholic Church has regarded as exclusively her own, [is that] of governing the passions of the human heart".[2]

---

[1] Virgil, *Eclogues*, 2. "Each one is attracted by his own delight."
[2] J. H. Bridges, *Essays and Addresses*, p. 107 (Chapman and Hall, 1907). See also the very excellent article by Richard O'Sullivan, K.C., in the July number, 1936, of the *Dublin Review*, entitled "The Social Theories of Sir Thomas More".

William Tyndale
From the portrait in the Hall of Hertford College

7

Tyndale

AND NOW for a time the interest of our story passes from Sir
Thomas More to William Tyndale; for these two famous men
can never be separated for long in any account of the beginnings
of the English Reformation. I so well remember going one winter's
morning, now many years ago, to the British Museum intent upon
seeing that very old and rare volume, the second edition of Sir Thomas
More's *Dialogue Concerning Tyndale*, printed in beautiful Black-Letter
Secretary type and published in 1531. And as I entered the Reading
Room, there, straight in front of me, I saw the name of William
Tyndale inscribed in letters of golden eminence upon the inner circum-
ference of the Dome in honourable company with those of other
notable men who at different times and in different ways had helped to
fashion our mother tongue. But at the same time I also noticed, and
with much regret, that the name of Sir Thomas More was not to be
seen within that golden circle. Surely it should have been there? For
did not Doctor Johnson, in the preface to his Dictionary, devote eight
folio pages to selections from More's *English Works* on the plea that "of
the works of Sir Thomas More it was necessary to give a larger specimen both because our language was then in a great degree formed and
settled, and because it appears from Ben Jonson that his works were
considered models of pure and elegant style"?

But to return to Tyndale and his earlier days. He was thought to have
belonged to a yeoman family living in the neighbourhood of Stinch-
comb Hill in Gloucestershire, just below the western spur of the Cots-
wolds. More recent research, however, has led his latest biographer[1] to
conclude that his forebears lived not on the eastern side of the River
Severn, but in Monmouthshire, on the western side of that great river.
In either case the Tyndale Monument which commemorates his birth
at North Nibley stands where it ought not. We may further presume
on the same good authority that the date of his birth was not in 1494,
as previously held, but in 1491 or 1492.

[1] J. F. Mozley, *William Tyndale* (1937), to whose generosity in a detailed correspondence
I am indebted for these latest conclusions.

Coming now to his own writings, we find some interesting self-evidence as to his appearance and disposition. "God hath made me", he says, "evil favoured in this world, and without grace in the sight of men." And this is borne out by an engraving to be found in Holland's *Heroologia* (1620), and reproduced as the frontispiece of Mr. Mozley's book. He further describes himself as "speechless and rude, dull and slow witted".[1] Yet this diffident and self-belittling man was one "whose choice of words", as found substantially surviving in the Authorised Version of the New Testament, "has for four hundred years exercised a supreme influence upon English prose".[2]

This silent being of homely appearance, buttoned up within himself and, as we may infer, almost companionless in his youth, needed surely a friend older than he was–say an understanding priest or some member of a religious order, experienced in the ways of prayer, who might have led him almost imperceptibly to a knowledge of himself and of his God-given capacities for the contemplative life. We have, indeed, words of his own, sufficient of themselves, to indicate how potential a kingdom of God lay undisclosed within his soul.

God is a spirit [he writes] and will be worshipped in spirit; that is, though He is present everywhere, yet He dwelleth lively and gloriously in the minds of angels only, and hearts of men that love His laws and trust in His promises. And wheresoever God findeth such a heart, there He heareth prayer in all places indifferently. So that outward place neither helpeth or hindereth except (as I said) that a man's mind be more quiet from the rage of worldly business, or that something stir up the word of God and the example of our Saviour more in one place than another.[3]

Perhaps in this connection an opinion may be permitted that just as the earlier troubles of Erasmus came from a "forced vocation" to the monastic life, so those of Tyndale's later years may have arisen from a "missed vocation" to the contemplative life, either in some religious community, or perhaps to an even greater seclusion like that of St. Jerome, who at the end of the fourth century retired from Rome to Bethlehem, and there devoted himself, for the remainder of his days, to the spiritual direction of others, and to the translation of the Scriptures into the Latin version known as the Vulgate.

---

[1] Tyndale, *Works*, vol. i, Introd., p. lv, Letter to John Frith.
[2] Professor R. W. Chambers, *Man's Unconquerable Mind*, pp. 190–1. Tyndale was substantially responsible for about 90 per cent of the Authorised Version.
[3] Tyndale, *Works*, vol. iii, p. 64 (Parker Society).

The spiritual life, as lived throughout the Christian centuries, has never been, nor was ever meant to be, wholly individualistic. The Church has always insisted that while each individual soul has been created for the society of God, it is not good for man to be alone. And just as the human family has been the unit of the natural life, so, too, in differing forms, has it been that of the supernatural. As a recent historian has pointed out, life in mediæval times should be mainly regarded as a collection of societies rather than of individuals, and that for better or worse it is as a collection of societies that it must be judged.[1] Nor was it because men in those times were individually more helpless, but because they were socially inspired by an active Christian faith. How could those who tried to love God fail at the same time to try to love their neighbours? They gathered in groups in order the more safely, the more easily, the more justly and the more charitably to carry out their common tasks. And so within the common unity of Christendom we find an abundant and prosperous diversity of social communities founded and continuing for the good of the common life–and all this in obvious contrast to what later became an over-stressed conception that nothing should intervene between the individual soul and God, the Christian idea being that everything should so intervene, and thereby be sanctified and blessed to its proper use. In those mediæval ages, as distinguished from the ages that followed them, the natural and the supernatural were intermixed, interfused, interpenetrated and inter-twined, so that, although separable, they were never separated, each serving the other and united in their service. It was understood then that distinction need not lead to disunity where charity–the love of one's neighbour–and justice–the respect for his rights–prevented it from so doing. Life, then, was more coloured, and perhaps less whitewashed, than it is now: there was more unity but less uniformity, and differ-ences, though pronounced, and often most violently so, were less spiritually and socially disintegrating, both among nations and kindreds, than at present. Christendom was an organised whole by virtue of its united faith–faith that was held by all, although, of course, practised in varying degrees. But for all its faith, resting upon a settled belief, it was no period of minted individualism. Because of its faith, it was often riotously happy; and again because of its faith it was often miserably unhappy through its own realised failure to be faithful; but, taken all in

---

[1] *The Legacy of the Middle Ages*, art. "The Christian Life," by Professor F. M. Powicke, p. 28 (Oxford, the Clarendon Press).

all, it was a brighter world than ours, with brighter people in it, enlightened as it was by the sun of a real faith, shining more visibly than
it now does, but shining nevertheless upon the unjust as well as upon
the just.

And now someone may be inclined to say, "But would you really
like to have lived in times so mediæval?" I answer unhesitatingly, "By
all that's reasonable, I would." O to have been in England then, when
God was there, and when, in His great humility and condescension, He
came down upon every altar in every parish church of the ten thousand
in the land! But you may say, "God is still here." Yes, indeed He is; but
who believes it and rejoices in that belief? Just a few scattered souls up
and down the length of the country, the remnant of an Israel of God.

But to return to Tyndale. Accepting 1491 as the approximate date of
his birth, and 1506 as that of his entry at Magdalen Hall, we infer that
he remained at Oxford until about 1519, and then migrated to Cambridge, where he stayed until 1521, the year in which Luther's writings
were publicly burned at that University. We are thus met by the
important consideration that for sixteen years continuously he resided
at one or other of the two great Universities at a time when they, and
indeed the country at large, were entering upon that bewildering
conflict of religious thought which led to our English Reformation.

We know pretty well the course of studies he would have followed
at Oxford from the time of his entry, the taking of his B.A. degree in
1512 and his M.A. in 1515. In fact he has told us about it himself but
surely with some prejudice.[1]

First, they nosel [their young men] in sophistry and in *benefundatum*
[logic]. And there corrupt they their judgments with apparent arguments, and with alleging unto them texts of logic, of natural *philautia*,
of metaphysic, and moral philosophy, and of all manner of books of
Aristotle, and of all manner doctors which they yet never saw. Moreover, one holdeth this, another that; one is a Real, and another a
Nominal. What wonderful dreams have they of their predicaments,
universals, second intentions, quiddities, haecceities, and relatives. . . .
When they have in this wise brawled eight, ten or twelve years and,
after that their judgments are utterly corrupt, they then begin their
divinity; not at the scriptures, but every man taketh a sundry doctor;
which doctors are as sundry and as divers, the one contrary unto the
other, as there are divers fashions and monstrous shapes, none like
another, among our sects of religion. Every religion, every university,
and almost every man hath a sundry divinity.[1]

    [1] Tyndale, *Works, The Obedience of a Christian Man* (1528), vol. i, pp. 157-8.

Our evidence as to Tyndale's personal life at this period is scanty enough. He himself is silent; but Foxe, in his *Acts and Monuments*, tells us that

William Tyndale . . . was . . . brought up from a child in the univer-sity of Oxford, where he by long continuance grew up and increased, as well in the knowledge of tongues and other liberal arts, as especially in the knowledge of the scriptures, whereunto his mind was singularly addicted; in so much that he, lying in Magdalen hall, read privily to certain students and fellows of Magdalen college some parcel of divinity, instructing them in the knowledge and truth of the scriptures.

Demaus, an authoritative biographer, holds that "one thing is certain, the seed [of Protestantism] however or whenever sown, took deep root in his mind. He seems to have subjected all his religious beliefs to a searching examination, and to have applied to them with rigorous logic the standard he found in Holy Scripture. His progress was more rapid and definite than that of his great contemporaries Latimer and Cranmer; and he never exhibited the same reluctance to abandon opinions or practices which had nothing to plead in their favour but custom and the practice of ages. . . . In Tyndale almost from the outset of his career as a public teacher, there is to be noted a clear-ness, a boldness, and withal a freedom from the trammels of ecclesias-tical tradition which produce in the reader's mind a profound admira-tion of the vigour and originality of his intellect."[1]

Foxe then goes on: "Thus he in the university of Oxford increasing more and more in learning, and proceeding in degrees of the schools, spying his time, removed from thence to the university of Cambridge."[2]

He had evidently grown dissatisfied with Oxford, and rather, I think, from intellectual than from religious causes. Oxford, just then, was in a turmoil over the introduction of Greek studies, to which the authorities there seemed very much averse, while at Cambridge, as we know, owing to the influence of Erasmus, they had been accepted as part of the regular university curriculum. And thus at Cambridge Tyndale would find himself in a more congenial atmosphere.

But before leaving Oxford, he was ordained as a priest.

When did his ordination take place?

Mr. Mozley speaks of finding an entry in the Hereford ecclesiastical register to the effect that on June 10th, 1514, the bishop held an ordina-

---

[1] Demaus, *William Tyndale*, p. 41.
[2] Wordsworth, *Eccles. Biog.*, vol. ii, p. 187.

tion at Whitborne at which William Hychens (Tyndale), Hereford
diocese, was granted letters dimissory for the other sacred orders. But
no further trace of his name has as yet been found in the episcopal
registers. Mr. Mozley's opinion, kindly communicated to me, is that
Tyndale's "ordination as a priest is not likely to have been later than
1515". And again, "the conclusion which I come to is that Tyndale was
born in 1491 or 1492 and was ordained priest about 1515", being then
about twenty-three.

It would seem, then, that Demaus had placed Tyndale's doubts about
the Catholic faith too early, and that his wish to leave Oxford had
another cause. At the time of his ordination as a priest, say 1515, and for
some years afterwards he could hardly have been unorthodox, and
what really drove him from Oxford to Cambridge was, as we have
already said, the uncongenial atmosphere arising in the older University
over the introduction of classical studies, which led to those quarrels
between "Greeks" and "Trojans", which, by order of the King himself,
More was sent to Oxford to settle in 1518. Tyndale retained a very
vivid recollection of all this, and, strange to say, in one of his friendlier
passages with More, written about 1531, thirteen years later, he says:
"Remember ye not how within this thirty years and far less, and yet
dureth unto this day, the old barking curs, Dun's disciples, and the like
draff called Scotists, the children of darkness, raged in every pulpit with
their fists for madness, and roaring out with open and foaming mouth,
that if there was but one Terence or Vergil in the world, and that same
in their sleeves, and a fire burning before them, they would burn them
therein, though it should cost them their lives; affirming that all good
learning decayed, and was utterly lost, since men gave them unto the
[classical] Latin tongue?"[1]

In contrast to this, we have a letter written by Erasmus about classical
learning at Cambridge at about the same time:

About thirty years ago nothing was taught at Cambridge but
Alexander (Hales), the *Parva Logicalia*, as they called those old "dic-
tates" of Aristotle, and the questions of Scotus. In process of time good
letters were introduced; the study of Mathematics was added, and a new
or at least a renovated Aristotle. Then came some acquaintance with
Greek, and with many authors whose names were unknown to the
best scholars of a former time. Now I ask what has been the result to the
University? It has become so flourishing that it may vie with the first

[1] Tyndale, *Works*, vol. iii, *An Answer to Sir Thomas More's Dialogue*, p. 75.

schools of the age, and possesses men with whom those old teachers appear mere shadows of theologians. . . . Are your friends displeased that in the future the Gospels and Apostolic Epistles will be read by more persons and with more attention? Are they grieved to see even this portion of time allotted to studies on which all our time would be well bestowed? And would they prefer that our whole life should be consumed in the useless subtleties of "Questions"? Is it not well to recall such divines to the original sources?[1]

And again in 1518, the year before Tyndale's arrival, he writes: "In utraque traduntur Graecae litterae, sed in Cantabrigiae *tranquille*".[2]

As Demaus has been careful to say, "There is no doubt that until he left England, and became acquainted with Luther, Tyndale looked up to Erasmus as his religious guide."[3]

But when, in 1519, Tyndale reached Cambridge, he encountered a generation that knew not Erasmus, but was warming its hands at the fiercer fires of Martin Luther. And, as I have said before,[4] it would be only fair to Erasmus to bear this in mind.

But at this time things were happening at Rome calculated in their effects to reach not only Germany, but England itself. The extravagance, and consequent covetousness, of the papal court was at its worst, so that men as devoted to the Holy See as they were to the Church itself, were saddened and very apprehensive.

Vainly did Aleander in 1516 tell Leo X. that he much feared a revolt on the part of Germany. . . . But no heed was paid to his warning and, in face of the growing fermentation, the Pope committed the error of proclaiming an indulgence for the building of the new basilica of St. Peter's on an even more extensive scale than that proclaimed under Julius II.[5]

Cardinal Ximenes, the greatest of the Spanish prelates, protested, as did the Catholic University of Louvain. And then, to make the matter far worse, Albert of Brandenberg, a young prince of only twenty-five, in order to obtain two other Sees, as well as the one he already had, was compelled by the Roman Curia to pay a fee of 14,000 ducats, together with an extraordinary tax of 10,000 more for this privilege.

To indemnify him, Albert was entrusted with the proclamation of St. Peter's Indulgence in the ecclesiastical province of Mayence and Magdeburg, including the diocese of Halberstadt, and throughout the

---

[1] F. M. Nichols, *Epistles of Erasmus*, vol. ii, pp. 331–2.
[2] P. S. Allen, *Erasmi Epistolae*, tom. iii, p. 546.
[3] Demaus, *William Tyndale*, p. 242.
[4] P. 61.   [5] Pastor, *History of the Popes*, vol. vii, p. 328.

territory of the House of Brandenberg. Half the proceeds were to go towards defraying the expenses of St. Peter's, and the other half to the Archbishop of Mayence. . . . Though the term simony has been applied to this case, it is not quite borne out by the facts. Still the whole thing, looked at from every point of view, was a disgraceful affair for all concerned. That it, together with other causes, led to the impending catastrophe, appears to us like a judgment from heaven.[1]

The following year, 1517, Cooper in his *Annals of Cambridge* speaks of as "the only year in the sixteenth century that he can find nothing worthy of record". And yet in this same year the whole University was startled by an event as notable and significant as any in its history."[2] The occasion of it was this same Indulgence of which we have just spoken. Little could Bishop Fisher have anticipated, when he ordered it to be posted upon the gates of the common schools at Cambridge, that it would herald the coming Reformation in England, even as Luther, when he posted his theses upon the door of the Castle church at Wittenberg, heralded the Reformation in Germany. For at Cambridge, on the very night that the Indulgence was affixed, "a young Norman student, Peter de Valence by name, wrote over the chancellor's proclamation, *Beatus vir cujus est nomen Domini spes ejus, et non respexit in vanitates et insanias falsas ISTAS*. When with the morning the words were discovered, the excitement was intense. Fisher summoned an assembly, and, after explaining and defending the purpose and nature of indulgences, named a day, on or before which the sacrilegious writer was required to reveal himself and to confess his crime and avow his penitence under pain of excommunication.[3]

There is a significant likeness between these two events, happening in the same year, the one at Wittenberg and the other at Cambridge, having the same cause and tending towards the same result.

At any rate, as Mr. Mullinger says, the event "was notable and significant", and must still have been talked about when Tyndale himself arrived in Cambridge in 1519.

Of the friendships he made while there nothing certain is known. Latimer and Cranmer were in residence, but at that time had not yet joined the reformers. Gardiner was there, too, but was less likely to have come across him. Robert Barnes, the prior, and Coverdale, were

---

[1] Pastor, *History of the Popes*, vol. vii, pp. 331–3.
[2] J. B. Mullinger, *University of Cambridge*, p. 556.
[3] *Ib.*, pp. 556–7. It is said, but on doubtful authority, that Peter de Valence repented of his action and received absolution.

at the Augustinian house, and there was John Lambert, all three of whom he came to know on the Continent in later years. Possibly, too, John Frith was there, John Frith who was Tyndale's close disciple and dearest friend at the very last. But, just then, Tyndale seems not to have been at all forthcoming, fearing perhaps to court publicity, and, as far as we can judge, without ambition for place, power or even friendship, desirous only to find a means and condition of life in which unknown and undisturbed he could devote himself to the study of the Scriptures in order to translate them into his own mother tongue.

We do know, however, that he was very unfavourably impressed by the visit of Cardinal Wolsey in 1520 in all the pomp and glory of his high prelatry. And then in 1521, when Luther's writings were burnt in public by the University authorities, he may have thought it better to leave Cambridge and resort "to one Master Welch, a knight of Gloucestershire, there to become a schoolmaster to his children".[1]

There, at Chipping Sodbury, as Mr. Mozley delicately puts it, "we have reason to believe that he was ill at ease in the routine duties of the priesthood".[2] The situation may be left to unfold itself in the quaint words of old Thomas Fuller, not a great admirer of his. Tyndale, he says, "being schoolmaster to Mr. Welch, a bountiful housekeeper in Gloucestershire, to his house repaired many abbots of that country and clergymen, whom Tyndale so welcomed with his discourse against their superstitions, that afterwards they preferred to forbear Master Welch's good cheer rather than have the sour sauce therewith–Master Tyndale's company."[3]

He further annoyed his fellow-priests in the diocese by local preaching of a kind that brought complaints about him to the ears of his vicar-general:

After that, when there was a sitting of the bishop's commissary or chancellor, and warning was given to the priests to appear, Master Tyndale was also warned to be there. . . . So he being there before them, they laid sore to his charge, saying he was an heretic in sophistry (casuistry), an heretic in logic, an heretic in his divinity, and so continueth. But they said unto him: You bear yourself boldly of the gentlemen here in this country, but you shall be otherwise talked with. Then Master Tyndale answered them: *I am content that you bring me where you will into any country within England, giving me ten pounds a year to live*

[1] Foxe, Wordsworth's *Ecclesiastical Biography*, vol. ii, p. 102.
[2] *William Tyndale*, p. 25.
[3] Fuller, *Church History of Britain*, vol. ii, p. 102.

with, *so you bind me to nothing, but to teach children and preach.* Then they had nothing more to say to him, and thus he departed, and went home to his master again.[1]

The words I have put into italics are of a grave significance; for they could have but one meaning: Tyndale, a priest, no longer desired to say Mass.

So he returned to Chipping Sodbury, where of course, had he wished, he could have said Mass in the chapel adjoining the Manor House of Sir John Welch, some remains of which are still to be seen. But, as Foxe goes on:

> . . . being molested and vexed in the country by the priests, he was compelled to seek another place: and so coming to Sir John Welch . . . saying: "Sir, I perceive I shall not be suffered to tarry long here in this country, neither shall you be able, though you would, to keep me out of the hands of the spiritualty, and also what displeasure might grow thereby to you by keeping me." . . . So that, in fine, Master Tyndale with the good will of his master, departed; and eftsoons came up to London, and there preached according as he had done before, and specially about the towne of Bristowe, and also in the said towne, in the common place called S. Austines Greene.
> At length he bethinking himself of Cuthbert Tunstall then bishop of London, and specially for the great commendation of Erasmus, who in his *Annotations* so extolleth him for his learning, thus cast within himself, that if he might attain unto his service he was a happy man. And so coming to sir Henry Gilford, the kings controller, and bringing with him an oration of Isocrates, which he had then translated out of the Greek into English, he desired to speak to the said bishop of London, and to go himself with him. Which he did likewise, and delivered his epistle to a servant of his, named William Hebilthwaite, a man of his acquaintance. But God, who secretly disposeth the course of things, sawe that was not the best for Tyndale's purpose, nor for the profit of his soul; and therefore gave him to find little favour in the bishops sight. The answere of whom was this, that his house was full; he had mo[re] than he could well finde, and advised him to seeke in London abroad, where he said he could lacke no service.[2]

The rebuff which Tyndale then received from the Bishop of London shattered, for the time being, his hopes, and must have hastened his decline into unorthodoxy. Nor could he ever forgive or forget that severe setback. Writing six or seven years later in his *Practice of Prelates*,

---

[1] Foxe, *Acts and Monuments* (1563), quoted by Mozley, *William Tyndale*, pp. 29-30.
[2] Foxe, Wordsworth's *Ecclesiastical Biography*, vol. ii, pp. 192-3.

he could find nothing better to call Bishop Tunstall than "that still Saturn, the imaginer of all mischief".[1]

Foxe then continues:

And so remained he in London the space of almost a year, beholding and marking with himself the course of the world, and especially the demeanour of the preachers, how they boasted themselves and set up their authority and kingdom; beholding also the pompe of the prelates, with other things which greatly misliked him: in so much that he understood, not only there to be no room in the bishop's house for him to translate the new testament: but also there was no place to do it in all England. And therefore finding no place for his purpose within the realm, and having some aid and provision by God's providence ministered unto him by Humphrey Monmouth (a great merchant of London) and certain other good men, he took his leave of the realme and departed into Germany.[2]

Tyndale arrived at Hamburg in the spring of 1524, and, as More puts it, "gat him to Luther straight".[3] Luther was then living at Wittenberg; and Mr. Mozley, by a happy discovery, finds that a certain *Gulielmus Daltici ex Anglia*, who matriculated at the University of Wittenberg on May 27th, 1524, was no other than William Tyndale himself.[4] He remained there nine or ten months, and then paid a visit to Hamburg to get a sum of £10 which had been sent to him from England.

By this time his New Testament was, no doubt, nearly ready.

At Hamburg, having received some money that had come from England, he returned to Wittenberg, where he was joined by one Roye, a friar Observant from Greenwich, an untrustworthy, not to say dangerous person. But, finding that Wittenberg was too far from the coast to allow of easy communication with England, Tyndale, together with Roye, moved on to Cologne, a much more convenient city on the great waterway of the Rhine. A printer was discovered, and all seemed to promise well, when John Cochlaeus, a friend of both Erasmus and of More, happened to pass through the city, and in casual conversation, probably with Roye, heard that three thousand copies of Tyndale's translation of the New Testament were to be conveyed to England as soon as printed. Cochlaeus at once obtained a decree from

[1] Tyndale, *Works*, vol. ii, p. 321.
[2] Foxe, *Wordsworth's Ecclesiastical Biography*, vol. ii, pp. 193-4.
[3] More, *E.W.*, *Dialogue Concerning Tyndale*, bk. iv, c. 17, p. 283 B, and bk. iii, c. 8, p. 227 A.
[4] Mozley, *William Tyndale*, p. 53.

the Senate forbidding the printers to go on with their work; and so
Tyndale and Roye, taking with them the sheets already in print, were
obliged to fly up the Rhine to Worms, and there find another
printer. Cochlaeus took the further precaution of writing to Henry
VIII, to Wolsey and to Fisher, suggesting that a strict watch be kept
upon all the English ports where Tyndale's translation might possibly
find an entry.

Of this Cologne fragment in quarto, which included St. Matthew's
Gospel and probably the beginning chapters of St. Mark, only eight of
the ten sheets remain, and, together with the prologue and glosses, are
now to be seen in the British Museum. In the prologue Tyndale appro-
priates nearly half of Luther's introduction to his own translation, but
it is largely increased by Tyndale's additions. The text, too, glossed on
the outer and inner margins with two sets of notes, is also greatly
indebted to Luther, and altogether of such an unorthodox character as
to compel the English bishops to condemn it and to do their best to
prevent its circulation.

Henry VIII also received another warning from his almoner, Edward
Lee, later to become Archbishop of York. Writing from Bordeaux, he
says:

Please it your highness to understand that I am certainly informed,
as I passed in this country, that an Englishman, your subject, at the
solicitation and instance of Luther, with whom he is, hath translated the
New Testament into English, and within a few days intendeth to arrive,
with the same imprinted, in England.[1]

The printing of Tyndale's octavo edition at Worms, then a Lutheran
stronghold, was completed without interference. It gave just the plain
text, together with a short epistle to the reader.

It was generally held that the quarto edition, begun at Cologne, was
finished at Worms; but Mr. Mozley gives us reason to suppose that it
was not finished, and that Tyndale only printed one New Testament at
Worms, the same octavo edition of which only two copies remain;
"but being unwilling to lose his labour on the Cologne fragment, he
decided to send this also to England, a little in advance of the complete
(octavo) book, as a herald of its coming".[2]

It may be supposed that orthodox translations of the Bible were as
rare abroad as they were in England; but this was not so. Before the end
of the fifteenth century Bibles were printed in Spanish, Italian, French,

---

[1] *L. & P.*, iv, 1802.   [2] *William Tyndale*, pp. 73-4.

Dutch, German and Bohemian, all of them, of course, being secondary versions of the Vulgate. But in England, since the time of Wyclif and the Lollards, the bishops had been very nervous about encouraging translations at all, even orthodox ones. Erasmus, writing to his friend Tunstall, then Bishop of London, in 1525, admires his zeal for the Church (in suppressing heresy); but hopes he will not be like some who, in their earnestness, pull up the wheat with the cockle.[1] There can be no question, however, that when, in the spring of 1526, Tyndale's New Testament had an entry into this country the bishops found reasonable cause for anxiety; and this was not diminished by the numbers imported and the rapidity with which, by means of a secret organisation, they were distributed. Spalatin, a German scholar, records in his diary under August 1526 that "the English in spite of the active opposition of the king were so eager for the gospel . . . that they would buy a New Testament even if they had to give a hundred thousand pieces in money for it". But, in truth, the price of an octavo copy was not ruinous. "For the Worms octavo we hear of prices ranging from 4s. to 1s. 8d.; and the small pirate editions seem to have fetched about a shilling or less. Reduce these sums to modern values," says Mr. Mozley, "you could get a Testament from anything between 15s. and £3 10s., just the sort of price which thousands of working men to-day pay for a bicycle or a wireless set."[2] By April of that year 6000 copies had come from Worms and were being sold in England.

But just before the importation of Tyndale's Testament there had been trouble about heresy. Dr. Barnes, a Cambridge Augustinian prior, had preached an heretical sermon at Christmas, 1525, and on February 11th, 1526, in company with four German merchants of the Steelyard, had borne a faggot at Paul's Cross and listened to a sermon preached by Bishop Fisher. The accused then walked to the fire there enkindled and cast into it their faggots, while basketfuls of Lutheran books were thrown in too. In the summer of 1527 the circulation of the Testament had so increased that the bishops met to consider the matter, as we learn from the preface to Henry VIII's reply to Luther. On October 25th Tunstall summoned the London booksellers and warned them a second time against the importation of Lutheran books, his first warning, two years before, having proved ineffectual. He also issued an injunction to his archdeacons, informing them that the circulation of "the holy gospel

---

[1] P. S. Allen, *Erasmi Epistolae*, vol. iii, 1369, pp. 294–5.
[2] Mozley, *William Tyndale*, p. 80.

of God" had been endangered by the intermingling therewith of heretical glosses. On November 3rd Archbishop Warham addressed the bishops of his province in exactly the same words, and another burning of heretical books took place at Paul's Cross, where Tunstall preached, and spoke of Tyndale's Testament as "naughtily translated". Still later on, the King, who, for reasons connected with the annulment of his marriage with Katherine of Aragon, had taken the censorship into his own hands, issued a further prohibition. But something even more positive had to be done.

On March 7th, 1528, Tunstall granted to his friend More a licence to read and keep certain publications in English of an heretical nature in order that he might write an answer to them also in the vernacular tongue. The most dangerous of these were by Tyndale; and thus there arose, between More and Tyndale, that prolonged controversy which we may now consider.

The causes which in their accumulated effect brought about that great historic change known as the English Reformation were so many and so various, and from time to time have been so differently emphasised by a multitude of writers who did not witness what they had to interpret, that the true proportions of the problem still remain obscure. It can hardly be wrong, therefore, if we return to contemporary witnesses, not only for the evidence of what they saw, but also for their own interpretation of it. For these same events were witnessed by two very distinct groups of men. One group was Catholic in the pre-Reformation sense of that word, and remained so; while the other had been Catholic but did not remain what it had been. Of the former group Sir Thomas More was the most conspicuous layman; while of the latter William Tyndale was a no less able ecclesiastic; and between these two the first great English vernacular controversy upon the doctrines and discipline of the ancient faith took place. As the writer of the article on Tyndale in the *Dictionary of National Biography* remarks:

This contest of Tyndale and More was the classic controversy of the English Reformation. No other discussion was carried on between men of such pre-eminent ability and with so clear an apprehension of the points at issue.[1]

In this contest, so long drawn out, Tyndale's New Testament may be called, without offence, the first offensive gesture; while More's

[1] *D.N.B.*, art. "Tyndale," vol. lvii, p. 427.

Dialogue Concerning Tyndale may be said to have concluded the first round; for a duel it was from beginning to end, and one in which each protagonist was called upon, at the last, to sacrifice his own life for what he believed to be supremely true.

But before we follow the controversy in detail, it would be useful for us to take account of three important treatises written by Tyndale to which More makes reference in the course of his argumentation.

In the year 1528 Tyndale published his *Parable of the Wicked Mammon*, or, as he calls it elsewhere, "my book of the justifying of faith". It is an exposition of Luther's key doctrine of Justification by Faith, and is a clue not only to Luther's theological mind, but also, and perhaps even more, to his tempted and tortured nature—a nature, indeed, so very unlike Tyndale's that we may wonder how Tyndale came to be enamoured of such a doctrine. But perhaps with him it came to express his own longing for union with God rather than any exaggerated sense of delivery from the bondage of sin. The very word *atonement*, at-one-ment, which he introduces for the first time into our own English theological language, seems to bear this out.[1]

A few quotations from *The Parable of the Wicked Mammon* will give us Tyndale in his more devotional and less controversial mood.

Through faith God is one with thee, and thou received to mercy, and art become the son of God, and heir annexed with Christ of all the goodness of God; the earnest whereof is the Spirit of God poured into our hearts.[2]

As man feeleth God to himself, so is he to his neighbour.[3]

Christ is thine, and all his deeds are thy deeds. Christ is in thee, and thou in him, knit together inseparably.[4]

Neighbour is a word of love; and signifieth that a man should ever be nigh, and at hand, and ready to help in time of need.[5]

Prayer is a mourning, a longing, and a desire of the spirit to God-ward for that which she lacketh, as a sick man mourneth and sorroweth in heart, longing for health. Faith ever prayeth.[6]

Faith, the mother of all good works, justifieth us before we can bring forth any good work; and the husband marrieth his wife before he can have any lawful children by her. Furthermore, as the husband marrieth not his wife that she shall continue unfruitful as before, but contrariwise to make her fruitful; even so faith justifieth us not, that is to say, marrieth

---

[1] Strange to say, More uses this same word in his *Life of Richard III* (E.W., p. 40 F), but in an untheological sense, meaning an ordinary reconciliation. See also *Times Literary Supplement*, June 4th, 1925, p. 374.

[2] Tyndale, *Works*, vol. i, p. 71.

[3] P. 77.   [4] P. 79.   [5] P. 85.   [6] P. 93.

us not to God that we shall continue unfruitful as before, but that He should put the seed of the Holy Spirit in us to make us fruitful."[1]

Thou canst never know or be sure of thy faith but by thy works; if works follow not . . . thou mayest be sure thy faith is but a dream.[2]

The next treatise written by Tyndale, and also published, in 1528, was his *Obedience of a Christian Man*. In 1928, Dr. Hensley Henson, preaching in the University church at Cambridge, began his sermon with these words: "Just four centuries have passed since Tyndale published the most famous of his works, *The Obedience of a Christian Man*, a composition to which the historian of English religion will ascribe a critical importance."[3] St. Thomas More spoke of it as the book "whereby we be taught to disobey the doctrine of Christ's Catholic Church and set His holy sacraments at nought";[4] but admitted that its author, "before he gat himself to Luther in Germany, was well-known for a man of right good living, studious and well-learned in scripture, and in divers places in England very much liked and did good with preaching".[5] It may be affirmed, I think, that *The Obedience of a Christian Man*, whether in good repute or bad, stands as a sign in the way at one of the cross-roads of our national and religious life. One may go further and say that it was a magazine from which subsequent reformers took most of their explosive doctrines.

And what gives it still greater importance is the influence it undoubtedly exercised upon Henry VIII, through the urgent persuasion of Anne Boleyn. Strype tells us the story on good authority:

Upon the lady Anne Boleyn waited a fair young gentlewoman, named Mistress Gainford; and in her service also was retained Mr. George Zouch. This gentleman of a comely sweet person, a Zouch indeed, was a suitor in way of marriage to the said young lady and among other love tricks once he plucked from her a book in English, called Tyndale's *Obedience*, which the lady Anne lent her to read. About this time the Cardinal [Wolsey] had given commandment to the prelates, and especially Dr. Sampson, dean of the King's chapel, that they came not abroad; that so much as might be, they might not come to the King's reading. But this which he most feared fell out upon this occasion. For Mr. Zouch (I use the words of the MS.) was so ravished with the spirit of God speaking now as well in the heart of the reader,

---

[1] Tyndale, *Works*, vol. i, pp. 15–6.
[2] P. 60.
[3] *The Church Times*, February 3rd, 1928.
[4] More, *English Works*, *The Confutation of Tyndale*, p. 341 G.
[5] More, *Dialogue Concerning Tyndale*, bk. i, c. 1, p. 7; *E.W.*, p. 108 H.

as first it did in the heart of the maker of the book, that he was never
well but when he was reading of that book. Mistress Gainford wept
because she could not get the book from her lover; and he was as ready
to weep to deliver it. But see the providence of God! Mr. Zouch standing in the chapel before Dr. Sampson, ever reading upon this book, and
the dean never having his eye off the book in the gentleman's hands,
called him to him, and then snatched the book out of his hand, asked
his name, and whose man he was. And the book he delivered to the
Cardinal.

In the meantime the lady Anne shewed herself not sorry nor angry
with either of the two. But said she, "Well, it shall be the dearest book
that ever the dean, or Cardinal, took away."

The noble woman goes to the King, and upon her knees she desireth
the King's help for the book. Upon the King's token the book was
restored. And now bringing the book to him, she besought his Grace,
most tenderly to read it. The King did so, and delighted in the book.
"*For*," saith he, "*this book is for me and all kings to read*."[1]

This saying of Henry VIII's which I have printed in italics reminds me
of another, spoken by Sir Thomas More one day at Chelsea to Thomas
Cromwell:

Master Cromwell, you are now entered into the service of a most
noble, wise and liberal prince: if you follow my poor advice, you shall
in your counsel-giving unto his Grace, ever tell him what he ought to
do, but never what he is able to do. . . . For if a lion knew his own
strength, hard it were for any man to rule him.[2]

Tyndale's treatise on *Obedience* told the lion the secret of his own
strength; and hard indeed were it, after that, for any man to rule him.
For, as Stubbs puts it in another way, not only did Henry VIII, in the
exercise of his power, wish to be the king, the whole king, and nothing
but the king, but, with regard to the Church in England, "he wished to
be the pope, the whole pope, and something more than the pope".[3]

It may therefore be of interest to trace out from the *Obedience* itself
the plan or blue-print of what already was shaping itself in the mind of
the King, not forgetting, however, that there was also a good deal in
the book not at all accordant with the royal mind.

It is true that Henry VIII had quarrelled with the Pope; but in his
inmost mind he seems to have thought that he had no quarrel with the

[1] *Ecclesiastical Memorials*, vol. i, p. 112.
[2] Roper, *Life of Sir Thomas More* (ed. Hitchcock), pp. 56-7.
[3] Stubbs, *Essays on Mediæval and Modern History*, p. 301. Also cf. Gairdner, *Lollardy and the Reformation*, vol. i, p. 305.

H

Catholic religion; and he was assured that with himself as Supreme Head it would go on in England much as before, and perhaps even better than before.[1] It may fairly be said that in his own estimation he was never a Protestant; and in his will, dated only a month before his death, he directs that after his demise his body shall be removed to "his college at Windsor, and the service of *Placebo and Dirge*, with a sermon and Mass on the morrow . . . devoutly to be done and solemnly kept".[2]

In writing his book of *Obedience*, Tyndale went all the way with Henry VIII, in so far as he wished to transfer the spiritual obedience of Englishmen from the Pope to himself. But he went much further than Henry VIII in wishing to discredit, and finally to destroy, the practice of the Catholic religion throughout the country. And this will become evident as we follow the course of his thought.

In his preface he encourages those who are prevented from reading "the word of their soul's health"; and in the prologue he defines his attitude towards the spiritual powers that be: "Forasmuch as our holy prelates and our ghostly religious [that is, the monks and the friars] which ought to defend God's word, speak evil of it . . . therefore have I made this little treatise that followeth."[3]

Tyndale first describes the nature and necessity of obedience on the part of children to their parents, of wives to their husbands, and of servants to their masters. Then he comes to the consideration of obedience in its principal exercise–namely, that unto kings, princes and rulers.

"There is no power but of God"; by power understand the authority of kings and princes. "The powers that be are ordained of God"; yea, though he be pope, bishop, monk or friar, "they that shall resist shall receive unto themselves damnation." Why? For God's word is against them, which will have all men under *the temporal sword*. . . . With good living ought the spiritualty to rid themselves from the fear of the temporal sword; and not with craft, and with blinding the kings, and bringing the vengeance of God upon them, and in purchasing license to sin unpunished.

Furthermore, though he [the king] be the greatest tyrant in the world, yet is he unto thee a great benefit of God, and a thing wherefore thou oughtest to thank God highly.[4]

[1] But see Froude, *History of England*, vol. iv, p. 212, seemingly on Foxe's authority.
[2] *Ib.*, p. 233.
[3] Tyndale, *Works*, vol. i; *Doctrinal Treatises* (Parker Society), p. 163.
[4] *Ib.*, p. 179.

It is not surprising that when Henry VIII read this "little treatise", he found in it some very comfortable doctrine, especially as, at the time, he was quarrelling with the Pope.

In another section Tyndale supports his stark theory of an absolute royal power by saying that the law was given as a witness against sin and to express God's abhorrence of it.

Governors are ordained of God. If they are evil, it is because of our sins, and a sign of God's anger. . . . Resistance to evil rulers only deepens the bondage of sin; submission will lead God to deliver his children. . . . A Christian in respect of God is but a passive thing.

Christ saith unto Peter, "Put up thy sword into his sheath; for all that lay hand upon the sword shall perish with the sword"; that is, whosoever without commandment of the temporal officer, to whom God hath given the sword, layeth hand on the sword to take vengeance, the same deserveth death in the deed-doing. God did not put Peter only under the temporal sword, but also Christ himself. . . . If then the head be under the temporal sword, how can the members be excepted?[1]

Again Tyndale justifies kingly tyranny by saying:

If thy rulers were always kind, thou shouldst not know whether thine obedience were pure or no; but if thou canst patiently obey evil rulers in all thing that is not to the dishonour of God, and when thou hurtest not thy neighbours, then art thou sure that God's Spirit worketh in thee, and that thy faith is no dream nor any false imagination.

Then follows some good counsel:

Dearly beloved, avenge not yourselves, but give room unto the wrath of God: for it is written, "Vengeance is mine, saith the Lord. Therefore if thy enemy hunger, feed him; if he thirst, give him to drink; for in so doing, thou shalt heap coals of fire upon his head"; that is, let not another man's wickedness make thee wicked also, "but overcome evil with good"; that is, with softness, kindness, and all patience win him, even as God with kindness won thee.

But a few lines later he returns to his constantly recurring theme:

As the law is a terrible thing, even so is the king: for he is ordained to take vengeance, and hath a sword, and not peacock feathers [as the pope hath]. Fear him, therefore, as thou wouldst look on a sharp sword that hanged over thy head by a hair.[2]

Was not that sword an ever-present and very real menace in Henry VIII's time?

[1] Tyndale, *Works,* vol. i; *Doctrinal Treatises* (Parker Society), p. 188.
[2] *Ib.,* pp. 193–4.

Evil rulers then are a sign that God is angry and wroth with us. Is it not a great wrath and vengeance that the father and mother should hate their children, even their flesh and their blood? or that a husband should be unkind to his wife, or a master unto the servant that waiteth on his profit? or that lords and kings should be tyrants unto their subjects and tenants, which pay them tribute, toll, custom, and rent, labouring and toiling to find them in honour and to maintain them in their estate? Is not this a fearful judgment of God, and a cruel wrath, that the very prelates and shepherds of our souls which were wont to feed Christ's flock with Christ's doctrine, and to walk before them in living thereafter, and to give their lives for them, to their ensample and edifying, and to strengthen their weak faiths, are now sore changed, that if they smell that one of their flock do but once long or desire for the true knowledge of Christ, they will slay him, burning him with fire most cruelly? What is the cause of this? . . . Verily it is the hand of God to avenge the wickedness of them that have no love or lust unto the truth of God when it is preached. . . .[1]

Let us receive all things of God, whether it be good or bad: let us humble ourselves under his mighty hand, and submit ourselves unto his nurture and chastising, and not withdraw ourselves from his correction. Read Hebrews xii for thy comfort; and let us not take the staff by the end, or seek to avenge ourselves on his rod, which is the evil rulers. . . .[2]

Whensoever the children of Israel fell from the way which God had commanded them to walk in, he gave them up under one tyrant or another. As soon as they came to the knowledge of themselves, and repented, crying for mercy, and leaning unto the truth of his promises, he sent one to deliver them, as the histories of the Bible make mention.

A Christian man, in respect of God, is but a passive thing; a thing that suffereth only, and doth nought; as the sick, in respect of the surgeon or physician, doth but suffer only. . . . Now if the sick resist the razor, the searching iron, and so forth, doth he not resist his own health, and is cause of his own death? So likewise is it of us, if we resist evil rulers, which are the rod and scourge wherewith God chastiseth us; the instruments wherewith God searcheth our wounds; and bitter drinks to drive out the sin and to make it appear, and caustics to draw out by the roots the core of the pocks of the soul that fretteth inward.[3]

Then follows a sentiment, often repeated by Tyndale, that adversity in its varying forms does but help to show forth, utter and bring to light secret and inward sin, in that it may be recognised and the more easily overcome. "A Christian man knoweth every thing how to live, yet is the flesh so weak, that he can never take up his cross himself, to

[1] Tyndale, *Works*, vol. i, p. 195.   [2] P. 196.   [3] P. 197.

kill and mortify the flesh: he must have another to lay it on his back."[1]

He concludes this section by saying that, as he has just described the obedience of them that are under power and rule, even so in what is to come he will declare how the rulers themselves, which God shall vouchsafe to call unto the knowledge of the truth, ought to rule.

His first instruction is to kings:

The most despised person in the realm ought to be treated as if he were the king's brother and fellow-member with him in the kingdom of God and of Christ. Let the King, therefore, not think himself too good to do service to such humble people nor seek any other thing in them than a father seeketh, yea than Christ sought in us. Though that the king, in temporal regiment, be in the room of God, and representeth God Himself, and is without comparison better than his subjects; yet let him put off that, and become a brother, doing and leaving undone all things in respect of his commonwealth, that all men may see that he seeketh nothing but the profit of his subjects."[2]

Nor is he afraid to venture a keen thrust at the King's own weaknesses by warning him, in the words of Moses, not to have too many wives, lest his heart be turned away: for women (and pride) are the common pestilence of all princes. Read the stories and see.[3]

Tyndale then exhorts all princes "to rule their realms with the help of *laymen* that are sage, wise, learned, and expert. Is it not a shame above all shames and a monstrous thing, that no man should be found able to govern a worldly kingdom save bishops and prelates, that have forsaken the world and are taken out of the world, and appointed to preach the kingdom of God? . . . To preach God's word is too much for half a man: to minister a temporal kingdom is too much for half a man also. Either requireth a whole man. One cannot well do both."[4]

This good counsel may have had some effect; for More was made Chancellor at the end of the following year.

He uses a powerful argument against the exercise of secular authority by the spiritualty.

One cannot do both [he says]. He that avengeth himself on every trifle is not meet to preach the patience of Christ, how that a man ought to forgive and suffer all things. He that is overwhelmed with all manner of riches, and doth seek more, daily, is not meet to preach poverty. He that will obey no man is not meet to preach how we ought

[1] Tyndale, *Works,* vol. i, p. 198.　　　[2] Pp. 202–3.
[3] P. 204.　　　　　　　　　　　　　　[4] Pp. 206–7.

to obey all men. Peter saith, Acts vi, "It is not meet that we [the spiritualty] should leave [preaching] the word of God, and serve tables." Paul saith in the sixth chapter of first Corinth, "Woe is me if I preach not." A terrible saying, verily, for popes, cardinals and bishops! If he had said, "Woe be unto me if I fight not and move princes to war, or if I increase not St. Peter's patrimony", as they call it, it had been a more easy saying for them.[1]

And here he touches upon one of the weakest spots in the pre-Reformation Church, and in words that remind us of what Father Bridgett has written in his *Life of St. John Fisher*, "Neglect of preaching was perhaps the greatest evil in the 15th century, and the source of every other."[2] It has been remarked too that the sermon, so neglected by the Catholic clergy, very shortly afterwards became the most effective weapon of the Reformers. On this point, at any rate, Tyndale and Fisher were at one, although upon every other they were at bitter difference, as we have had occasion to realise in many a page of the *Obedience*.

Mark, I pray you [he writes], what an orator is Rochester. . . . Martin Luther hath burned the pope's decretals; a manifest sign, saith he, that he would have burned the pope's holiness also, if he had had him! A like argument, which I suppose to be rather true, I make: Rochester and his holy brethren have burnt Christ's testament; an evident sign, verily, that they would have burnt Christ himself, if they had had him![3]

Finally:

I had almost, verily, left out the chiefest point of all. . . . Rochester will have love to go before, and faith to spring out of love. Thus antichrist turneth the root of the tree upwards. I must love a bitter medicine (after Rochester's doctrine), and then believe that it is wholesome, and that the bitterness shall heal me: when, by natural reason, I first hate a bitter medicine until I am brought in belief that it is wholesome, and that the bitterness shall heal me; and then afterward love it, of that belief. Doth the child love the father first, and then believe that he is son or heir? or rather, because he knoweth that he is son or heir and beloved, therefore loveth again? . . . Because we are sons, therefore love we. Now by faith we are sons, therefore love we, as John saith in the first chapter of his gospel: "He gave them power to be the sons of God, in that they believed on his name." We are all sons of God by the faith which is in Jesus Christ.[4]

[1] Tyndale, *Works*, vol. i, p. 222. [2] P. 105.
[3] P. 221. [4] P. 222.

See in my book of the Justifying of Faith (*The Parable of the Wicked Mammon*) and there shalt thou see all things abundantly. How faith justifieth before God in the heart; and how love springeth of faith and compelleth us to work; and how the works *justify before the world*, and testify what we are, and certify that our faith is unfeigned, and that the right Spirit of God is in us.[1]

So therefore, though Rochester be a beast faithless, yet ought natural reason to have taught him, that love springeth out of faith and knowledge; and not faith and knowledge out of love.[2]

Wicked sinners have no faith. It is another thing to believe that the king is rich, and that he is rich unto me, and that my part is therein; and that he will not spare a penny of his riches at my need. When I believe that the king is rich, I am not moved; but when I believe that he is rich for me, and that he will never fail me at my need, then love I; and of love am ready to work unto the uttermost of my power.[3]

But let us return at the last unto our purpose again. *What is the cause that laymen cannot now rule*, as well as in times past, and as the Turks yet do? Verily because that antichrist [the Pope] with the mist of his juggling hath beguiled our eyes . . . and hath taught Christian men to dread not God and his word, but himself and his word, not God's law and ordinances, princes and officers which God hath set to rule the world, but his own laws and ordinances, traditions and ceremonies, and disguised disciples.[4]

Tyndale then goes on to attack the Mass, and carries, not his criticism, but rather his mockery of it beyond all bounds.

What helpeth it . . . that the priest, when he goeth to mass, disguiseth himself with a great part of the passion of Christ, and playeth out the rest under silence, with signs and proffers, with nodding, becking and mowing, as it were jackanapes, when neither he himself, neither any man else wotteth what he meaneth?[5]

And that Tyndale's mockery of the holy action of the Mass effected what he wished may be seen from the list of "Articles to be followed and observed, according to the injunctions" of Edward VI in 1549, the second of which enjoins:

That no minister do counterfeit the popish mass, as to kiss the Lord's table; washing his fingers at every time in the communion; blessing his eyes with the paten, or crossing his head with the paten; shifting of the book from one place to another; laying down and licking the chalice of the communion; holding up his fingers, hands, thumbs, joined towards his temples; breathing upon the bread, etc.

[1] Tyndale, *Works*, vol. i, pp. 222–3.   [2] P. 223.
[3] P. 224.   [4] P. 224.   [5] P. 226.

We see, too, how, with this charge of "disguise", Tyndale, at a stroke, does away with all vestments used in the Holy Sacrifice or at other times.

God anointed his son Jesus with the Holy Ghost, and therefore called him Christ; which is as much as to say as anointed. Outwardly he disguised him not; but made him like other men, and sent him into the world to bless us, and offer himself for us a sacrifice of a sweet savour.

Whosoever goeth about to make satisfaction for his sins to Godward, saying in his heart: This much have I sinned, this much will I do again; or this-wise will I live to make amends withal; or this will I do to get heaven withal; the same is an infidel, faithless and damned in his deed-doing, and hath lost his part in Christ's blood.[1]

There is a word called in Latin *sacerdos*, in Greek *hiereus*, in Hebrew *cohan*, that is a minister, an officer, a sacrificer or a priest. . . . And in the English should it have had some other name than priest. . . . Of that manner is Christ a priest for ever; and all we priests through him, and need no more any such priests on earth, to be a mean for us unto God.[2]

This last sentence is condemned as heresy. As More puts it:

Tyndale teacheth plainly that the blessed sacrament is, in the mass, no sacrifice, none host, nor none oblation; by which abominable heresy he taketh quite away the very special profit and fruit of all the mass.[3]

By a priest then [continues Tyndale], in the New Testament, understand nothing but an elder to teach the younger.[4]

At the conclusion of this section Tyndale describes the clergy as "unlearned in the secrets of the faith", men at once "stubborn and headstrong, and who set not a little by themselves. But, alas, we have about 20,000 of them that know no more scripture than is written in their portesses [breviaries]; and among them he is exceedingly well learned that can turn to, his service," that is, find his place easily.[5]

Tyndale, it would seem, would have discarded much in the practice of religion, which for centuries had given it order, beauty, gravity, decorum and devotion. "Is not that shepherd's hook, the bishop's cross, a false sign? Is not that white rochet? . . . What other things are their sandals, gloves, mitres, and all the whole pomp of their disguising, than false signs in which Paul prophesied they should come?"[6] And what added to his anger was that so many of these things were connected with the generous offerings of the faithful. Nothing, he says, can be

---

[1] Tyndale, *Works*, vol. i, p. 228.   [2] P. 255.
[3] More, *E.W.*, *Confutation*, p. 390 H.   [4] Tyndale, *Works*, vol. i, p. 256.
[5] *Ib.* p. 229.   [6] *Ib.* p. 252.

done unless the laity must pay for it. "They [the clergy] will lose nothing. Why? It is God's; it is not theirs. It is St. Hubert's rents, St. Alban's lands, St. Edmund's right, St. Peter's patrimony, say they, and none of ours." Much they get for so little painstaking on their part—offerings at weddings, offerings at buryings, offerings to images, offerings of wax-lights and candles, offerings to brotherhoods and pardoners.

What get they also by confessions? Yea, and many enjoin penance, to give a certain [sum] for to have so many masses said, and desire to provide a chaplain themselves; soul-masses, dirges, month-minds, year-minds, All-souls day and trentals. The mother church and the high altar must have something in every testament. Offerings at the priests' first masses, the hallowing, or rather conjuring of churches, chapels, altars, super-altars, chalices, vestments, copes, altar-clothes, surplices, towels, basins, ewers, ships [incense-boats], censers, and all manner of ornament, must be found them freely; they will not give a mite thereunto. Last of all, what swarms of begging friars are there! The parson sheareth, the vicar shaveth, the parish priest polleth, the friar scrapeth, and the pardoner pareth; we lack but the butcher to pull off the skin.[1]

Then comes a last counsel meant, unmistakably, for the King himself:

The kings ought, I say, to remember that they are in God's stead, and ordained of God, not for themselves, but for the wealth of their subjects. . . . Therefore ought they to pity them, and to rid them from such wily [priestly] tyranny, which increaseth more and more daily.[2]

And here we may leave this book of "Obedience", which taught disobedience to so many, so opposed as it is to what Tyndale calls pope-holiness, and so partial to what, on the contrary, perhaps, we may be allowed to call king-holiness, the king in question being Henry VIII.

The third important treatise of Tyndale's was his *Practice of Prelates*, published towards the end of 1530. It was intended, in the first place, to be a defence of the marriage of Queen Katherine; for, unlike other English reformers, Tyndale took the pains to inform himself on the matter, and be it said "to his credit, he was entirely against the divorce".[3] But when the book appeared this vexed question occupied only a few pages at the end. "I did my diligence", wrote Tyndale, "a long season to know what reasons . . . should make for the divorcement; but I

---

[1] Tyndale, *Works,* vol. i, pp. 237–8.
[2] Pp. 239–40.
[3] Gairdner, *Lollardy and the Reformation,* vol. i, p. 376.

could not come by them."[1] Wolsey, he contends, originated the miserable business, and so angry is he with the Cardinal on this account that the book becomes largely a tirade against prelacy. "Thomas Wolf-see" is the nickname he gives to the Cardinal in order to call his readers' attention to that great prelate's weakness for ecclesiastical preferment.[2]

Gairdner considers the treatise "a very absurd quasi-historical review of the misdeeds of prelates", adding "that it was naturally offensive to Henry VIII who was at that time persuing his great aim of a divorce through thick and thin".[3] Mr. Mozley is constrained to admit that the *Practice of Prelates* was "that work of Tyndale which we could most readily spare".[4] But, like the other two treatises, it helps us to understand the controversy which he was then carrying on with St. Thomas More. A few typical passages may be better than further comment.

In his preface "to the Christian reader" he writes, "Take heed . . . wicked prelates, blind leaders of the blind; indurate and obstinate hypocrites, take heed!"[5]

Whatsoever soundeth to make for your bellies, and to maintain your honour, whether in the scripture, or in your own traditions, or in the pope's law, that ye compel the lay-people to observe; violently threatening them with your excommunications and curses, that they shall be damned both body and soul, if they keep them not. And if that help you not, then ye murder them mercilessly with the sword of the temporal powers; whom ye have made so blind that they be ready to slay whom ye command, and will not yet hear his cause examined, nor give him room to answer for himself.[6]

He reproves them, not without cause, for neglecting to preach, which is their proper business.

Prelates appointed to preach Christ may not leave God's word and minister temporal offices; but ought to teach the lay people the right

---

[1] Tyndale, *Works*, vol. ii, p. 332.

[2] In 1514 Wolsey became Bishop of Lincoln with Tournai as well, and later in the year Archbishop of York. "In virtue of his legatine authority he enjoyed the spiritualities of all English bishoprics during vacancy, and 'farmed' the bishoprics of Salisbury, Worcester, and Llandaff to five non-resident aliens who merely received fixed stipends from their sees. It was almost unprecedented for an English archbishop to hold an English bishopric *in commendam* and it was a still more flagrant abuse for a secular priest like Wolsey to hold such an improper *commendam* as St. Alban's said to be the richest abbey in England." A. F. Pollard, *Wolsey*, pp. 173–4. In justice to Wolsey, it should be said that pluralism was the custom of that time. Even so good a man as Dean Colet held many benefices.

[3] *Lollardy and the Reformation*, vol. i, p. 376.

[4] *William Tyndale*, p. 169.

[5] *Tyndale, Works*, vol. ii, p. 242.   [6] P. 243.

way, and leave all temporal business to them. Christ called his disciples unto him, and said: "Ye know that the lords of the heathen people have dominion over them; and they that be great do exercise power over them. Howbeit, it shall not be so among you. . . . Wherefore the officers in Christ's kingdom may have no temporal dominion or jurisdiction, nor execute any temporal authority or law of violence."[1] The world, truly, can see no other way to rule than with violence; for there no man abstaineth, but for fear; because the love of righteousness is not written in their hearts.[2]

From all this we cannot but gather that Tyndale, though in character unexceptionable, and brave to a fault, was in disposition over-serious, narrow in mind, untimely in discussion and irritable in controversy, growing more and more averse to Catholic belief and practice as the years went on, a very close student of the Scriptures, but in the interpretation of them inclined to abound in his own sense rather than in that of "the old holy fathers and doctors of the Church".

[1] *Tyndale, Works,* vol. ii, p. 247.　　[2] P. 249.

8

More's Dialogue Concerning Tyndale

WE COME now to the great vernacular religious controversy between William Tyndale and Sir Thomas More, which, on More's side, begins with *A Dialogue Concerning Heresies and Matters of Religion made in 1528 by Sir Thomas More* or, as we may call it, *The Dialogue Concerning Tyndale,* to distinguish it from his better-known *Dialogue of Comfort against Tribulation,* written six years later, when he was a prisoner in the Tower of London. It consists of four books, with a short preface, and runs to some 170,000 words, its immediate occasion being the distribution throughout the country of Tyndale's English version of the New Testament.

It begins with a prefatory note in which More explains that a right worshipful friend of his had sent him a confidential Messenger to ask his advice on certain matters of faith which, though very certain in themselves, were just then being called in question. After he had delivered his mind unreservedly and at great length to this Messenger, he thought it well to write out what he had said, and finally, lest it should be misreported, to publish it. But before doing this he had taken great care to have the advice of certain friends who were expert theologians. We may say, therefore, that what is published in the *Dialogue* is authoritatively representative of the Catholic doctrine held at the time upon all matters arising in dispute between men of the old faith and those of the new. In doctrine More speaks as the mouthpiece of the Church; but the sentiments and comments that accompany his doctrinal statements are, of course, his own. His own, too, is the expression, undoubtedly severe, of his hatred and loathing of the heretical opinions he brings under review. Here, indeed, we get the light and shade of a picture drawn very true to his time; for in a world, rightly deserving the name of Christendom, sustained, enlightened and warmed by the sun of high spiritual certitude, absence of light and shade would be impossible. That which obscured the sun, though it were but a passing cloud of heresy, must needs leave its shadow upon a land that previously had rejoiced in the sunlight.

More strongly objected to Tyndale not because he translated the New Testament, but because his translation was unauthorised and unorthodox. Older translations, he said, were still in existence, and a new one, favoured by the King and approved by the more influential clergy, was said to be forthcoming. Erasmus in 1515 had put in a plea for vernacular translations; but the appearance in 1522 of Luther's heretical version had, at any rate for the time, "clouded the practice of translation with the suspicion of heresy". Yet More spoke cautiously in its favour:

The fear [which some of the clergy had of an authorised translation] nothing feareth me; but whosoever would of their malice and folly take harm of that thing that is of itself ordained to do all men good, I would never, for the avoiding of their harm, take from other the profit which they might take, and nothing deserve to lose. *For else, if the abuse of a good thing should cause the taking away thereof from another that would use it well, Christ should himself have never been born.*[1]

Surely no sounder argument for the publication of an authorised version of the New Testament has ever been used? Moreover, it explains and justifies More's disagreement, on the one hand, with those who wanted no vernacular translation at all, and his opposition, on the other, to men like Tyndale and Luther, who were distributing translations that were not only unauthorised, but were also deliberately subversive of Catholic teaching. More continues:

My mind giveth me that his Majesty is of his blessed zeal so minded to move this matter of an authorised version unto the prelates and clergy, among who I have perceived some of the greatest and best of their own minds well inclinable thereto already, that we lay people shall in this matter, ere long time pass, except the fault be found in ourself, be well and fully satisfied and content.[2]

The sad irony was that in 1537, eight years later, his Majesty was moved, "of his blessed zeal", to authorise a vernacular translation; but it was after More's martyrdom, and the translation was Tyndale's own, revised by Miles Coverdale for his second edition.

But before we come to a detailed examination of More's *Dialogue* we may speak of its general character, and perhaps, too, of the character of the period in which it was written. The men and women we come across in our reading of the *Dialogue* had some qualities worth our attention. They were, for instance, a people honest with each other and with themselves in a way that ordinary people of to-day have

---

[1] *E.W., Dialogue*, bk. iii, c. 16, p. 241 G.   [2] *Ib.*, p. 241 G.

perhaps less occasion to be; for in the confessional they learned to know themselves as they truly were, facing with an always difficult but certainly genuine candour their own sins and failings and inordinate desires, and, what was more, realising them in all their dreadful consequences as visited upon our Lord Himself in the sufferings of His earthly life and His passion and death upon the Cross. Certain passages in the *Dialogue* occur as an illustration of this. In one place More is talking about the idea then, and perhaps always, popular, that people should go less to church and pray more in private. "If churches and congregations of Christian people were once abolished and put away," he says, "we were like to have few good temples of God in men's souls." [1] Or again, the Messenger brings forward a charge of idolatry against people who venerate the saints and pray before statues. "What is idolatry?" he exclaims:

It is not, as heretics lay to the charge of good people, reverence to the saints or honour to their images, but doing as do those heretics themselves, making our belly or beneath our belly, or goods, or our own blind affection towards other creatures, or our own proud affection and dotage towards ourself, our mammots and idols very false. [2]

Again he speaks of the crucifix:

If then ye set aught by the name of Jesus, written or spoken: why should ye set naught by his image painted or carven that representeth His holy person to your remembrance, as much, and more too, than doth His name written? . . . And yet these heretics forbear not villainously to handle and cast dirt upon the holy crucifix, an image made in the remembrance of our Saviour Himself, and not only of His most blessed person, but also of His bitter passion. [3]

Then, as now, many were "naught", as More would have said, and few were "aught" to speak of; but men and women in those times, realising their natural frailty and repeated weaknesses, asked help from heaven. To them God was stronger than man, grace than sin, and love than lust. Such was their humility, a very different thing from that clammy and revolting vice Dickens has taught us to despise in the person of Uriah Heep. Whatever humility then was, it was not a mask. It was rather a tearing away of the mask that hid a man from himself. It consisted, by the grace of God, in getting so clear a sight of one's own condition that one knew what manner of man one was—and

[1] *E.W.*, *Dialogue*, bk. i, c. 3, p. 30.　　[2] *Ib.*, c. 7, p. 41.　　[3] *Ib.*, c. 2, p. 21.

was not. It was, too, the foundation virtue of all solid piety. It taught men to be less willing to criticise others. "To say the truth," writes More, "I am of myself so little mistrusting that he were like very plainly to show himself naught whom I should take for bad."

Or, in another place, where the Messenger is criticising the clergy, More replies:

Now where ye say that ye see more vices in them than in yourself, truth it is that everything in them is greater because they are bounden to be better. But else, the things they misdo be the selfsame that we sin in ourself—which vices that, as ye say, we see more in them than in ourself, the cause is, I suppose, for we look more upon theirs than on our own; and fare, as Aesop saith in a fable, that every man carrieth a double wallet on his shoulder; and into the one that hangeth at his breast he putteth other folks' faults and therein he toteth [looketh] and poteth [upon] often. In the other, he layeth all his own, and swingeth it at his back, which himself never listeth to look in; but other that come after him cast an eye into it among. Would God we were all of the mind that every man thought no man so bad as himself. For that were the way to mend both them and us.[1]

More believed that the reversal of these two wallets was an essential part of true conversion.

But if humility was the foundation of piety, *charity* was its inspiration. It is probable that, since the Reformation, no word in our language has suffered so sad a change in popular meaning as this word "charity". And Tyndale did much to bring about the change. Charity in its social sense was in More's day a high and holy virtue, holy in its exercise and holy in the unashamed humility with which it was accepted. But now there is nothing more detested by humble folk than "charity". For after the Reformation it came to be administered in a way so detestable that it put a stigma upon anyone who was obliged to receive it. Dr. Johnson gave it four meanings in his Dictionary—"tenderness, goodwill, alms given to the poor, and the theological virtue of universal love", illustrating its meaning by a quotation from Hooker: "Concerning *charity* the final object whereof is that incomprehensible beauty which sheweth in the countenance of Jesus Christ the Son of the living God." But even in this last sense, spiritual as it is, it falls short of its fullest spiritual meaning.

In the eighth chapter of the third book of the *Dialogue*, More accuses

---

[1] *E.W.*, *Dialogue*, bk. iii, c. 11, p. 215; cf. also c. 13, p. 229.

Tyndale of having changed the word *charity* into the word *love* in his translation of the New Testament with the deliberate intention of discrediting the current teaching of the Church. "For although charity", he says, "be always love, yet is not, ye wot well, love always charity". He then discusses with the Messenger the difference between the two words as then commonly understood. "But now, whereas charity signifieth in Englishmen's ears not every common love, but a good, virtuous and well-ordered love, he that will (as Tyndale doth) studiously flee from that name of good love, and always speak of 'love' and leave out the 'good', I would surely say that he meaneth naught." He concludes, therefore, that Tyndale has altered it "in order to minish the reverent mind that men bear to charity, and therefore he changeth the name of holy virtuous affection into the bare name of love, common to the virtuous love that man beareth to God and to the lewd love that is between some worthless fellow and his mate".[1]

Charity meant to More, and to every other Catholic, that degree of supernatural love for God enjoyed by each particular soul in a state of grace.

And this supernatural state is one to which a man by his own efforts can never attain, one which is entirely beyond his deserts, and in which he is raised to the dignity of an adopted son of God and is endowed by grace with the powers befitting his new status.

Charity, then, is the key-word of the Catholic faith; and Tyndale's object, as More points out (and Tyndale did not deny in his *Answer* to More), was to displace it by the commoner word "love", and thus to make way for the key-word of Protestantism, which was *faith*—a faith, as they believed, sufficient in itself for salvation, without works and without charity.[2]

One last consideration upon the difference between natural love and supernatural charity, and upon the way the one may be changed into the other. We are taught by the divine authority of the Church that, as children of Adam, we are all *naturally selfish*—not naturally bad, but naturally selfish and self-centred. But we are also taught that if we make prayer our constant habit, and use all the other means of grace that God has given us, we may become by degrees *supernaturally unselfish*.

[1] E.W., *Dialogue*, bk. iii, c. 8, pp. 221 D to 222 B.
[2] Cf. E.W., *Dialogue*, bk. iv, c. 2, pp. 282 ff., where More discusses with the Messenger the difference between *faith* as defined by the Church and by Luther; and its connection with *charity* and *good works*.

Naturally speaking, a man has one tingling centre of reality, and that is himself. He may speak of God, and argue about God, and even dream about God; but, for all that, he is more real and personal to himself than God is to him. But with a man of prayer, who uses all the available means of grace, exactly the opposite is the case. He gradually becomes unselfish by virtue of the charity of God. He has now two centres of personal reality, God and himself; and, of the two, God is the more real. God becomes more intimately real and personally present to him than he is personally present and real to himself. And if there is one true thing to be said about a man who makes prayer and the use of the available means of grace his main and determining activities, it is that he is unselfish; nay, more, that he is becoming supernaturally selfless. He is a man becoming more and more emptied of self, and more and more filled with the divine charity of God. Such a man is ready, as none else are ready, to become the fitting, because selfless, instrument of the divine purpose as it works itself out in the world.

Thus it was that More, seeing the importance of this distinction, strenuously opposed Tyndale's substitution of the word *love* for the word *charity* in rendering the New Testament into English.

And there is one more note of pre-Reformation Christian piety in England to which we may call attention—*unity*.

Unity, whether individual or institutional, is always the outward and visible sign of an inwardly well-ordered life. But there is more than one kind of unity—a unity of faith as well as a unity of practice. Children, who utterly and always believe in their mother and father and in the truth of what their mother and father tell them, may not, however, always do what their mother and father tell them to do. And as in the natural family so in the great supernatural family of the Church. The obedience of the faith is one thing, and the obedience of practice another. Because the children of the Church are not always good men and women they are not always at unity with the Church in practice; but, on the other hand, as faithful children of the Church, they are always one with the Church in faith. *Unity of faith*, therefore, was a mark of the pre-Reformation Catholic piety, as it has been, and will always be, its mark throughout the ages. And this was a thing that More felt bound, at all costs, to defend; it was also a thing which he clearly realised that Tyndale was likely to destroy.

We now pass to the *Dialogue* in a more particular way. As its name tells us, it was cast in the form of a discussion between two people—the

I

Messenger, "wise, more than meanly learned, [with] a very merry wit",[1] being one, and Sir Thomas More, to whom the Messenger has been sent for information on all matters of the faith just then in question, the other. The Messenger raises all these issues in turn, while More answers them with care and in detail, but also with "a very merry wit, and to the best of his knowledge, ability and wide experience. His argument may be likened to a tree with many branches—the trunk being the divinely-given, divinely-inspired and divinely-preserved Catholic Church. By this authority the Church, through the ages, has been able to determine rightly, and rightly to interpret, the Scriptures and also to declare what is true and what untrue in all matters of faith and practice as from time to time they may be called in question. If this tree stood, all stood with it; but if it fell, nothing else could remain standing in the Christian way of life. The Church, then, was the supreme Teacher. The reformers proclaimed, on the contrary, that each individual, independently of the Church, was able to teach himself, having private judgment in all doctrinal matters. Treating, therefore, of the *Dialogue* in its logical rather than in its chronological order, we will begin with this most important issue.

The Messenger wants to know More's mind on the recent burning of Tyndale's Testament, "lately translated and, as men say, right well, which maketh man marvel much of its burning".

To this More makes reply:

It is, quod I, to me a great marvel that any good Christian man, having any drop of wit in his head, would anything marvel or complain of the burning of the book, if he know the matter. . . . For so hath Tyndale, after Luther's counsel, corrupted and changed it from the good and wholesome doctrine of Christ . . . that it was a clean contrary thing.

That were a marvel, quod your friend, that it should be so clean contrary; for to some that read it, it seemed very like.

It is, quod I, nevertheless contrary, and yet the more perilous. For like as to a true silver groat as false copper groat is nevertheless contrary, though it be quicksilvered over, but so much the more false in how much it is counterfeited the more like to the truth.

Why, quod your friend, what faults were there in it?

To tell you that, quod I, were in a manner to rehearse you all the whole book wherein there were founden and noted wrong and falsely translated above a thousand texts by tale.

[1] *E.W.*, 107 G.

I would, quod he, fain hear some.[1]

More then points out certain key-words changed by Tyndale in his translation:

> *Priests* to *seniors*,
> *Church* to *congregation*,
> *Charity* to *love*,
> *Grace* to *favour*,
> *Penance* to *repentance*,
> *Confession* to *knowledge*,
> *Contrite* to *troubled*.

The Messenger replies that he does not like these changes, but suggests that Tyndale (or Hychens as he is otherwise called) had no malicious purpose in changing them. More then asks him if he would like copies of the New Testament so changed to get about.

Nay in good faith, quod he, that would I not, if he use it very often.

With that, quod I, ye hit the nail on the head. For surely, if he changed the common knowen word into the better, I would well allow it. If he changed it into as good, I would suffer it. If somewhat into worse, so that he did it seldom, I would wink at. But now when he changeth the knowen usual names into so far worse, and that not repeateth seldom, but so often and so continually inculketh that almost in the whole book his lewd change never changeth. In this manner could no man deem but that the man meant mischievously.

In faith, quod he, so is it not unlikely.

That, quod I, when ye see more, ye shall say it much more than likely. For now is it to be considered that at the time of this translation Hychens was with Luther in Wittenberge, and set certain glosses in the margin, framed for the setting forth of the ungracious sect.

By saint John, quod your friend, if that be true that Hychens were at the time with Luther, it is a plain token that he wrought somewhat after his counsel, and was willing to help matters forward here.

But now, quod I, the cause why he changes the name of *charity*, and of the *church*, and of *priesthood*, is no very great difficulty to perceive. For since Luther and his fellows among other their damnable heresies have one that all our salvation standeth in faith alone, and toward our salvation nothing force of good works, therefore it seemeth that he laboureth of purpose to minish the reverent mind that men bear to charity, and therefore changeth the name of holy virtuous affection into the bare name of love.

And for because that Luther utterly denieth the very Catholic church

---

[1] *E. W.*, *Dialogue*, bk. iii, c. 8, pp. 207, 211.

in earth, and saith that the church of Christ is but an unknowen congregation of some folk, here two and three, no man wot where, having
the right faith which he calleth only his new forged faith, therefore,
Hychens in the new testament cannot abide the name of the *church*, but
turneth it into the name of *congregation*, willing that it should seem to
English men, either that Christ in the Gospel had never spoken of the
church, or else that the church were a congregation as they might have
occasion to say that a congregation of some heretics were the church
God spake of.

Now as touching the cause why he changed the name of *priest* into
senior, ye must understand that *Luther and his adherents hold this heresy
that all holy order is nothing*. And that a priest is nothing else but a man
chosen among the people to preach, and that by choice to that office he
is a priest by and by without any more ado, and no priest again when so
ever the people chose another in his place, and that a priest's office is
nothing but to preach. For as for saying mass, and hearing confession,
and absolution thereupon to be given, all this, he saith, that every man,
woman and child may do as well as any priest. Now doth Hychens
therefore to set forth this opinion withal after his master's heresy, put
away the name of priest in his translation, as though priesthood were
nothing.[1]

As we follow the discussion we are impressed by the Messenger's
desire to limit his faith by the Scripture, or rather to his own interpretations of it, very frequently of an anti-clerical kind. For him, the Bible is
a field for private interpretation, while More sets over against this the
Church's claim to interpret the Bible for the benefit of her children who
otherwise could but interpret it variously, and so bring about disunion.
More then goes on:

Christ said, "I am with you till the end of the world," not "I shall
be". For He never left behind Him a book of His own making. Nor did
He mean that neither part nor portion of holy Scripture should be not
lost, since some parts are lost already, more, peradventure than we can
tell of; and of what we have, the books in some part corrupted with
mis-writing. He saith also that His Father, and He should send the Holy
Ghost, and also that He would come Himself. Whereto all this, if He
meant no more but to leave the books behind them and go their way?
Christ is also present among us bodily in the holy sacrament. And is He
there for nothing? The Holy Ghost taught many things, I think, unwritten, and whereof some parts were not comprised in the scripture
yet unto this day, as the article which no Christian man will doubt of,
that our Blessed Lady was a perpetual Virgin, as well after the birth of
Christ as afore.[2]

[1] More, *E. W., Dialogue* bk. iii, c. 8, p. 227 F.   [2] *E.W.*, bk. i, c. 20, pp. 146–7.

But suppose, for the sake of argument, that Christ had continued with His Church none otherwise but only by leaving His Holy Scripture to them, and that all faith were only therein; then should it yet follow that as far as the necessity of our salvation requireth, God giveth the right understanding thereof [to the Church]. . . . And thereupon followeth farther that the Church cannot err in the right faith . . . and thereon also that all texts of holy scripture interpreted against the Church's interpretation can nothing avail.

More regrets that the Messenger pays little heed to the traditional interpretations of the Fathers, despises philosophy and almost all the seven liberal arts, and points to the harm that happens sometimes to fall to young men of a like temper; and he shows that in the study of the Scripture "the sure way is, with virtue and prayer, first to use the judgment of natural reason, whereunto secular literature helpeth much. And, secondly, the comments of holy doctors. And thirdly, above all thing, the articles of the Catholic Church received and believed through the Church of Christ".

As to the old holy doctors, first their wits were as much as our new men's; their diligence as great, their study as fervent, their devotion hotter, their number far greater, their time continued longer by many ages persevering. . . . Here might I lay you the holiness of their life and the plenty of their grace well appearing thereby, and that our Lord therefore opened their eyes and suffered and caused them to see the truth. And albeit, He used therein none open miracle nor sensible revelation, whereof as ye say none allege or pretend the proof of their opinions in their interpretations of holy scripture; yet used He the secret supernatural means by which His grace assistant with good men that labour therefor, by motions insensible to themself, inclineth their assent unto the true side; and that thus the old holy fathers did in the point that we speak of, and in such other, perceive the right sense of holy scripture so far at leastwise as they well knew that it was not contrary to their belief.

The Messenger now objects to More's reliance upon *natural reason, which he calls the enemy of faith.*
More proves that reason is servant to faith and not enemy, and must with faith and interpretation be concurrent. He agrees with the Messenger as to the pre-eminence, necessity and profit of Holy Scripture, but shows nevertheless that "*many things have been taught by God without writing. And many things so remain yet unwritten of truths necessary to be believed*". Luther, indeed, says that because a thing is not commanded by

Scripture, we may choose whether we will do it or leave it. This one point, More insists, is the very foundation and ground of all Luther's heresies. And in this Luther only follows the heretics of previous ages, who in "the high pride of their learning in scripture, wherein they followed their own wits and left the common faith of the Catholic Church, preferring their own gay glosses before the right Catholic faith of all Christ's Church, which can never err in any substantial point that God would have us bounden to believe".

The Messenger presses the point that "he could not believe the Church, if he saw the Church say one thing, and the holy scripture another thing; because scripture is the word of God".

More replies that "the faith is the word of God as well as the scripture, and therefore as well to be believed. Moreover, faith and scripture well understanden can never be contrary. Furthermore, if a doubt arise in any man's mind concerning anything found in scripture with regard to any necessary article of faith, that man hath a sure undoubted refuge provided him by the goodness of God to bring him out of all perplexity, in that God hath commanded him in all such doubts to believe the Church."

The Messenger still pressing his point, More concludes that "whereas God would that the Church should be your judge, ye would now be judge over the Church in the understanding of scripture".

More further makes it clear that "*saving for the authority of the Church, men could not know what scripture they should believe. . . .* Ye, therefore, that would believe the Church in no thing, nor give credence to the tradition of the Church but if it were proved by scripture, now see it proved to you that ye cannot believe the scripture [itself] unless it were proved to be scripture by the judgment and tradition of the Church."[1]

"Be you satisfied," then says More, "that the faith of the Church is a right rule with you to the study of the scripture, to shape you the understanding of texts, and so to take them as they may agree therewithal?"

Be it so, quod he.

Then are you, quod I, also fully satisfied in this, that where ye would not believe the Church telling a tale of her own, but only telling you scripture, ye now perceive that in such things as we spoke of . . . ye must believe and may be sure that since the Church cannot in such things

---

[1] Cf. St. Augustine, "For my part, I should not believe the gospel, except as moved by the authority of the Catholic Church," *Against the Epistle of Manichaeus*, chap. 5.

err, it is very true all that the Church in such things telleth you. And that it is . . . the word of God, though it be not in the scripture?

That appeareth well, quod he.[1]

Having convinced the Messenger that the "comen knowen Catholic Church" was divinely and infallibly inspired to determine

What the Faith was,
What the Scripture was, and
How the Scripture was to be interpreted in accordance with the Faith,

More was now, the more easily, able to convince him of the truth of the particular doctrines and practices of the Church to which the Messenger had previously taken exception. Not, however, until he had brought forward the theory, then so much in favour among the reformers, that "the very Church" was not the *visible* Church, but an invisible one known only to God and consisting only of those souls predestinate to salvation.

More meets this objection:

Marry, quod I, this gear groweth from worse to worse. And in very deed is this point their sheet anchor. For first they see plainly that they must needs grant that the very Church can neither be deceived in the right faith, nor mistake the holy scripture, nor misunderstand it to the introduction of infidelity and false belief. And this ground find all heretics themself so sure and fast, that they perceive well except they would openly and utterly deny Christ altogether, it cannot be undermined. And since they manifestly see that, and as evidently see therewith, that the Church (which is the very Church indeed) damneth all their ways, whereof since the Church cannot err in discerning truth, it must needs follow that they mistake themself all the whole matter, and be quite in a wrong way, *therefore they be driven to deny for the Church the people that be known for the Church.* And so they seek another, they neither know what nor where, [and] build up in the air a church all so spiritual that they leave therein at length neither God nor good man. And, first, where they say that there be none therein but they that be predestinate to be saved; if the question were of the Church triumphant in heaven, then said they well. But we speak of the Church militant here on earth.

Luther saith that his unknown church must be a sinless church, since Christ prophesied that "the gates of hell should not prevail against it"; and the gates of hell do prevail against every man that sinneth against any church that containeth such men, to wit the Catholic Church as we

[1] *E.W.*, bk. i, cc. 20-31, pp. 147-76, *passim*.

commonly know it. If this be so [says More] what church can we find
on earth that doth not sin? And thus he that would both have the church
to be only a secret unknowen sort of folk that do not sin yet confesseth
that there be no such.[1]

Then follows one of the most beautiful passages ever written by
St. Thomas More.

The Church, therefore [he concludes], must needs be the comen
knowen multitude of Christian men, good and bad together, while the
Church is here on earth. For this net of Christ hath for the while good
fishes and bad. And this field of Christ hath for the while corn and
cockle, till it shall be at the day of doom purified, and all the bad cast
out, and only the good then remain. Christ Himself said to His apostles,
"Now be you clean, but not all," and yet were they all of his Church,
albeit that one of them was, as our Saviour said, a devil. And if there
were none of the Church but good men, as long as they were good,
then had Saint Peter been once no part of the Church after that Christ
had appointed him for chief. But our Lord, in this mystical body of the
Church, carried His members, some sick, some whole, and all sickly. . . .
But when the time shall come that this Church shall whole change her
place and have heaven for her dwelling instead of earth, after the final
judgment pronounced and given, when God shall with His spouse, this
Church of Christ, enter into the pleasant wedding chamber to the bed
of eternal rest; then shall these scalde and scab pieces scale clean off, and
the whole body of Christ's holy Church remain pure, clean and glorious
without wen, wrinkle or spot, which is (and for the while, I ween, will
be, as long as she is here) as scabbed as ever was Job, and yet her loving
spouse leaveth her not, but continually goeth about by many manner
medicines, some bitter, some sweet, some easy, some grievous, some
pleasant, some painful, to cure her.[2]

But the Messenger, before capitulation, tries one more *cul-de-sac*.
Since the Church "is this knowen multitude of good men and bad, of
whom no man knoweth which be one sort and which the other . . . it
may, peradventure, be that the good sort of the Church be they that
believe the worship of images to be idolatry, and the bad sort, they that
believe the contrary."

"If that be so," More asks, "are those good men that commit idolatry
while they are in the Church?"

"Surely not," answers the Messenger.

"Then," More replies, "if your friends, not believing in images, pay

[1] *E.W., Dialogue,* bk. ii, c. 3, p. 181 C.   [2] *Ib.,* c. 4, p. 185 C.

devotion to them in our various churches, they are idolaters, and therefore their opinions are nought."

After this stroke the Messenger owns that he is "even at the hard wall,"[1] and so this part of the discussion is brought to an end.

We have given some space to what is worthy of more detailed study in the *Dialogue* itself; for it shows how Tyndale's strong contention against the supreme authority of the "comen knowen Catholic Church" exactly suited the present pressing necessities of the King–as Henry himself admitted when he said of Tyndale's *Obedience of a Christian Man* that it was a book for him and all kings to read. On the other hand, it shows how More was brought inevitably, for conscience's sake, into conflict with the royal will, the writing of this dialogue being but one of the many and successive steps he felt bound to take in defence of the supreme authority of the Church. And it was followed in due course by his resignation of the Chancellorship, his refusal to attend the coronation of Anne Boleyn, to take the oath and sign the Acts of Supremacy, and finally, by his imprisonment in the Tower of London, his trial, his condemnation and his death.

The main argument of the *Dialogue* just given may briefly be summarised as follows: The Catholic Church, "that most glorious society and celestial city of God's faithful, which is partly seated in the course of these declining times, and partly in the solid estate of eternity", is the only infallible source of divinely-revealed truth. And what the Church proclaims as divinely true, whether in faith or morals, must be accepted obediently by her children not because they understand it to be true, but because she has told them that it is true.[2] For the Church existed and proclaimed the truths of divine revelation before the Scriptures were written; and ever since the Scriptures were in writing she has proclaimed other truths as divinely true which are not contained in Scripture. Moreover, the very Scriptures themselves were determined by the Church. And what God gave her the power to determine aright, He also has given her the power to interpret aright. It is therefore wrong to set up the Scriptures in opposition to the Church, as did the reformers; for to the Church the Scriptures owe not only their existence, but also their true interpretation. The position is therefore very simple. The Church is the Church of God; and

---

[1] *E.W., Dialogue*, bk. ii, c. 4, p. 187 D.
[2] *Ib.,* bk. iii, c. 1, p. 205 A, "And so believe you the Church, not because it is truth that the Church telleth you; but ye believe the truth of the thing, because the Church telleth it."

because she is the Church of God she cannot err; and because she cannot err, she must be obeyed by every one of her true children. As More himself puts it to the Messenger, "Ye must believe and may be sure, that since the Church cannot err, all that the Church telleth you is very true; and that it is the word of God, though it be not in scripture."[1]

The idea of the Catholic Church, so vividly present to the mind of St. Augustine between the years 413 and 426 when he wrote his *De Civitate Dei*, and also to Sir Thomas More when he lectured upon that same treatise in 1501, has, since the Reformation, become for many a somewhat indistinct and confused reality, if indeed a reality at all. But now, as in the times of St. Augustine and of St. Thomas More, the Church really exists, and to many throughout the world has still that great and glorious reality St. Augustine so splendidly put into words. What then, does it stand for? First of all for eternal truth.   Beyond and above the partial and imperfect and passing apprehensions of frail, because fallen, man there is *a divine order of being* ever present to the mind of God—a divine order of being that was put into perfect practice, and lived out in human form in the person of our Lord Jesus Christ, the Way, the Truth and the Life. That Way, that Truth, that Life did not end on Calvary; for Christ rose from the dead and ascended into heaven. And then, at Whitsuntide, His Holy Spirit came down upon earth and there created and possessed the outward form and inward being of the Catholic Church. And the Church Militant then and there constituted is still upon the earth, and will never fail so long as the world continues. Like our Lord, it is in the world and the world comprehends it not; like our Lord, too, it comes to its own and its own receive it not; like Him, it lives and works and sorrows and suffers among men; and wherever it is, He is. The passing spirit of every age tries to create a Christ of its own; but the next age repudiates it as a false Christ; for only the presence of the Holy and Eternal Spirit, which neither changes nor deceives, can bring Christ back to the hearts of men. But if they will but pray for its coming, it will come; and with it they will find our Lord, and will live and rest and work with Him in unity and peace and fruitful obedience.

Apart from all questions of doctrine, one has often thought that what divides us from the religious practices and customs of our forefathers is a different way of conveying the facts of the Christian life which we all hold in common. In the days before the invention of printing the

---

[1] *E.W.*, *Dialogue*, bk. i, c. 31, p. 176 G.

written word did not count for so much as it does to-day. The historical events of our Lord's life on earth were then represented in outward show, dramatically. Then there happened in our country, and still happens abroad, in addition to the great liturgical solemnities of the ecclesiastical year, a whole cycle of popular representations in which the Gospel scenes of the Passion and Resurrection were dramatically reproduced and socially enacted in city and countryside, in which all took part, irrespective of age, occupation or degree, as may still be seen, for instance, in Spain. So when More wrote that "images be laymen's books" he was stating a simple fact, now well worth thinking over. And long after the introduction of the printed word, books were only for the learned, and not for the great majority, who could neither write nor read. "If", he says, "the having of the Scripture in English be a thing so requisite of precise necessity that the people's souls must needs perish unless they have it translated into their own tongue, then the greater part of them must needs perish unless the preacher further provide that all people shall be able to read it when they have it. For of the whole people, far more than *four-tenths* could never read English."[1]

But although this was so, More wished for a vernacular translation of the Scriptures which could be read by the clergy and by laymen as well. His views on the method of such study, and of the personal disposition of mind and body which should accompany it, are of interest, as showing the hopes and desires which he shared with men like Fisher, Colet and Erasmus for the renewal of a devout and scholarly study of the New Testament. A careful reading of all that More and the Messenger have to say on the subject from the twenty-first to the end of the thirty-first chapter of the third book of the *Dialogue* will make it clear to us that what the reformers wanted was not by any means a "higher criticism" impugning biblical and Church authority by the use of reason, but a sort of biblical superstition exalting the written word over human reason and Church authority alike. "It was the belief of 'known men' [that is, the new and subversive teachers] in their own infallibility as the interpreters of Holy Writ, and the treatment of human reason as the enemy of the faith that made these zealots think themselves superior to all exterior authority whatever."[2] To quote More's summary given in the twenty-second chapter of the first book of the *Dialogue*:

Because the Messenger has in the beginning shewed himself desirous

[1] *E.W.*, bk. i, c. 25, pp. 156–62.
[2] James Gairdner, *Lollardy and the Reformation*, vol. i, p. 517

and greedy upon the text of scripture with little force of the old fathers'
glosses, and with dispraise of philosophy and almost all the seven liberal
sciences, the author sheweth that in the study of the scripture the sure
way is, with virtue and prayer, first to use the judgment of natural
reason, whereunto secular literature helpeth much. And secondly, the
comments of holy doctors. And thirdly, above all things, the articles of
the Catholic faith received and believed through the Church of Christ.[1]

The Messenger dissuades the student from leaning to the commenta-
tors, nor should he use his natural reason which is "an enemy to the
faith".

More replies that natural reason so far from being "an enemy to the
faith" is "servant to faith . . . and must with faith and interpretation of
the scripture needs be concurrent". While insisting upon the pre-
eminence, necessity and profit of Holy Scripture, he nevertheless shows
that:

. . . many things have been taught by God without writing. And
many great things so remain yet unwritten of truths necessary to be
believed. And that the new law of Christ is the law so written in the
heart that it shall never be out of the Church. And the law there written
by God is a right rule to interpret in his holy scripture. And therefore is
holy scripture . . . the highest and best learning that any man can have,
if one take the right way in the learning. It is, as a good holy saint (St.
Gregory) saith, so mervaylously tempered, that a mouse may wade
therein, and an Olyphaunt be drowned therein. For there is no man so
low but [if only] he will seek his way with the staff of faith in his hand,
and hold fast and search the way therewith, and have the old holy
fathers also for his good guides, going on with good purpose and a
lowly heart, using reason and refusing no good learning, with calling of
God for wisdom, grace and help, that he may well keep his way and
follow his good guides, then shall he never fall in peril, but well and
surely wade through, and come to such end of his journey as himself
would well wish.

But surely, if he have a high heart and trust upon his own wit, as he
doth, look he never so lowly, that setteth all the old holy fathers at
nought, that fellow shall not fail to sink over ears and drown. And of all
wretches worst shall he walk that, forcing little of the faith of Christ's
Church, cometh to the scripture of God to look and try therein whether
the Church believe aright or not. For either doubteth he whether Christ
teach His Church true, or else whether Christ teacheth it at all or not.
And then he doubteth whether Christ in his words did say true, when
He said He would be with His Church till the end of the world. And

---

[1] *E.W., Dialogue,* bk. i, c. 22, p. 149 D, G.

surely the thing that made Arius, Pelagius, Faustus, Manichaeus, Dona-
tus, Elvidius and all the rabble of the old heretics to drown themself in
those damnable heresies, was nothing but high pride of their learning in
scripture, wherein they followed their own wits and *left the common
faith of the Catholic Church*, preferring their own gay glosses before *the
right Catholic faith of all Christ's Church, which never can err in any substantial point that God would have us bounden to believe.*[1]

While discussing the reasons which induced the clergy to burn
Tyndale's New Testament, the Messenger, in the eleventh chapter of
the third book, suggests that, since in other countries the clergy allow
vernacular translations, the reason why it is not allowed in ours must be
either that "our people be the worst of all people, or else our clergy be
the worst of all clergies". To this More replies:

For where ye touch the vice of the clergy in general, I can and will
with few words answer you. But as for the other which toucheth the
men, as where ye accuse the clergy in their persons of very vicious
living . . . I will keep no schools with you. For, as I told you in the
beginning, since we talk but of men's learning, I will not meddle of
men's living. . . . But yet where ye speak of other countries making an
argument that our clergy is the worst of all other, I wot well the whole
world is so wretched that spiritual and temporal everywhere all be
bad enough, God make us all better. But yet for that, I have myself seen
and by credible folk have heard, like as ye say by our temporalty that
we be as good and honest as anywhere else; so dare *I boldly say that the
spiritualty of England, and specially that part in which ye find most fault,
that is to wit that part which we commonly call the secular clergy, is in learning
and honest living well able to match (saving comparisons be odious, I would
say further) and far able to overmatch, number for number, the spiritualty of
any nation Christian.*[2]

More then puts his finger upon what he considers the main cause of
such ignorance and evil living to be found among the clergy of his own
time.

I wot well there be . . . many lewd and nought. And surely wheresoever there is a multitude it is not without miracle well possible to be
otherwise. But now if the bishops would once take unto priesthood
better laymen and fewer (for of us they be made) all the matter were
more than half amended.[3]

Again he writes: "Verily were all bishops of my mind (as I know

[1] *E.W., Dialogue*, bk. i, c. 25, p. 162 H–163 A, B.
[2] *Ib.*,bk. iii, c. 11, pp. 24–5.
[3] *Ib.*, bk. iii, c. 11. p. 225 C.

some that be) ye should not of priests have the plenty that ye have";
and again:

> The time was, I say, when few men durst presume to take upon them
> the high office of a priest, not even when they were chosen and called
> thereto. Now runneth every rascal and offereth himself for able. And
> where the dignity passeth all princes, and they that lewd be desireth it
> for worldly winning, yet cometh that sort thereto with such mad
> mind that they reckon almost God much bounden to them if they
> vouchsafe to take it. But were I Pope . . .
> By my soul, quod the Messenger, I would ye were, and my lady
> your wife Popess too.
> Well, quod I, then should she devise for the nuns. And as for me,
> touching the choice of priests, I could not well devise better provisions
> than are now by the laws of the Church provided. But for the number,
> I would surely see such a way therein that we should not have such a
> rabble, that every mean man must have a priest in his house to wait
> upon his wife, which no man almost lacketh now to the contempt of
> the priesthood.[1]

The Messenger thinks that matters would be bettered if the clergy
had wives of their own. More then discusses this difficult question. He
does not agree with Tyndale's contention "that chastity is an exceeding
seldom gift".

> Though chastity be a great gift [he says], but what if a man should
> deny him that yet it is a seldom gift? For though it be rare and seldom
> in respect of the remnant of the people that have it not, yet is it not
> seldom indeed for many men to have it. And Christ said that all men
> take it not; but he saith not that no man taketh it; not that few men
> take it. And highly he commendeth them that for his sake do take it.[2]

In conclusion, he points out that even among the Jews, who most
magnified generation, chastity was thought both to God and man a
thing meet and convenient for priests who served in the temple by
course. "And then how much more specially now to the priests of Christ,
which was born of a virgin, and lived and died a virgin himself, and
exhorted all his to do the same. Whose counsel (of perfection) in this
point, since some be content to follow, and some to live otherwise,
what were, I say, more meetly than to take into Christ's temple to serve
about the sacrament only such as be of that sort that are content and
minded to live after the cleanness of Christ's holy counsel."[3]

[1] E.W., *Dialogue*, bk. iii, c. 11, pp. 219–20.
[2] *Ib.*, c. 13, p. 231 B.　　　[3] *Ib.*, p. 232 G, H.

One of the great differences between Catholics and non-Catholics has always been in this very matter of clerical celibacy. The Church has always taught that in the sphere of moral obedience all are bound to keep the commandments, or precepts of the Church, as they are generally called, to distinguish them from the counsels of perfection which are not binding on all, but only on those who *voluntarily* and for a special purpose are called by God to serve Him in the priestly or monastic life. The Puritans did not believe in this distinction, although it had been made by Christ Himself; and they showed their disbelief by ignoring it in theory and in practice. They held that no one called to the clerical life was called of necessity to celibacy, and in fact, contrary to all previous custom, no matter to what special office a cleric was called, it need not and should not entail any kind of celibacy at all.

This distinction between the precepts and the counsels is, when we come to think of it, but the application of a principle acknowledged and necessary in ordinary life. A soldier, a lawyer, a miner, each one of them according to his special calling, needs to practise a special self-limitation or self-denial in order the more perfectly to carry it on. So, too, in the life of the Church. To repeat More's words: "What way were more meet than to take into Christ's temple to serve about the sacrament only such as be of that sort that are content and minded to live after the cleanness of Christ's holy counsel?"[1]

Therefore it is that the Church teaches that state differs from state in religious function and in spiritual dignity, and also in the kind of training in self-denial that goes with it. Yet, at the same time, she teaches that the sanctity of any particular soul depends, *not* upon the dignity of its religious duty or state, but upon the loving endeavour with which it strives to attain to the spiritual perfection within its reach, no matter how humble that may be. St. Thomas More, from early life even to his last days, longed to embrace the monastic state: but he was not called to it. Nevertheless he strove to attain to the perfection within his reach as a layman and finally attained it through martyrdom.

To More, the end and purpose of the spiritual life was simple–the union of the soul with God–but the way to God was difficult. "We may not look", he tells us, "at our pleasure to go to heaven in feather beds, it is not the way. For our Lord himself went thither with great pain, and by many tribulations, which is the path wherein he walked

---

[1] *E.W., Dialogue*, bk. iii, c. 13, p. 232 H.

thither, and the servant may not look to be in better case than his master."[1]

Life, he thought, could not be made easier by casting off or neglecting those habits of self-discipline or denial which our Lord had proclaimed to be necessary. To him the reformers were teaching a false simplicity and altogether lowering the standard of the spiritual life, and that, not only by discarding the counsels of perfection to which only a few were called by God Himself, but also by neglecting the ordinary means towards personal holiness which were binding on all alike. As he held, the Church laws, though necessary to the growth, order, regularity of the Christian life, were not to be compared in hardness or difficulty with the laws laid down by Christ Himself, as for instance in His Sermon on the Mount, wherein so many times He improved upon the precepts of the Old Law by the words, "But I say unto you", and what followed them in each particular case.

But said the Messenger, "Christ came to call us unto the law of liberty", meaning thereby to take away the band of those ceremonial laws so dear to the Scribes and Pharisees. And he continues, "Therefore saith our Saviour, of that law that He calleth us unto, 'My yoke is fit and easy, and my burden light.' Whereby it appeareth that He meant to take away the strait yoke and put on a more easy; and to take off the heavy burden and lay on a lighter. Which He had not done if He would load us with a fardel full of men's laws, more than a cart can carry away."

The laws of Christ [replies More] be made by Himself and His Holy Spirit for the governance of His people, and be not in hardness and difficulty of keeping anything like to the laws of Moses. . . . You would, I ween, rather be bounden to many of the laws of Christ's Church than to the circumcision alone. Not to as much ease as we ween that Christ called us, yet be not the laws that have been made by His Church of half the pain or half the difficulty that His own be, which Himself putteth in the gospel though we set aside the counsels. It is, I trow, more hard not to swear at all than to forswear, to forbear each angry word than not to kill, continual watch and prayer than a few days appointed. Then what anxiety and solicitude is there in forbearing every idle word? What an hard threat, after the worldly account, for a small matter. . . What ease would you call this, that we be bound to abide all sorrow and shameful death and all martyrdom upon pain of a perpetual damnation for the profession of our faith? Trow ye that these easy words of

---

[1] Roper, *Life of Sir Thomas More*, ed. Hitchcock, pp. 26–7 (E.E.T.S.).

His easy yoke and light burden were not as well spoken to His apostles
as to you, and yet what ease called He them to? Called He not them to
watching, fasting, praying, preaching, walking, hunger, thirst, cold and
heat, beating, scourging, prisonment, painful and shameful death? The
ease of His yoke standeth not in bodily ease, nor the lightness of His
burden standeth not in the slackness of any bodily pain—but it standeth
in the sweetness of hope, whereby we feel in our pain a pleasant taste of
heaven.[1]

And surely there can be little doubt that More practised those divine
precepts which he had so clearly set forth. As Roper tells us:

> Sir Thomas More's custom was daily, if he were at home, besides his
> private prayers with his children, to say the seven Psalms, litany, and
> suffrages following; so was his guise nightly, before he went to bed,
> with his wife, children, and household to go to his chapel and there
> upon his knees ordinarily to say certain psalms and collects with them.
> And because he was desirous for godly purposes sometime to be
> solitary, and sequester himself from worldly company, a good distance
> from his mansion house builded he a place called the new building,
> wherein there was a chapel, a library, and a gallery, in which, as his use
> was upon other days to occupy himself in prayer and study together,
> so on Friday there usually continued he from morning till evening,
> spending his time only in devout prayers and spiritual exercises. . . .
> Thus delighted he evermore not only in virtuous exercises to be occu-
> pied himself, but also to exhort his wife, children and household to
> embrace and follow the same.[2]

Reading passages of this description we come to understand that
Luther and Tyndale and those that followed them destroyed, or wanted
to destroy, the technique of the most difficult of all arts—the art of human
sanctity—and that as revealed by divine inspiration and shown forth in
saintly practice within the Church throughout the fifteen hundred
years that separated our Lord's own earthly life from theirs. And in so
doing they destroyed not only the bonds of religious unity which had
kept Christendom together, but those of national and international
unity as well. The high standards of the spiritual life had been applied
successfully during those centuries not only to innumerable individual
souls, but also to all the societies and states of the then known world.
The ages of St. Thomas Aquinas, of Dante, of St. Bernard and of St.
Francis of Assisi were not without "sweetness and light"; for they had

---

[1] *E. W.*, *Dialogue*, bk. i, c. 18, p. 142 F.
[2] Roper, *Life of Sir Thomas More*, ed. Hitchcock, pp. 25–6 (E.E.T.S.).

as it were behind them a great and strong executive power which spread order, beauty, colour and magnificence with a royal profusion over Christendom as a whole. As Lord Acton[1] has shown, it was a time too of very successful constitutional, communal and civic experiment. Of course there was failure and wickedness and bloodshed in high places as well as low. But that there will always be wherever there is life, and, as it then was, a life so abundantly in evidence.

Then came the Reformation—with the result that Europe lost much of the best of what it had previously gained at so great a cost. And may it not be questioned whether it got instead anything at all comparable in high spiritual and social value with what it had lost? Perhaps the answer may be given in a phrase from Matthew Arnold: "It got *provincialism* and lost *totality*."

After More had convinced the Messenger that the Church was the final and infallible authority in all matters of faith and scriptural interpretation, he had less difficulty in winning him back to an approval of all the remaining Catholic customs, observances and practices to which he had previously taken exception.

He is arguing with the Messenger that the faith will never fail in the Church in spite of the failures and treacheries of poor weak human nature. St. Peter, for instance, although Head of the Church, himself denied our Lord; but still our Lady stood firm.

Yet stood still the light of faith in our Lady, of whom we read in the gospel continual assistance to her sweetest Son, without feeling or flitting. And in all other we find either fleeing from Him, one time or other, or else doubt of His resurrection after His death, His dear mother only except. For the significance and remembrance whereof the Church yearly in the Tenebrae Lessons leaveth her candle burning still when all the remnant, that signifieth His apostles and disciples, be one by one put out.[2]

We have spoken of the unity that is a supernatural outcome of true spiritual obedience and charity within the household of the faith. But there is another privilege that comes quietly and almost unconsciously, but none the less really, to those children of the faith that practise these virtues. It is a familiarity with God and His saints in a realised family relationship—not a familiarity that breeds contempt, but one that carries with it a full measure of spiritual happiness. It brings to the soul a

---

[1] *Freedom and other Essays*, p. 39.　　[2] *E. W., Dialogue*, bk. i, p. 143 H.

deeper awe, a holier reverence, a more intimate communion with God and with each several Person of the Holy Trinity, and also, in a lower manner and in a different way, with His saints. For the saints are still in communion with us here on earth and we with them. They no longer belong, as we do, to the Church militant and compassionate on earth, not, as do the holy souls, to the Church suffering and patient in Purgatory; but they are now in heaven as part of the Church triumphant–and not only triumphant in heaven, but most powerfully helpful to us who still struggle here below. To speak humanly–for the Church ever draws her children "with the cords of Adam"–it is difficult for acquaintances or even less intimate friends of any ordinary earthly family to learn very quickly, if at all, the deeper intimacies and familiarities of the family itself, the members of which, individually, they may know quite well. Communion with the saints, like that between members of a family, is something more than mere acquaintance. Could any acquaintance of any family ever mistake the father for any of his children or the mother for any of hers? And yet there are those who fear that honouring the saints may be confused with the worship of God Himself. A little knowledge is perilous; but the more we know, the better we love, and love can distinguish where hate divides.

When the reformers came, then, with their hard, self-centred and exclusive individualism of the spirit, More, and men like More, blazed up into holy anger as they saw such people forbidding the communion of saints on the plea of a greater reverence for God; for More, and for men like him, the saints were the objects of a just, pure, deep and intimately familiar affection. More translated from Pico della Mirandola the twelve properties or conditions of a lover; and the seventh of these was "to love all things that pertaineth unto his love". He also translated a little verse enlarging thereupon which, by way of analogy, shows us what a soul on earth may feel for a saint in heaven.

> There is no page or servant, most or least,
> That doth upon his love attend and wait . . .
> Nor none so small, or trifle or conceit . . .
> Straight but that if to his love it hath been near
> That lover hath it precious, sweet and dear.[1]

But More could be as humorous and witty as he was tender and affectionate about the things that were dear to his soul. The Messenger is doubtful as to whether, after all, he ought to venerate the saints. More

[1] E.W., *Twelve Rules of John Picus*, p. 30.

implies in his answer that some do not venerate the saints because of their distance from God, whereas they ought to venerate them because of their nearness to Him. And that brings to mind one of More's "merry tales". A man was asked in confession whether he believed in the devil or not. "Believe in the devil, quod he, Nay, nay, sir, I've work enough to believe in God."[1]

Or again on the subject of images: "Even dogs understand the difference between a real animal and a wooden representation of it, for no dog is so mad but he knoweth a very coney[2] from a coney carved and painted."[3]

With regard to the reformers, More writes in the *Dialogue* not only about Tyndale in particular, but also about Bilney, Richard Hunne and Luther. Dr. Gairdner has written very fully about Bilney, and Miss Jeffries Davis, in the *Victoria County History of London*, has gone with convincing thoroughness into the case of Richard Hunne.

Then they discuss the question of Luther when one day More is talking to the Messenger in his garden at Chelsea.

The clergy, says the Messenger, will not have Luther's books read because they fear that in them they will read of the faults of the clergy which be therein put out with great plainness. And also men think it reasonable "that all were heard that can be said touching the truth to be knowen concerning the matters of our salvation; to the intent that, all heard and perceived, men may for their own surety the better choose and hold the right way."

From the outset the Messenger makes it clear that, according to the new Protestant teaching, each one should examine the Scripture for himself, and then use his own private judgment upon it.

More replies that if, indeed, it were at all "doubtful whether the Church of Christ were in the right rule of doctrine or not, then were it necessary to give them all good audience that could and would anything dispute on either part, for it or against it. But if it so be, as indeed it is, that Christ's Church hath the true doctrine already, and the self-same that St. Paul would not give an angel of heaven audience to the contrary,[4] what wisdom were it now to show oneself so mistrustful and wavering ... that we should give hearing not to an angel from heaven, but to a fond friar, to an apostate, to an open incestuous lecher, a plain limb of the devil, and a manifest messenger of hell?"[5]

---

[1] *E.W., Dialogue*, bk. ii, c. 11, p. 197 H.   [2] Coney, rabbit.
[3] See whole of *E.W., Dialogue*, bk. i, c. 2.   [4] *Galatians*, i. 8.
[5] *E.W., Dialogue*, bk. iv, c. 1, pp. 247–8.

More then excuses himself for his violent language against Luther:

If ye would haply think that I use myself too sore to call him by such odious names, ye must consider that he spareth not both, untruly and without necessity, in his railing books to call by as evil them whom his duty were highly to reverence, whereas I do, between us twain, but call him as he hath shown himself in his writing, in his living, and in his mad marriage. And yet I neither do it, nor would, were it not that the matter self of reason doth require it. For my part, it is of necessity to tell how nought he is, because that the worse a man is the more madness were it for wise men to give his false fables harkening against God's undoubted truth by his Holy Spirit taught unto the Church, and by such multitude of miracles, by so much blood of martyrs, by the virtuous living of so many blessed confessors, by the purity and cleanness of so many chaste widows and undefiled virgins, by the wholesome doctrine and agreement of all Christian people this fifteen hundred years confirmed.[1]

Plain speech and strong action against what is doctrinally or morally reprehensible has always co-existed with deep religious conviction from our Lord's time until now. It should not surprise us, however, who live in an age less deeply religious, to read what More has written in defence of his own strong language against Luther. "Even vigorous persecution or keen exclusiveness of feeling have–*pace* Lord Acton–saved mankind, at certain crises of its difficult development, convictions of priceless worth."[2]

"I pray you," continues the Messenger, "let me hear some of Luther's opinions."

First, he began [says More] with pardons and with the Pope's power, denying finally any of both to be of any effect at all. And soon after to show what good spirit moved him, he denied all the seven sacraments, except baptism, penance, and the sacrament of the altar, saying plainly that all the remnant be but feigned things and of none effect. Now these [sacraments] that he leaveth for good, it is good to see how he handleth them. For in *penance* he saith that there needeth neither contrition nor satisfaction. Also he saith that there needeth no priest for the hearing of confession: but that every man, and every woman too, is sufficient to hear confession and assoil [give absolution], and do all that belongeth to a confessor as is a priest.[3]

Now in earnest, quod the Messenger, this a much, merry, mad

[1] E. W., bk. iv, c. 1, p. 247 P, G.
[2] Von Hugel, *Essays and Addresses*, First Series, p. 91.
[3] E. W., *Dialogue*, bk. iv, p. 249 B, C.

invention of Luther. But now, if I might after Luther's way be confessed to a fair woman, I would not let to be confessed weekly.[1]

Yes, yes, quod More, a woman can keep counsel well enough. For though she tell a gossip, she telleth it but in counsel yet, nor her gossip to her gossip neither, and so when all the gossips in the town know it, yet it is but counsel still. And therefore I say it, not for any harm that would come by them, but for the novelty thereof.

Now in earnest, quod your friend, this was a much merry mad invention of Luther, and Luther is in a manner as mad as Tyndale. For it were as good almost to have no confession at all as to set women to hear it.

Forsooth, quod I, if it had been wisdom and not against God's will, it would of likelihood have been founden by some good men before these days, in this long time of so many hundred years. Howbeit he goeth near enough to take it all away. And divers of his scholars do now deny it utterly. And himself leaveth little substance and little fruit therein. For he would that we should not care much for any full confession of all deadly sins nor be very studious in the gathering of our faults to mind, nor pondering the circumstances, nor the weight and gravity thereof, nor taking any sorrow therefor. Now these things taken away, and *the sacrament of penance* left such as he would have it, consider in yourself what fruit were any man likely to find in it?[2]

Forsooth, quod I, and he handleth *the sacrament of baptism* not much better. For he magnifieth baptism but to the suppression of penance and all good living. For therein he teacheth that the sacrament's self hath no virtue at all; but the *faith* only.[3]

More then goes on to catalogue "Luther's conclusions and most shameful opinions":

Item, he teacheth that only faith sufficeth to our salvation with our baptism, *without good works*. He saith also that it is sacrilege to go about to please God with any works and not with faith only.

Item, that no man can do any good work.

Item, that the good and righteous man alway sinneth in doing well.

Item, that no sin can damn any Christian man, but only lack of belief. For he saith that our faith suppeth up all our sins how great soever they be.

Item, he teacheth that no man hath no free will, nor can anything do therewith, not though the help of grace be joined thereunto; but that everything that we do, good and bad, we do nothing at all there in our self, but only suffer God to do all thing in us, good and bad, as wax is wrought into an image, or a candle by the man's hand, without anything doing thereto itself.

---

[1] *E.W.*, *Dialogue*, bk. iv, p. 249 B, C.   [2] *Ib.*, p. 250 C, D.   [3] *Ib.*, p. 250 F, G.

Item, he saith that God is as verily the author and cause of the evil will of Judas, in betraying Christ, as of the good will of Christ in suffering of His passion.

In *matrimony*, he saith plainly that it is no sacrament; and so saith Tyndale too.

Item, if a man be not able to do his duty to his wife, he is bounden secretly without slander to provide another to do it for him.

Forsooth, quod the Messenger, this was courteously considered of him, he is a very gentleman, I warrant you.

In the *sacrament of order*, he saith that priesthood and all holy orders be but a feigned invention.

Item, that every Christian man and Christian woman is a priest.

Item, that every man may consecrate the body of Christ.

That is a shameful saying, in good faith, quod the Messenger.

Abide ye, quod More, and ye shall hear worse yet. For he saith further that every woman and child may consecrate the body of our Lord.

Surely, quod the Messenger, then is the man mad outright.

He saith, quod More, further yet, that the canon of the Mass is false . . . that the host in the Mass is none oblation nor sacrifice . . . that the Mass with his canon is sacrilege and abomination. And though much of this concerneth his damnable heresies touching the blessed sacrament of the altar, yet he saith many lewd doctrines more. . . .

Ye see now how he handleth all the blessed sacraments. But now hath he other wild heresies at large. For he teacheth against scripture and all reason that no Christian is or can be bounden by any law made among men, nor is bounden to keep any . . . he teacheth that there is no purgatory, that all men's soul lie still and sleep till the day of doom . . . that no man should pray to the saints not set by any holy relics nor pilgrimages, nor do any reverence to images.[1]

More afterwards shows that there is no constancy in Luther's teachings, as he alters them to suit the necessities of his own changing religious, political and moral circumstances.

Since by reason, writes More, Luther cannot prove the reasonableness of his doctrines, he refuses to stand by reason at all, and proclaims "that the matters of our faith be above reason and that reason hindereth us in our faith; and that he would stand to nothing but only scripture nor to that neither but if it were very plain and evident. But now if it were in question whether the scripture were evident for him or against him, therein would he stand to no man's judgment but his own."[2]

In the tenth chapter of the fourth book[3] More deals with the

---

[1] *E.W., Dialogue*, bk. iv, c. 2, pp. 249 B to 251 F.
[2] *Ib.*, c. 6, p. 257.   [3] *Ib.*, c. 10, p. 261.

"detestable article of the Lutheran sect whereby they take away man's free will, and ascribe all things to destiny". Such teaching is of present interest, since certain modern psychologists seem to hold the same doctrine. This, says More, is a blasphemy against God Himself, our Father, and utterly against all the goodness of His Godhead, since they "lay all the weight and blame of our sin to the necessity and constraint of God's ordinance, affirming that we do no sin of ourself by any power of our own will but by the compulsion and handiwork of God. And that we do not sin ourself, but God doth the sin in us Himself—and thus with this blasphemous heresy alone lay more villainous rebuke to the great majesty of God than ever any ribald laid unto another."[1]

Then follows a very long and careful examination of Luther's principal heresy, his *doctrine of justification by faith alone*.[2]

And this [says More in conclusion] they call the liberty of the gospel, to be discharged of all order and of all laws, and do what they list, which, be it good or bad, be, as they say, nothing but the works of God wrought in them. But they hope by this means God shall for the while work in them many merry pastimes. Wherein, if their heresy were once received, and the world changed thereby, they should find themself sore deceived. For the laws and orders among men, with fear of punishment once taken away, there were no man so strong that could keep his pleasure long, but that he should find a stronger take it from him. But after that it were once come to that point, and the world once ruffled and fallen into wildness, how long would it be, and what heaps of heavy mischiefs would there fall, ere the way were found to set the world in order and peace again![3]

The foregoing words are something more than the commonplace ending of an argument, and are worthy of careful consideration. Sir Thomas More, the More who wrote the *Utopia*, wrote them when heavy with the foreboding of evil things to come—things that he attributed directly to Luther's new religion of *uncurbed individualism*. Was it not the teaching of Luther, and of Tyndale his disciple, that taught Tudor and Stuart alike to exercise an uncurbed monarchical individualism in the sphere of politics and religion? And since then, even down to our own day, has it not encouraged an uncurbed individualism in industry that only now at last begins to suffer its proper abatement? The question of *the curb* has always been a difficult one, whether considered in its individual or in its social aspect, and whether applied

---

[1] *E.W.*, *Dialogue*, bk. iv, c. 10, p. 261.
[2] *Ib.*, cc. 11, 12.   [3] *Ib.*, c. 12, p. 274 E, F, G.

in the realm of faith, morals, politics or industry. Since man is a fallen creature, ever tempted to uncontrol, he needs the curb; and he needs its *compulsory* application *from without* just at the moment when he reaches the "breaking-point. For are not all human vows, laws and contracts so many ways of surviving with success this breaking-point, this instant of potential surrender" to moral or doctrinal or political or industrial license and disorder? "It is then that the Institution [of Church or State] upholds a man and helps him on to firmer ground."[1]

But suppose that a man refuses the curb? Suppose that he breaks his vow, or disobeys the law, or disowns the contract, or throws over his religious obedience, and encourages others to do the same? Then, in so far as he is wrong, the curb must be applied with yet sterner force; and, if he persists, it must needs reach the limits of its application in some sort of final sentence, either excommunication by the Church or capital punishment by the State—and this for the good of the greater number. Only so can the spiritual and social orders be maintained. Such at any rate was More's theory when as Chancellor, and without any personal exercise of cruelty on his own part, he held heresy to be the worst kind of sedition possible in a Catholic State.

If we read carefully the thirteenth, fourteenth and fifteenth chapters of the fourth book of the *Dialogue* we shall find this theory of More's amply confirmed.

Professor A. F. Pollard wrote of Cranmer, when in a position somewhat similar to that of More. He did not "deny the necessity of recourse to extreme penalties against obstinate disbelievers in the real presence. Toleration was in the sixteenth century no more part of the Protestant creed than it was of Roman Catholicism: Protestants as well as Catholics thought that only one form of truth could be true, and that form must be preserved at all costs."[2]

This statement of Professor Pollard's requires, however, some qualification in More's case. For More there were two kinds of State: a Catholic State and a State that was not Catholic. In a Catholic State he believed that all manifestations of heresy should be treated as seditious, with the severe penalties that were customary in every Catholic country at that time. But in a State that was not Catholic he believed that religious toleration was not merely expedient, but a matter of just necessity. As Roper tells us, he foresaw that England might cease to be a

---

[1] G. K. Chesterton, *What's Wrong with the World*, p. 53.
[2] *Thomas Cranmer*, p. 122; cf. also R. W. Chambers, *Thomas More*, p. 282.

Catholic country and be broken up into various religious sects and denominations, and in that event toleration in religious matters would be the only reasonable course. "Son Roper," he said, "I pray God that some of us, as high as we seem to sit upon the mountains, treading heretics under our feet like ants, live not the day that we gladly would be content to be at a league and composition with them, to let them have their churches quietly to themselves, so that they would be content to let us have ours quietly to ourselves."[1]

More clearly foresaw a time when religious toleration might prevail; but he did not welcome it; for the price of such toleration, he again foresaw, would be the sectarian disunity of Christendom; and he did not wish to sacrifice what he believed to be the greater good for what, under the circumstances of religious disunity and indifference, could hardly be called a good at all. He supremely desired that England should be, and should remain, Catholic; and as long as it was so, and in order to keep it so, he did not wish the State to tolerate what to him was intolerable, a false Christianity, as distinguished from the only one, true, Catholic Church of Christ.

But if, as he feared, England might cease to be Catholic—a catastrophe he prayed God he might never live to see—he then understood that there was only one reasonable policy left for the State to adopt, that of religious toleration.[2]

And now that so undesirable a catastrophe has taken place, we may be sure that St. Thomas More prays for the return of his country and ours to the Catholic faith and still believes, as he wrote in the *Utopia*, that "though there be one religion which alone is true, and all other vain and superstitious, yet did he well foresee (so that the matter were handled with reason, and sober modesty) the truth of its own power would at the last issue out and come to light".[3]

---

[1] Roper, *Life of Sir Thomas More*, ed. Hitchcock, p. 35.
[2] Lord Acton, *Freedom and other Essays*, "The Protestant Theory of Persecution".
[3] *Utopia*, trans. G. C. Richards, Fellow of Oriel College (Oxford, Blackwell), p. 108.

9

The Supplication of Souls

WHEN THE *Dialogue Concerning Tyndale* came out in 1528, More was fifty years of age and Chancellor of the Duchy of Lancaster. In 1529 he became Lord Chancellor, in that Reformation Parliament, which was to last for seven years and to bring about such momentous changes in the religious life of the country. In the same year he turned aside from his controversy with Tyndale to answer a pamphlet called the *Supplication for the Beggars*, written by one Simon Fish, a lawyer and friend of Tyndale's, in exile beyond the sea. It advocated, and indeed it suggested to Henry VIII, the wholesale confiscation of Church property and endowments in order, as Simon Fish said, at first, that they might be devoted to the relief of the poor.

Foxe, in his *Acts and Monuments* (1563)[1] gives us an account of Simon Fish:

After that the light of the gospel, working mightily in Germany, began to spread its beams in England, great stir and alteration followed in the hearts of many, so that coloured hypocrisy and false doctrine and painted holiness began to be espied more and more by the reading of God's Word. The authority of the Bishop of Rome and the glory of his Cardinals were not so high but such as had fresh wits, sparkled with God's grace, began to espy Christ from antichrist, that is true sincerity from counterfeit religion. In the number of whom was the said Master Simon Fish, a gentleman of Gray's Inn. It happened the first year that this gentleman came to London to dwell (1526) that there was a certain play or interlude made by one Master Roo of the same Inn, gentleman, in which play partly was matter against the Cardinal Wolsey. And when none durst take upon him to play that part which touched the said Cardinal, this aforesaid Mr. Fish took upon him to do it. Hereupon great displeasure ensued against him upon the Cardinal's part; insomuch as he, being pursued by the said Cardinal, the same night that this tragedy was played, was compelled by force to void his own house, and

---

[1] Edited by Cattley, of whom Mr. Mozley writes in *John Foxe and His Book*, p. 181: "Cattley had not only done his work badly but made the mistake of trying to defend what was indefensible." But how well Foxe could write!

so fled over the sea unto Tyndale. Upon occasion whereof, the next year following, this book was made. And so, not long after, was sent over to the lady Anne Boleyn who then lay at a place not far from the Court. This book, her brother seeing in her hand, took and read, and gave it her again, willing her earnestly to give it to the King; which thing she did. This was, as I gather, about 1528.

The King, after he had received the book, demanded of her who wrote it. Whereunto she answered and said, a certain subject of his, one Fish, who was fled out of the realm for fear of the Cardinal. After the King had kept the book in his bosom three or four days, as is credibly reported, such knowledge was given by the King's servants to the wife of the said Simon Fish, that she might boldly send for her husband without all peril or danger. Whereupon she, thereby encouraged, came first and made suit to the King for the safe return of her husband. Who, understanding whose wife she was, showed a marvellous, gentle and cheerful countenance towards her, asking where her husband was. She answered, if it like your grace, not far off. Then saith he, fetch him and he shall come and go safe without peril, and no man shall do him harm; saying, moreover, that he had much wrong that he was from her so long, who had been absent now the space of two years and a half. In the mean time the Cardinal was deposed, and Master More set in his place of the Chancellorship.

Thus Fish's wife, being emboldened by the King's words, went immediately to her husband (being lately come over, and lying privily within a mile of the Court) and brought him to the King; which appeareth to be about A.D. 1530. When the King saw him and understood he was the author of the book, he came and embraced him with loving countenance. After long talk for the space of three or four hours as they were riding together in hunting, the King at length dismissed him, and bade him take home his wife, for she had taken great pains for him, who answered the King again and said he durst not so do for fear of Sir Thomas More, then Chancellor, and Stokesley, then bishop of London. This seemeth to be about A.D. 1530.

The King taking the signet off his finger, willed him to have him recommended to the Lord Chancellor, charging him not to be so hardy as to work him any harm. Master Fish, receiving the King's signet, went and declared his message to the Lord Chancellor, who took it as sufficient for his own discharge, but he asked him if he had anything for the discharge of his wife. For she, a little before, had by chance displeased the friars by not suffering them to say their gospels in Latin in her house as they did in others, unless they would say them in English. Hereupon the lord Chancellor, though he had discharged the man, yet not leaving his grudge towards the wife, the next morning sent his man for her to appear before him; who, had it not been for her young daughter, who lay sick of the plague, had been like to come to much trouble. Of which plague her husband (the said Master Fish) deceasing within half a year, she afterwards married one Master James Bainham, Sir Alexander Bainham's son, a worshipful knight of Gloucestershire; which aforesaid Master James Bainham not long after was burned.[1]

Foxe, too, tells another story of how the book came to the notice of the King.[2]

Now cometh an other note of one Edmund Moddys, the King's footman, touching the same matter.

This M. Moddys being with the King in talk of religion, and of the new books that were come from beyond the seas, said, if it might please his grace to pardon him, and such as he would bring to his grace, he should see such a book as was marvel to hear of. The King demanded what they were. He said, two of your merchants, George Elyot and George Robinson. The King pointed a time to speak with them. When they came afore his presence in a privy closet, he demanded what they had to say, or to show him. One of them said that there was a book come to their hands, which they had there to show his grace. When he saw it, he demanded if any of them could read it. Yea, said George Elyot, if it please your grace to hear it. I thought so, said the King, for if need were, thou canst say it without book.

The whole book being read out, the King made a long pause, and then said, if a man should pull down an old stone wall and began at the lower part, the upper part thereof might chance to fall upon his head: and then he took the book, and put it into his desk, and commanded them upon their allegiance, that they should not tell any man, that he had seen the book, &c.[3]

The *Supplication for the Beggars* was a petition addressed to the King from "the wretched hideous monsters on whom scarcely for horror any eye dare look, the foul unhappy sort of lepers and other sore people, needy, impotent, blind, lame, and sick, that live only by alms". Their number, it was said, had "so sore increased that all the alms of all the well disposed people of this your realm are not half enough to sustain them, but that for very constraint they die for hunger".[4]

And what was the cause of their increasing destitution? It arose, so Fish contended, because in time past there had craftily crept into the realm another sort of beggars, not impotent, but strong, holy and idle

[1] Foxe, iv, pp. 657–8, *q.v.* Introd., *Supplication for the Beggars* (E.E.T.S., pp. vi–vii).
[2] The King might have wished to hear of the book from more than one source.
[3] Foxe, *Ib.*, p. viii.
[4] *A Supplication for the Beggars*, pp. 1, 2.

vagabonds, who with the craft of Satan had increased and become a
kingdom. "These are not the herds but the ravenous wolves going in
herd's clothing, devouring the flocks–bishops, abbots, priors, deacons,
archdeacons, suffragans, priests, monks, canons, friars, pardoners and
sumners." They had got possession of more than a third part of the
realm–the best manors, lands, and territories, with the tenth part of all
the corn, meadow, pasture grass, wood, colts, calves, lambs, pigs, geese
and chickens," and vast wealth besides by probates, offerings at
pilgrimages and so forth.

Then follows the astonishing statement that there were 52,000 parish
churches in England, and allowing ten households in a parish, that
would make 520,000 households, each of which contributed (as Fish
alleged) a penny a quarter to each of the orders of friars, making a sum
total of £43,333 6s. 8d. sterling.[1]

And what, says Fish, did these "holy thieves" (the clergy both secular
and regular) do with all their riches?

Truly nothing but exempt themselves from the obedience of your
grace. Nothing but translate all rule, power, lordship, authority,
obedience and dignity from your grace unto them! Nothing but that
all your subjects should fall into disobedience and rebellion against your
grace and be under them, as they did unto your noble predecessor King
John; who because he would have punished certain traitors that had
conspired with the French King to have deposed him from his crown
and dignity (among whom a clerk called Stephen, whom afterwards,
against the King's will, the Pope made bishop of Canterbury, was one),
interdicted his land. For this matter your most noble realm wrongfully
(alas for shame!) hath stood tributary, not unto any kind of temporal
prince but unto a cruel, devilish, blood-supper, drunken with the
blood of the saints and martyrs of Christ, ever since.[2]

Simon Fish, we cannot but infer, attacked the doctrine of purgatory
mainly because it served, as he thought, to enrich the clergy. His zeal,

---

[1] Some years ago I went into this matter with Dr. Coulton, and, helped by his kindness,
came to the conclusion that there were something like 10,000 parish churches at that time.
Mandell Creighton (*History of the Papacy*, vol. i, pp. 379–80) says that at the Council of
Constance a discussion took place (1417) in which the French ambassadors laid before the
Council a protest against the English nation being allowed to vote. The ambassador of the
"King of England and France" retaliated that eight kingdoms were subject to the English
crown and that the realm of the English king contained 110 dioceses, while that of the
French king had only 60. France had not more than 6000 parish churches, England (which
then included two-thirds of France) had 52,000. Simon Fish may have got his figures from
the same original source. But, of course, the figures are fantastic.

[2] *A Supplication for the Beggars*, pp. 4, 5.

after all, was rather to bring about the downfall of the Church than to relieve the poor. As he says at the end of his tract:

Wherefore, if your grace will build a sure hospital that shall never fail to relieve us all, your poor bedemen, so take from them [the clergy] all these things. Set these sturdy loobies abroad in the world, to get wives of their own, to get their living with their labour in the sweat of their faces, according to the commandment of God, Genesis iii, to give other idle people, by their example, occasion to labour. Take these holy, idle thieves to the carts, to be whipped naked about every market town till they fall to labour, that they by their importunate begging, take not away the alms that good Christian people would give unto us sore, impotent, miserable people, your bedemen.[1]

One other great grievance, too, he had against the clergy–namely, that they lived unmarried, and so deprived the King of the children who in time would grow to strengthen his realm both in peace and war.

He then brings his tract to an end by naming the positive benefits that will accrue to the realm if his advice find favour with the King.

Then shall, as well, the number of our foresaid monstrous sort, as of the bawds, whores, thieves, and idle people decrease. Then shall these great yearly exactions cease. Then shall your sword, power, crown, dignity, and obedience of your people, be not translated from you. Then shall you have full obedience of your people. Then shall the generation of your people be increased. Then shall your commons increase in riches. Then shall the gospel be preached. Then shall none beg alms from us. Then shall we have enough, and more than shall suffice us; which shall be the best hospital that ever was founded for us. Then shall we daily pray to God for your most noble estate long to endure.[2]

Perhaps it may be of interest to compare this rosy forecast of good things to come to the poor, as a result of the wholesale appropriation of ecclesiastical property, with the actual outcome of Simon Fish's policy as witnessed by later evidence. Fish's *Supplication for the Beggars*, short and vigorous in its style, was a model for a series of pamphlets which give us an insight, though not an unprejudiced one, into the religious and social conditions of the time: such were a *Supplication to our most sovereign Lord Henry the Eighth* (1544), a *Supplication of the Poor Commons* (1546), *Certain Causes gathered together wherein is showed the decay of England, only by the great multitude of sheep* (c. 1550), and two attributed to Henry Brinklow, *The Complaynt of Roderyck Mors* (c. 1545), and the

---

[1] *A Supplication for the Beggars*, pp. 14, 15 (E.E.T.S.)   [2] *Ib.*

Lamentation of a Christian against the City of London (1545). In this last, printed sixteen years after Simon Fish's pamphlet, we have recorded the bitter experiences of the poor who had exchanged their former land-lords for the new owners of monastic lands.

Those who retained their [small] farms found, instead of the certainty of tenure and low rents of the Abbey lands, a merciless demand to know by what right, or by what lease, their farms were held; and their rents increased to such an extent that very few could pay them; and then they were left to choose between a vagabond's life and a felon's death, if they threw up their lands, and want and oppression if they retained them.[1]

This, too, is borne out by Starkey in his letter to Henry VIII on the *Condition of England* (1537), in which he says that the effect of the reformers' preaching "under colour of driving away man's tradition and popishness . . . had almost driven away all virtue and holiness", so that the people began to lose their belief in any doctrine, "and with the despising of purgatory, they began little to regard hell, heaven, or any other felicity hereafter to be had in another life".

He continues:

Albeit some men considering with themselves certain of your Acts succeeding this defection from Rome, as the acts of first fruits, of the tenths, and of the suppression of these monasteries and houses of religion, judge thereby plainly that the body of your realm in a few years shall succeed the same, yet when I consider your grace's high wisdom and prudence whereby your highness most clearly seeth how the wealth of all princes hangeth chiefly of the wealth of their subjects, and how penury ever breedeth sedition, and how the heaping of treasure without liberality, hath always brought in ruin and destruction of every commonalty . . . you will see and provide that they [your Acts] may proceed to such an end as by your high wisdom they were chiefly directed to. Wherefore considering that this worldly treasure is no such thing wherein any noble heart can take delight and pleasure, sure hope have I that your grace, whom I know so deeply can weigh the nature of things, will most liberally dispense this treasure to the aid, succour and comfort of your most loving obedient poor subjects.[2]

Savine, in his *Studies of Monastic Lands before the Dissolution*,[3] points to the contrast between conditions under the old monastic owners and

---

[1] Henry Brinklow, *Complaynt of Roderyck Mors*, Introd., pp. vii, viii (E.E.T.S.).
[2] *England in Henry VIII's Time*, Introd., p. liii (E.E.T.S.).
[3] *Oxford Studies in Legal and Social History*, ed. Vinogradoff, vol. i, p. 178.

their successors who cannot resist the temptation to turn their arable land into pasture. In the pre-dissolution days "when every man was contented with one farm, there was plenty of everything . . . but now in a town of twenty or thirty dwellings, the houses are decayed, the people gone, the church in ruins, and in many parishes nothing".

It will be gathered from the quotations just given that St. Thomas More rightly estimated the danger of such a pamphlet as Simon Fish's *Supplication for the Beggars*. "That it should have been thought worthy of an answer from the pen of Sir Thomas More seems really not a little humiliating," writes James Gairdner.[1] "But Sir Thomas knew the temper of the times, and how much mischief could be done by pure scurrility and gross exaggeration and lying. So, to defeat the *Supplication for the Beggars*, he drew up another supplication, very much in the same form, entitled the *Supplication of Souls*," in which we have touching evidence of his own personal devotion to the holy souls.

To all good Christian people. In most piteous wise continually calleth and crieth upon your devout charity and most tender pity for help and comfort, and relief your late acquaintance, kindred, spouses, companions, playfellows, and friends, and now your humble and unacquainted and half-forgotten suppliants, poor prisoners of God, silly souls in Purgatory here abiding and enduring the grievous pains and hot cleansing fire that fretteth and burneth out the rusty and filthy spots of sin, till the mercy of Almighty God, the rather by your good and charitable means, vouchsafe to deliver us hence.[2]

Speaking, then, as it were in their own persons, these holy suffering souls say that it was not their custom to disturb the sleep of their friends on earth in order to ask them for their prayers, but now, of late, there are sprung up certain seditious persons, which not only labour to destroy the clergy by whom they are much helped, but also to set forth such a pestilent opinion against themselves that people will cease to pray for them altogether, because they are taught by these same persons that there is no purgatory at all; and the very worst of these is that dispiteous and despiteful person which of late under the pretext of piety (God forgive him) made and put forth a book he names the *Supplication for the Beggars*.

Though this book, say the holy souls, touches them closely, yet they are more concerned about those still living upon earth, lest by means of

---

[1] *Lollardy and the Reformation*, vol. i, p. 522.
[2] More, *English Works* (1557), p. 288 D.

it they lose their belief in purgatory itself and many go straight to hell. The author of the book, who, because he is unknown, escapes earthly punishment, is not unknown to them, for they have several acquaintances of his in purgatory already, to whom God gave grace to repent at their death; and his performances have been reported here with exultation by his and their ghostly enemy, the devil.[1]

Who could ever have thought that any Christian man could for very piety have found it in his heart to seek and study the means whereby a Christian man should think it labour lost to pray for all Christian souls? But alack the while, we found soon after, that the falsehood and malice of the man, proved the devil true.

Then layeth (this beggar's proctor) the cause of all these poor beggars, both their increase in number and their default in finding, all this he layeth to the one only fault of the clergy, naming them in his bederoll (mighty sturdy beggars that they were), bishops, abbots, priors, deacons, archdeacons, suffragans, priests, monks, canons, friars, pardoners and summoners, idle holy thieves every one of them, who have begged so importunately that they have got into their hands the third part of the realm of England, besides tithes, privy tithes, probates of testaments and offerings, with Mass pence and mortuaries, blessing and cursing, citing, suspending and assoiling.[2]

Then cometh he particularly to friars, to whom he maketh, as he thinketh, a plain open reckoning that they receive by begging through the realm yearly £43,333 6s. 8d. sterling. Then showeth he that all this cast together amounteth yearly far above half of the whole substance of the realm.

Then cometh he at the last unto the device of some remedy for the poor beggars. What will he suggest? They should have no hospital provided for them, because, he saith, that therein the profit goeth to the priests. *What then is his remedy? That nothing should be given to the beggars but only that everything should be taken from the priests* and then set them abroad in the world ... to get their own living ... and finally to tie them to the carts to be whipped about every market town till they fall to labour.[3]

More, for his part, denies Fish's contention that the number of beggars has of late so sore increased and that private charity has lessened towards them.

As to that sum of £43,333 6s. 8d. said to have been collected quarterly by the friars from every household in the land, his calculations are based

---

[1] More, *English Works*, p. 289.   [2] *Ib.*, p. 290 B, D.   [3] *Ib.*, p. 291 D.

on the assumption that there are 52,000 parish churches in the country, whereas there were but about 10,000, as mentioned previously.

Fish accuses the clergy of inciting the people to disloyalty, sedition and even rebellion.

But [replies More] every child may see that the clergy would never be so mad as to be glad to bring the people to disobedience and rebellion against the prince by whose goodness they are preserved in peace, and were, in such rebellion of the people, likely to be the first that should fall in peril. King John is adduced by Fish to support his argument; [but More answers him that] no king of England could ever give away his realm to the pope, or make the land tributary to him by any legal method. What was given to the pope was given through the devout charity of the people and under no sort of legal compulsion.

Now goeth Fish still further and asketh the King, "Did not Doctor Horsey and his accomplices most heinously, as all the world knoweth, murder in prison that honest merchant Richard Hunne, for that he sued your writ of premunire against a priest that wrongfully held him in plea in a spiritual court for a matter whereof the knowledge belonged unto your High Courts? And what punishment hath he for it? After that he had paid, as it is said, six hundred pounds for him and his accomplices, as soon as he had obtained your most gracious pardon, he was immediately promoted by the captains of his kingdom with benefice upon benefice to the value of four times as much. Who is he of their kingdom that will not rather take courage to commit the like offence, seeing the promotions that fell to such men for their so offending, so weak and blunt is your sword to strike at one of the offenders of this crooked and perverse generation."[1]

A good deal has been written about this case of Richard Hunne; but More's final judgment on the matter is clear enough. "Hunne had a quarrel with the clergy. He was accused of heresy, and whilst in the bishop's prison, awaiting trial, he was found hanged. Had he added the crime of suicide to the crime of heresy? Or had the clergy added the crime of murder to that of false witness? More was certain that it was a case of suicide.[2] As Professor Chambers remarks, "It is noteworthy that so loyal a Londoner as More should represent the inviolability of the clergy as a sound principle, prescribed by the law of reason which governed Utopia. We must never forget that in Utopia the despotic supremacy of the State is balanced by the inviolability of a priesthood entirely exempt from State control."[2]

[1] E. W., pp. 297-8. cf. Chambers, *Thomas More*, p. 134.   [2] *Ib.*, p. 134.

To any reader it is obvious that Simon Fish was much more anxious to "down" the clergy than to raise up the beggars. As More writes:

He showeth himself that he nothing else intendeth but openly to destroy the clergy first, and after that covertly as many as have aught above the state of beggars. . . . He layeth that the living which the clergy hath is the only cause that there be so many beggars that be sick and sore. Very well and wisely, as though the clergy by their substance made men blind and lame. The clergy also is the cause, he saith, why they die for hunger, as though every layman gave to beggars all that he ever could, and the clergy gave them never a groat.[1]

"But now to the poor beggars. What remedy findeth their proctor for them?" He will allow them no hospitals "because they be profitable to priests. What remedy then? They must not be given money, nay, not a groat. What other thing then? Nothing in the world will serve but this . . . that everything shall be taken from the clergy. . . . Is not this a goodly mischief for a remedy? Is not this a royal feast to leave these beggars meatless, and then send more beggars to dinner with them?"[2]

We verily think that, if (the beggars) have as much wit as their proctor lacketh, they had liefer see their bill-maker burned than his supplication sped. For they may soon perceive that he mindeth not their alms, but only the spoil of the clergy. For so that the clergy lose it, he neither deviseth further, or further forceth, who have it. But it is easy to see whereof springeth all his displeasure. He is angry and fretteth at the spiritual jurisdiction for the punishment of heretics and burning of their erroneous books; for ever upon that string he harpeth, very angry with the burning of Tyndale's testament. For these matters he calleth them blood suppers, drunken in the blood of holy saints and martyrs. Ye marvel peradventure which holy saints and martyrs he meaneth. Surely by his holy saints and martyrs he meaneth their holy schismatics and heretics, for whose just punishment these folk that are of the same sect, fume, fret, froth and foam, as fierce and as angrily as a new hunted sow. And for the rancour conceived upon this displeasure cometh up all his complaint of the possessions of the clergy.[3]

More then argues that once the beggars have added to their number the clergy whom they have despoiled, they will then go on to demand that Merchants, Gentlemen, Kings, Lords and Princes shall submit to the same spoliation and, for the same reason as the clergy, should be sent to labour for their living in the sweat of their faces. In this way, too, the

---

[1] *E.W.*, p. 300 B.   [2] *Ib.*, p. 301 H.   [3] *Ib.*, p. 302.

beggars will grow to such a large and powerful party that they will rise in rebellion against the State itself, as indeed they have lately done in Germany, where in one summer some sixty thousand of them were slain.

He makes merry over Fish's fear that, because the clergy marry not, the whole realm for lack of subjects will fall into weakness and decay. If the clergy be, as the beggars' proctor saith, but a hundredth part of the whole population, he should also remember that there are other folk beside the clergy unmarried. How many servants, how many tall serving men, how many soldiers, sailors and other subjects of the King, how many women, too, prefer not to marry?

It will be a scandal to all good people that a married clergy should undertake to say Mass, to dispense the other sacraments and to preach from the pulpit.

Either he must mean to have it thus, which none honest man could endure to see, or else of which twain we wot never well whether is the worse, he intendeth to have all holy orders accounted as nothing, and to have no more sacraments ministered at all, but whereas, soon after Christ's Ascension, His Church buried the ceremonies of the Jew's synagogue with honour and reverence, so would he now that Christian people should kill and cast out on a dunghill the blessed sacrament of Christ with villainy, rebuke and shame. . . . And therefore here would his own high sore words have good place against himself. For this mischievous device of his is indeed "a great, broad, bottomless ocean sea full of evils", wherein would not fail the grievous shipwreck of the commonwealth, which God would soon forsake, if the people once forsook His faith and condemned His holy sacraments, as this beggars' proctor laboureth to bring about.[1]

The real secret matter, says More, that the beggars' proctor is afraid to speak of plainly, is nothing less than this, that the Church still teacheth and preacheth "the whole corps and body of the blessed faith of Christ, and the ministering of the blessed sacraments of our Saviour Christ. For the teaching and preaching of all which things the beggars' proctor or rather the devil's proctor, with other beggars who lack grace, and neither beg nor look for none, bear all this malice and wrath to the Church of Christ."[2]

There are only two ways, concludes More, for them to choose between in their contest against the Church, "either plainly to write against the faith and the sacraments or else to labour against the Church

[1] E. W., p. 307 C.   [2] Ib., p. 310 C.

alone, and get the clergy destroyed, whereupon they perceive well that the faith and sacraments would not fail to decay".[1]

They have tried the first way already:

. . . sending forth Tyndale's translation of the new testament in such wise handled as it should be a fountain and well-spring of all their whole heresies. For he had corrupted and purposely changed in many places the text, with such words as he might make it seem to the unlearned people that the scripture affirmed their heresies itself. Then came out in print that dialogue of friar Roy and friar Jerome, between the father and the son against the sacrament of the altar, and the blasphemous book entitled the burying of the Mass. Then came forth after Tyndale's wicked book of *Mammona*, and after that his more wicked book of *Obedience*. In which books, afore specified, they go forth plainly against the faith and holy scaraments of Christ's Church, and most specially against the sacrament of the altar, with as villainous words as the wretches could devise.[2]

Seeing, then, that this way did not prosper, they now determined to try a second way–that is, by forbearing to write so openly and directly against all the faith and the sacraments, and make one book specially against the Church, attributing false crimes to the clergy, and so have them destroyed.

To close the matter, when the Church and the sacraments have been set at nought, then will come the time to set forth the gospel of Luther and the testament of Tyndale.

Simon Fish's contention that at the beginning of the Church there were no clergy is just nonsense. "Now knoweth every man that the Christian clergy and the Christian faith came into the Christian people together."[3]

After reciting the evils that would follow upon taking the advice of "the beggars' proctor", the holy souls bring the first book of their *Supplication* to an end, saying that in their second and concluding one they hope to set forth their refutation of that uncharitable heresy wherewith Simon Fish would persuade good Christians to cease from praying for the holy souls because, as he says, purgatory itself has no existence.

In the second book, the holy souls set forth in simple argument the necessity for Purgatory, and beg continual remembrance from their friends on earth.

If there had never been any revelation on the subject we have only,

---

[1] *E.W.*, p. 310 D.   [2] *Ib.*, p. 310 E.   [3] *Ib.*, p. 312 D.

say they, to consider the immortality of the soul and the righteousness and goodness of God to see that Purgatory must needs exist. For, since God of His righteousness will not leave sin unpunished, nor will He in the case of converted souls punish them in hell for ever, there must be some way, even after they have been pardoned, of exacting from them the penalty of their sinfulness, either in this life, or, if they die before the penalty is fully paid, in the life after death.

But if, as the heretics do, in magnifying God's high goodness we should say that not only is all a man's sin forgiven, but also the pain and penalty thereof as well, we should be magnifying God's goodness at the expense of His justice, and give men great occasion and freedom to sin boldly without fear, nothing more being necessary than "to cry Him mercy, as one woman would that treadeth on another's train, this way, as we said, would give the world . . . courage not only to fall boldly to sin and wretchedness, but also careless to continue therein".[1]

And the consequence of such presumption is that the heretics are teaching men

. . . that three or four words ere they die shall sufficiently serve them to bring them straight to heaven, whereas, besides the fear that they should have lest they shall lack at last the grace to turn at all, and so for fault of those three or four words fall to the fire of hell, they must believe the further truth that though they may have the grace to repent and be forgiven their sin, and so be delivered of the endless pain of hell, yet they shall not so freely be delivered of purgatory, but that beside the general relief of Christ's whole passion extended unto every man, not after the value thereof, but after the stint and rate appointed by God's wisdom, great and long pain abideth them here among us (in purgatory), whereof their willingly taken penance in the world, and affliction there put upon them by God, and there patiently borne and suffered, with other good deeds there in their life done by them, and finally the merits and prayers of other good folks for them, may minish and abridge the pain which will else hold them here with us in fire and torments intolerable, only God knoweth how long–this thing, we say, as it is true indeed, so if the world well and firmly for a sure truth believe it, cannot fail to be to many folk a good bridle and sharp bit to refrain them from sin. . . .[2]

And therefore is this place of our temporal pain of purgatory not only consonant unto God's righteous justice, but also the thing that highly declareth His great mercy and goodness, not only for that pain

[1] Cf. Luther's saying, "Pecca fortiter, sed crede firmius". The first part of this saying is so often quoted without the last, which makes it so paradoxical.
[2] E.W., p. 316 B.

thereof, though great and sore it is, is yet less than our sin deserveth; but also most especially in that by the fear of pain to be suffered and sustained here, His Goodness refraineth men from the boldness of sin and negligence of penance, and thereby keepeth and preserveth them from pain everlasting.[1]

On the contrary side, easy forgiveness without any penalty to be paid for sins, however heinous, would encourage men to be presumptuous, and a boldness in sinning and an incitement to continue in the same, which would give occasion to many to run headlong down into hell. Wherefore, say the holy souls, it must needs follow that since the pain is always due to sin, and not always clean forgiven without convenient penance, or other recompense made in this life, and yet the man discharged of hell by his conversion, all the pain that remaineth must needs be sustained here in Purgatory.

And now there comes into question the scriptural authority upon which the doctrine of Purgatory rests.

The heretics make a great profession of their belief in the infallibility of Scripture; but, on examination, it proves rather to be a show than a reality. For when Scripture itself maketh against them, "they then with false, fond glosses of their own making do but mock and shift over in such a trifling manner that it may well appear they believe not scripture neither".[2] But since they rest so much on the authority of Scripture, let us see what the Scripture has to say about Purgatory itself.

"And first, it seemeth very probable and likely that good king Ezechias for none other cause wept at the warning of his death, given him by the prophet, but only for the fear of purgatory. . . . And therefore wept he tenderly and longed to live longer, that his satisfaction done here in this world in prayer, and in other virtuous deeds, might abolish and wear out all the pain that else were toward him here among us (in Purgatory)."[3] And so . . . our Lord of His high pity condescended and granted him the lengthening of his life for fifteen years, wherein by penance and good deeds he might be delivered from the pains of purgatory he would otherwise have had to endure hereafter.

Or again, have we not the words of Scripture written in the book of Kings? *Dominus deducit ad inferos et reducit,* Our Lord bringeth folk down to hell and bringeth them thence again.

But they that be in that hell where damned souls be, they be never delivered thence again. Wherefore it appeareth well that they whom

God delivereth and bringeth thence again, be in that part of hell that is called purgatory.[1]

Or once again:

What say the heretics to the words of the prophet Zacharias, *Tu quoque in sanguine testamenti tui eduxisti vinctos tuos de lacu in quo non erat aqua*, Thou hast in the blood of Thy testament brought out Thy bounden prisoners out of the pit or lake in which there is no water. In that they whom the prophet there speaketh of were bounden, we may well perceive that they were in a prison of punishment. And, in that he calleth them the prisoners of God, it is easy to perceive that he meaneth not any that were taken and imprisoned by any other than the damned spirits, the very jailers of God. . . . So that, as we show you, these words . . . do right well appear to be spoken of these poor imprisoned souls whom Christ after His bitter passion, by His precious blood wherewith He consecrated His Church in His new testament, delivered out of the lake of fire wherein they lay bounden for their sins.[2]

And as those already in hell were past deliverance, those delivered could only have been those then in Purgatory.

Lastly, we come to that place in the book of Maccabees that putteth Purgatory beyond all doubt. It will also show us why the book of Maccabees was excluded from the Protestant canon only on account of its clear witness to the doctrine of Purgatory.

It also gives rise to that very important question, On what authority does the Canon of Scripture rest?

Anglican authorities have said that as the book of the Maccabees was not included in the Jewish canon, it could not be included in the canon of the Scriptures given us by the Church. But they are met with another question put by More into the mouths of the holy souls. If you admit, on the one hand as canonical a book of Scripture admitted by the Jews, and deny, on the other hand, a book admitted by the Church, you evidently say "that the Spirit of God was more effectually present and assistant unto the synagogue of the Jews in the law of His prophet Moses than unto the Church of His own begotten Son in the law of Christ's gospel". The conclusion is obvious, "*For if these heretics deny for holy scripture any book that the Church of Christ accounteth for holy scripture, then deny they one of the great foundations of all Christian faith.*"[3]

Even Luther himself affirmed "that God hath given unto the Church

---

[1] *E.W.*, p. 317 E.   [2] *Ib.*, F, G.   [3] *Ib.*, p. 319 A.

of Christ that gift that the Church cannot fail surely and certainly to discern the words of God and the words of men; and that it cannot be deceived in the choice of holy scripture and rejecting of the contrary", and "that the noble doctor saint Austin saith very well, when he said that he should not have believed the gospel but for the authority of the Church".[1]

And surely [concludes More] if the Church might be so deceived in the choice of holy scripture, that they might take and approve for holy scripture any book (say that of the Maccabees) that were none, then stood all Christendom in doubt and unsurety whether saint John's gospel were holy scripture or not, and so forth of all the new testament. . . . And since yourself well perceiveth also, the Church of Christ receiveth and taketh and (as ye see by saint Jerome and the other holy doctors this thousand year) hath approved and firmly believed the holy book of Maccabees to be one of the volumes of holy scripture, and then in that book ye see so manifestly purgatory proved, that none heretic . . . can yet for shame say the contrary, but are by the plain open words of that holy book so driven up to the hard wall, that they can no farther but are fain to say that the book is no part of the scripture. . . .[2]

We then come to the proofs from the New Testament. First there are the words of Saint John (1 John v. 16): "*Est peccatum usque ad mortem, non dico pro eo ut roget quis*, There is, he saith, some sin that is unto death, I bid not that any man should pray for that."[3] This sin is that of those who die in desperation and impenitence, for which, of course, no prayers will avail.

Then appeareth it clearly that saint John meaneth that there be other which die not in such case, for whom men should pray because that prayer to such souls may be profitable. But that profit can no man take neither, being in heaven where it needeth not, nor being in hell where it booteth not. Wherefore it appeareth plain that such prayer helpeth only for purgatory, which they (the heretics) must therefore needs grant except they deny saint John".[4]

He quotes further from Saint John in the fifth chapter of the Apocalypse, and from Saint Peter, who speaks in the second chapter of the Acts in this way, *Quem Deus suscitavit solutis doloribus inferni*, in which our Lord, after His passion, descended into hell, meaning that He released, among others, those who were suffering the pains of Purgatory.

---

[1] St. Augustine, *Against the Epistle of the Manichees called Fundamental*, c. 5 trans.
[2] *E. W.*, p. 319 E.   [3] *Ib.*, G.   [4] *Ib.*, G, H.

In conclusion, say the holy souls:

... whereas we by plain scripture have proved you purgatory, yet, if there were therein not one text that anything seemed to say for it, but divers and many texts which as far as seemed unto the misunderstanders to speak against purgatory ... yet since the Catholic Church of Christ hath alway so firmly believed it for a plain truth, that they have alway taken the obstinate affirmers of the contrary for plain erroneous heretics, it is a proof full and sufficient for purgatory to any man that will be taken for a member of Christ's Church, and is alone a thing sufficient in any good Christian audience to stop the mouths of all the proud, high-hearted, malicious heretics, that anything would bark against us.[1]

They then go on to speak of Luther's new-fashioned doctrine, which, while it denies the existence of Purgatory, affirms that departed "souls unto doomsday do nothing else but sleep".[2] Purgatory, say the heretics, is the invention of the Pope, and that "no man may satisfy for another".

But if all that ever must avail any man must needs, as they say, be done by himself and no man's merit may be applied to the help of another, then were wiped away from all men all the merits of Christ's bitter passion, in which, though it be true that God died on the cross because of the unity of God and man in person, yet had His tender manhood all the pain for us and His impassible godhead felt no pain at all, whereof serveth also the prayers that every man prayeth for other? Wherefore did saint Paul pray for all other Christian men, and desire them all to pray for him also, and each of them for other, that they might be saved? And why is there so special a mention made in the Acts ... that at the delivery of saint Peter out of prison the Church made continual prayer and intercession for him? And think ye that if God have pity upon one man for another's sake, and delivereth him at another man's petition from a little pain or imprisonment in the world there upon earth, He hath not, at other men's humble and hearty prayer, much more pity upon such as lie in much more heavy pain and torment here in the hot fire of purgatory?[3]

The holy souls, in return for all that is done for them, do the same for us who are still alive on earth. For they pray "with great fervour of heart, and are so far forth in God's undoubted favour, that very few men living upon earth are so well heard"[4] as they.

And yet [say they] there is one thing more to be considered, namely, that these heretics rather hate priests for hatred of Christ's faith than

---

[1] *E.W.*, p. 324 F, G.   [2] *Ib.*, p. 325 G.   [3] *Ib.*, p. 327 B.   [4] *Ib.*, p. 328 D.

speak against purgatory for hatred of priests. Which though it seem to you dark at the first hearing, ye shall yet, if ye look well, very well perceive. For if it so were that this kind of people did speak against purgatory only for the hatred of the pope and the clergy, then would they grant that saved souls are yet purged in the fire here for their sins unsatisfied in the world; and it should then suffice them to say for their purpose that neither priest nor pope nor any man else, nor any man's alms or prayer can, in this place of punishment anything relieve us. . . . But yet they have a far farther purpose against all good Christian faith, they be not content . . . until they deny purgatory utterly . . . and if they would be once believed therein, then would they step yet farther and deny hell and all, and, after, heaven too.[1]

The holy souls now put forward an argument rather anticipating Pascal's famous wager. "Now suppose", say they, "that purgatory could in no wise be proved, and that some would say plainly that there were one, and some would say plainly, nay. Let us see whether sort of this twain might take most harm if their part were wrong."

First, he that believed there were Purgatory, and that his prayer and good works wrought for his friends' souls might relieve them therein, and because thereof used much prayer and alms for them; he could not lose the rewards of his good will, although his opinion were untrue. . . . But, on the other side, he that believeth there is none, and therefore prayeth for none, if his opinion be false, and that there be purgatory indeed, as indeed there is, he loseth much good, and getteth him also much harm, for he both feareth much the less to sin, and to lie long in purgatory, saving that his heresy shall save him thence, and send him down deep into hell. Wherefore it well and plainly appeareth, and every wise man well seeth, that it is the far surer way to believe in such wise as both parties agree to be out of all peril, than that way which so far the greater part, and much farther the better part, affirm to be undoubted deadly sin.[2]

After some trenchant and amusing talk as to the difference between the people who now disbelieve in purgatory and those who, throughout the Christian centuries, have always believed in it, we come at last to the particular points raised against it by Simon Fish himself. First, he contents himself with advocating the spoliation, beating and marriage of all the clergy, and, as a special appeal to Henry VIII, that all should be taken from them because they have broken "the statute made of mortmain, and have purchased still more land"[3] in defiance of that law, and that once they possess such lands they never given them up or sell them

---

[1] *E. W.*, p. 329 B, C.   [2] *Ib.*, F, G.   [3] *Ib.*, p. 332 F.

again. The fact is, on the contrary, for neither is there so much coming
to them as he would make out, while his tale that they never give up
or sell again what they have gotten is plainly untrue. London apart, in
which much property has gone into the hand of the city companies and
fellowships of crafts, there is now, nor has been for a good while, much
land passing into monastic possession, "except somewhat done in the
universities. And yet whoso consider those great (monastic) foundations
that have all this while been made anywhere, shall well perceive that
the substance of them be not all founded upon temporal lands, new
taken out of the temporal hands into the Church, but of such as the
Church had long before, and now the same translated from one place
unto another. And over this he shall find that many an abbey have the
great part thereof in benefices given in and empropriated unto them."
Nowadays, alas, when fervour and charity have so much cooled "there
is little fear that all the temporal lands shall come into the spiritualty".
Fish proves too much, and should learn that there is a mean way
between every whit and never a whit. "And now when the Church
pulleth not away the land from the owner by force, but hath it of his
devotion and his gift, given of his own offer unasked, and yet not without license of all such as the statute (of Mortmain) limiteth; where is
the great fault of theirs for which, lest they should take more in the
same manner, he would have they should lose all that they have
already?"[1]

But now, to leave all this matter of contention, let us come to the
purpose of our supplication, in which St. Thomas More's own great
devotion to the holy souls is so well shown forth.

Consider you [they say to their friends still on earth], consider you
our pains and pity them in your hearts, and help us with your prayers,
pilgrimages and other almsdeeds, and of all thing in special procure us
the suffrages and blessed oblation of the holy Mass, whereof no man
living so well can tell the fruit as we that here feel it (in purgatory).
The comfort that we have here except our continual hope in our Lord
God, cometh at seasons from our Lady, with such glorious saints as
either ourselves with our own devotion while we lived, or ye with
yours for us since our decease and departing, have made intercessors for
us. And among other, right especially be we beholden to the blessed
spirits of our own proper good angels, who when we behold coming
with comfort to us, albeit that we take great pleasure and greatly rejoice
therein, yet it not without much confusion and shamefacedness to

[1] E.W., p. 333 B.

consider how little we regarded our good angels, and how seldom we thought upon them while we lived. They carry our prayers to God and good saints for us, and they bring down the comfort and consolation to us with which they come and comfort us. Only God and we know what joy it is to our hearts, and how heartily we pray for you. And therefore, if God accept the prayer after His own favour borne towards him that prayeth, and the affection that he prayeth with, our prayer must needs be profitable, for we stand sure of His grace. And our prayer is for you so fervent that ye can nowhere find any such affection upon earth. And therefore since we lie so sore in pains and have in our great necessity so great need of your help, and that ye may so well do it, whereby shall also rebound upon yourself an inestimable profit, let never any slothful oblivion raze out of your remembrance, or malicious enemy of ours cause you to be careless, or any greedy mind upon your own good withdraw your gracious alms from us. Think how soon ye shall come hither to us, think what great grief and rebuke would then your unkindness be to you, what comfort, on the contrary part, when all we shall thank you. What help ye shall have here of your good sent hither. Remember what kin ye and we be together, what familiar friendship hath ere this been between us, and what sweet words ye have spoken, and what promise ye have made us. Let now your own words appear, and your fair promise be kept. Now dear friends, remember how nature and Christendom bindeth you to remember us. If any point now of your old favour, any piece of your old love, any kindness of kindred, any care of acquaintance, any favour of old friendship, any spark of charity, any tender point of pity, any regard of nature, any respect of Christendom be left in your breasts, let never the malice of a few fond fellows, a few pestilent persons borne toward priesthood, religion, and your Christian faith, raze out of your hearts the care of your kindred, all force of your old friends, and all remembrance of all Christian souls. Remember our thirst while ye sit and drink, our hunger while ye be feasting, our restless watch while ye be sleeping, our sore and grievous pain while ye be playing, our hot burning fire while ye be in pleasure and sporting, so might God make your offspring after remember you: so God keep you hence, or not long here, but bring you shortly to that bliss to which our Lord's love help you to bring us, and we shall set hand to help you thither to us.[1]

[1] *E.W.*, p. 338 to the end. Simon Fish made his peace with the Church before his death.

10

More as Lord Chancellor (1529–32)

THE *Supplication of Souls* came out in 1529, but before October 25th, when "the great seal was given to the most eminent layman in England, Sir Thomas More".[1] His first important duty in that high office was to make a speech at the opening of the Reformation Parliament on November 3rd in the presence of the King, and one that may be called the King's Speech in a very true sense, particularly as it contained, no doubt at the King's behest, a very unchivalrous reference to Cardinal Wolsey, his fallen predecessor. More expressed what we may believe was his own private feeling about Wolsey in a rather different way when he wrote, "Glorious was he, very far above all measure, and that was great pity; for it did harm and made him abuse many great gifts that God had given him."[2] More, indeed, could but remember how the proud and acquisitive spirit of Wolsey had given general scandal, and how "a London crowd had watched with deep disappointment the Cardinal's barge make for Putney instead of for the Tower [after his disgrace], and no news would have been more popular than the intelligence of his death".[3] Even Tyndale, unambitious and unacquisitive as he was, could make Wolsey an excuse for his unceasing denunciations of the clergy, not distinguishing, as More always did, between bad Catholics and good Catholicism. Professor R. W. Chambers considered that More's language about Wolsey was justified.

Wolsey's pro-French and anti-Spanish policy [he wrote] laid him open to the suspicion of having instigated the divorce, for the divorce was the natural corollary of that policy. More's circle believed this, and moreover they believed that Wolsey was moved by personal motives. More has left us nothing in writing on the subject; but we may well suppose that he had come to regard Wolsey as the evil genius of Henry VIII and, indeed, of England—the man who had impoverished his country by useless wars with France, and then embroiled her in war

---

[1] H. A. L. Fisher, *The Political History of England*, vol. v, p. 290.
[2] *Dialogue of Comfort*, ed. Hallett, p. 102.
[3] H. A. L. Fisher, *The Political History of England*, vol. v, p. 290.

with Charles V, representing England's traditional friends, the house of Burgundy. Those things Wolsey indisputably had done, and they were enough to have earned from More his strong disapproval. But if Wolsey, in addition to this, had put doubts about his union with Katherine into Henry's mind, then More would feel that Wolsey had endangered the unity of Christendom, and the salvation of Henry's own soul. The wonder is that here, and elsewhere, More deals as leniently with Wolsey as he does.

Besides, although More probably felt about Wolsey even more bitterly than he spoke, we must remember that he was speaking as Henry's servant.[1]

We may add, too, that More's reference in his "King's Speech" to the immediate necessity of ecclesiastical reform–of a kind that More himself could not approve of–shows that its main sentiments were the King's and not his own.

The temper of the new House of Commons may be inferred from some words uttered by St. John Fisher in the House of Lords in 1531:

My lords, you see daily what bills come hither from the Common house and all to the destruction of the Church, for God's sake see what a realm the kingdom of Bohemia was, and when the Church went down, then fell the glory of the kingdom, now with the Commons is nothing but "Down with the Church", and all this meseemeth is for lack of faith only.[2]

This utterance brought a protest from the Commons, who accused Fisher by Audley, their Speaker, before the King, for saying they were no better than heretics. After their departure the King sent for the Bishop of Rochester and others; on which Fisher excused himself.[3]

But to go back to 1529. On July 19th Clement VII had revoked Henry's cause to Rome; and the King was not slow to turn this unwonted event to his own advantage.

The divorce had been from the beginning, and remained to the end, a stumbling-block to the people. Katherine received ovations wherever she went, while the utmost efforts of the King could scarcely protect Anne Boleyn from popular insult. The people were moved, not only by a creditable feeling that Henry's first wife was an injured woman, but by the fear lest a breach with Charles should destroy their trade in wool, on which, said the imperial ambassador, half the realm depended for sustenance.[4]

---

[1] R. W. Chambers, *Thomas More*, pp. 242–3.
[2] *Hall's Chronicle*, fol. clxxxviii. Imprinted by Grafton, 1548.
[3] *Ib.*   [4] A. F. Pollard, *Henry VIII*, p. 250.

It would be well to remember that Parliament at that time was not representative of popular feeling. As Professor A. F. Pollard puts it:

There was discontent in abundance during Tudor times, but it was social and economic and not as a rule political. It was directed against the enclosers of common lands; against agricultural capitalists (as distinguished from the old monastic landlords) who bought up farms, evicted tenants, and converted their holdings to pasture; against large traders in towns who monopolised commerce at the expense of their poorer competitors. It was concerned, not with one tyrant on the throne, but with the thousand petty tyrants of the villages and towns, against whom the poorer commons looked to the King for protection. Of this discontent Parliament could not be the focus, for members of Parliament were themselves the offenders. "It is hard," wrote a contemporary radical, "to have these ills redressed by Parliament, because it pricketh them chiefly which be chosen for burgesses. . . . Would to God they would leave their old accustomed choosing of burgesses! For whom do they choose but such as be rich or bear some office in the country."

But for the time being . . . the interests of the King and of the lay middle classes coincided, both in secular and in ecclesiastical affairs. . . . Both thought the clergy too rich, and that ecclesiastical revenues could be put to better uses in secular hands. Community of interests produced harmony of action. Tyrants have often gone about to break parliaments, and in the end parliaments have generally broken them. Henry was not of the number. . . . He found them far too useful and he used them. He would have been as reluctant to break Parliament as Ulysses the bow which he alone could bend.[1]

Henry was cleverer than Wolsey in his treatment of Parliament. Wolsey had tried to browbeat them, Henry did nothing so foolish. Even when a member, in 1532, moved that Henry should take back Katherine to wife (and nothing could have touched him on a tenderer spot) he only argued the point with the Speaker. "Charles I, for a less offence, would have gone to the House himself to arrest the offender. . . . There is nothing to show that Henry VIII intimidated his Commons at any time, or that he packed the Parliament of 1529."[2]

Henry VIII was indeed very skilful in his dealings with Parliament, and the harmony which prevailed between him and it has been adduced as a proof of its servility.

That accusation [continues the same writer] can only be substantiated

---

[1] *Henry VIII*, pp. 256–8 *passim*.
[2] *Ib.* pp. 259–60. H. A. L. Fisher, writing four years later than A. F. Pollard, held that the 1529 Parliament *was* a packed one (*Political History of England*, vol. v, pp. 291–2).

by showing that Parliament did, not what it wanted, but what it did not want, out of deference to Henry. And that has never been proved. . . . The general harmony between King and Parliament was based on a fundamental similarity of interests, the harmony in detail was worked out, not by the forcible exertion of Henry's will, but by his careful and skilful manipulation of both Houses. No one was ever a greater adept in the management of the House of Commons, which is easy to humour but hard to drive. Parliaments are jealous bodies, but they are generally pleased with attentions, and Henry VIII was very assiduous in the attentions he paid his lay Lords and Commons.[1]

In all important matters he managed the business himself, and he constantly visited both Houses, and remained within their precincts for hours at a time. He issued no royal commands, but suggested policy, giving reasons for it, and was willing to discuss its reasonability. He was more like a modern leader of Parliament, and, like them, demanded most of its time for the measures he put forward. But all were not accepted, and their rejection did not, as now, involve the fall of the Government or a dissolution. Sixteenth-century members of Parliament were representatives rather than delegates, and together with the King decided what legislation was necessary. Of course the King and the Parliament did not always want the same things–it was a matter of give and take between them, partly by the Parliament doing what Henry wanted, and partly by Henry doing what Parliament wanted. Both Henry and the Parliament wanted to appropriate ecclesiastical property on a large scale, and neither Parliament nor Henry wanted any doctrinal changes to be made. Henry wanted to be supreme head of the Church in England, and Parliament seemed not unwilling that the Church of England should be subject to the royal power. To use a modern word, though hardly in its modern sense, they both wanted the Church to be *nationalised*; but by being nationalised it would "compromise its universal character, and become the Church of England, rather than a branch of the Church universal *in* England".[2]

The steps by which these great changes were wrought by the secular power have been well summed up by H. A. L. Fisher:

The Parliament which met on November 3, 1529, was destined to carry out a series of changes more profound and widespread than any which had yet been accomplished in the annals of English legislation. In the seven years of its existence it snapped the bonds which bound England to Rome, and established the royal supremacy over the English

---

[1] Pollard, *Henry VIII*, pp. 262–3.   [2] *Ib.*, pp. 265–8 *passim*.

Church. It dissolved the smaller monasteries and initiated a redistribution of national wealth which in scale and significance surpassed anything of the kind since the land settlement of the Norman conquest. It exalted the royal power to a pitch to which it had never previously attained, and it excited a protest which but for the moderation of its leaders would have endangered the throne. It determined articles of religious belief; it settled more than once the succession of the crown; it created new treasons and greatly abridged the liberty of the subject. It handled many grave social problems such as mendicancy, which it attempted to stamp out by severity, and the economic revolution which was emptying cottages and extending sheep-runs. It passed an Act which had the effect of obliterating that which was distinctive in the legal and administrative system of Wales; and working in an atmosphere of projects and projectors it considered some far-reaching plans, such as the abolition of entails, which it did not carry out. We have reached one of the few epoch-making periods in the history of English legislation.[1]

Up to this time Henry had not wanted to quarrel with the Pope, but only to use every means in his power to persuade him to do what he wished in the matter of Katherine of Aragon and Anne Boleyn. He had just taken into his service a man of unscrupulous ambition and great ability, Thomas Cromwell, who is thought to have brought him to his final break with Rome. Reginald Pole, speaking from personal knowledge of Cromwell and his friends, says "that they made no concealment of their desire to abolish papal power, to spoil the monks, and to exalt the monarch at the expense of the Church."[2]

Meanwhile More was to remain Lord Chancellor for three years—a period in which he did what he could to hold in check the enemies of the Church, and this the King sometimes pretended to do, but was not really doing.

When the Reformation Parliament was prorogued in December 1529, the first move had been made towards the subjection of the clergy; and, "whether or no, the matter should go no further, whether the power of the Pope should be abolished and the Church subjected to the uncontested control of the monarchy, was an issue dependent upon the action of the Curia in the great matrimonial cause".[3]

In January 1530 an embassy led by the father of Anne Boleyn, now the Earl of Wiltshire, and including such learned persons as Stokesley and Lee, was sent to Bologna to interview the Pope, who was there in order to place the imperial crown upon the head of Charles V—hardly a

---

[1] *The Political History of England*, vol. v, p. 291.   [2] *Ib.*, p. 295.   [3] *Ib.*, p. 300.

convenient moment for the negotiation of Henry VIII's unpleasant business. The immediate result was the citation of Wiltshire, as Henry's representative, to appear before the Roman Court; and there was little doubt that the verdict would be unfavourable to the English King. All that could be obtained was the postponement of the proceedings for six weeks.

Meanwhile the opinions of the Universities, at home and abroad were sought on the divorce. In February Gardiner and Fox were sent to Cambridge, and another deputation to Oxford, where in both cases, not without royal pressure, a verdict in favour of the King was given. In the same way, under the persuasion of Francis I, a favourable opinion was got from the French universities of Paris, Orleans, Angers, Bourges and Toulouse. In Italy, Bologna and Padua were also found favourable. In Germany, too, favourable answers were given; but in Spain, as might be expected, the opposite was the case.

But while secretly favouring unorthodoxy for his own ends, Henry was anxious to impress European Catholic opinion, and set out to exhibit himself as an upholder of orthodoxy by the persecution of English heretics.

In the spring of 1530 Lutheran writings were being widely circulated, together with Tyndale's translations of the Scripture with their heretical prologues, and were giving much cause for anxiety to the ecclesiastical authorities. Bishop Nix of Norwich writes to Archbishop Warham on May 14th:

After most humble recommendation I do pray your Grace to understand that I am accumbred with such as keepeth and readeth these erroneous books in English, and believe and give credence to the same, and teacheth others that they should do so. My Lord I have done that lieth in me for the suppression of such persons, but it passeth my power, or any spiritual man to do it. For divers saith openly in my diocese that the King's Grace *would* that they should have the said erroneous books, and so maintaineth themselves to the King. Whereupon I desired my Lord Abbot of Hyde to show this to the King's Grace, beseeching him to send his honourable letters under his Seal down to whom he pleases in my diocese, that may show and publish that it is *not* his pleasure that such books should be had or read, and also punish such as saith so . . .
The said Abbot departed from me on Monday last; and since that time I have had much trouble and business with others in like matter; and they say that wheresoever they go, they hear say that the King's pleasure is, the New Testament in English should go forth, and men

should have it and read it. . . . Wherefore I beseech your good Lordship to advertise the King's Grace . . . that a remedy may be had.

For now it may be done well in my diocese, for the gentlemen and the commonalty be not greatly infected, but merchants and such that hath their abiding not far from the sea. The said Abbot of Hyde can show you of a curate, and well learned in my diocese, that exhorted his parishioners to believe the contrary to the Catholical faith. There is a college in Cambridge call Gunwell Hall, of the foundation of a bishop of Norwich. I hear of no clerk that hath come out lately of that college but savoureth of the frying pan, though he speak never so holily.

What, then, did the King do about it? The following passage from Hall,[1] who writes in his record of the twenty-second year of the reign, dating from April 22nd, 1530, tells us a good deal:

In the beginning of this year, the King, like a politic and prudent prince, perceived that his subjects and other persons had, divers times within four years past, brought into his realm great number of printed books of the New Testament, translated into the English tongue by Tyndale, Joye, and others, which books the common people used and daily read privily; which the clergy would not admit, for they punished such persons as had read, studied or taught the same, with great extremity; but because the multitude was so great, it was not in their power to redress their grief. Wherefore they made complaint to the Chancellor [Sir Thomas More], which leaned much to the spiritual men's part in all causes; whereupon he imprisoned and punished a great number; so that for this cause a great rumor and controversy rose daily among the people. Wherefore the King, considering what good might come of the reading of the New Testament with reverence and following the same, and what evil might come of the reading of the same if it were evil translated, and not followed; came into the Star Chamber the five and twentieth day of May, and there commoned with his Council and the Prelates concerning this cause; and after long debating, it was alleged that the translation[s] of Tyndale and Joye were not truly translated and also that in them were prologues and prefaces which sounded to heresy and railed against the Bishops uncharitably. Wherefore all such books were prohibited, and the commandment given by the King to the Bishops that they calling to them the best learned men of the universities, should cause a new translation to be made, so that the people should not be ignorant in the law of God. And notwithstanding this commandment, the Bishops did nothing at all to set forth a new translation; which caused the people to study Tyndale's translation; by reason whereof many things came to light, as you shall see hereafter.

[1] *Hall's Chronicle*, fol. clxxxii.

Gairdner, whose judgment on this quotation from *Hall's Chronicle* is of interest, said that it deserved our careful attention; for although Hall "was a sad special pleader in favour of the King", it witnessed, from the other side, to the facts enumerated by Bishop Nix as to the importation of Tyndale's books and the impossibility of suppressing them, but without mentioning the King's own connivance at their diffusion, and how Henry had cleverly laid upon the bishops the duty of making a new translation of the New Testament in order to counteract the mischief that was being done by Tyndale's translation, a duty which they were very slow to perform. Gairdner adds this further criticism of Tyndale's work:

The substantial benefit we have gained by a vernacular translation from the Greek very naturally hides from our view, after the lapse of ages, the indications of a perverse and bitter spirit running through the whole design. And Demaus, Tyndale's biographer, does not hesitate to say that not a single passage is overlooked from which any comment could be drawn against the doctrines and practices of the Pope and clergy.[1]

A list of books with the heresies contained in them was issued which included Tyndale's *Wicked Mammon* and the *Obedience of a Christian Man*, also the *Sum of Scripture*, the *Revelation of Antichrist*, and Simon Fish's *Supplication for the Beggars*, and "the translation of scripture corrupted by William Tyndale as well in the old testament and the new". Preachers were also instructed to inform their flocks of the decisions that had been made.

What Hall does not mention is that discretion was reserved by the King as to when and how it was advisable to give this translation to the public. Finally, a proclamation was issued in June forbidding the use, or even the keeping, of the heretical books denounced, and declaring that it was not expedient at that time to have the Scripture in English.[2]

Henry VIII now made a last effort to procure a papal judgment in his favour. In June 1530 a petition went forth in the name of the spiritual and temporal lords, including the signatures of twenty-three abbots, addressed to Clement VII, and stating that the unlawfulness of his marriage had been declared by a number of famous universities at home and abroad. The Pope replied with a dignified negative on September 27th.

[1] Gairdner, *Lollardy and the Reformation*, vol. ii, pp. 242-3.
[2] *L. & P.*, vol. iv, 6487. Quotation from the old edition, a new one has since appeared.

The next step taken by the King was an extraordinary and momentous one. When Wolsey had been proceeded against for *præmunire* in the King's Bench, he had thought it wise to confess to the charge against him; but in truth the proceedings were grossly unjust; for the Bulls he had procured from Rome constituting his legatine authority, and upon which the charge was based, had been obtained at the instance of the King himself. But now it was made to appear that his legatine jurisdiction obtained in this way had been a usurpation all along, and the whole body of the clergy were also included in the *præmunire* for having submitted to it.

Notice of proceedings in this matter had been given by the beginning of August, but apparently no positive steps had been taken for some time. On January 16, 1531, Parliament met again after prorogation, and five days later the Convocation of Canterbury did the same. The chosen scene of the deliberations was the chapter-house of Westminster Abbey, and the great question before them was whether they could compound with the king for their alleged offence. It had been proposed to give him a subsidy of £40,000, but they were made to understand they must increase the grant to two and a half times as much to secure their pardon. On this the vote was raised to £100,044 8s. 4d., and so passed both Houses on January 24, with a preamble stating that it was granted in consideration of the king's great services against heretics, without a word about the threat (of *præmunire*) by which it was really extorted. . . . On February 7, Henry notified to them that he declined to accept the gift without the insertion of certain clauses in the preamble, the most important of which acknowledged him as "Protector and Supreme Head of the English Church and Clergy", while another insinuated that he had the cure of his subjects' souls committed to him and a third expressly mentioned what they so studiously ignored–a general pardon for their transgression of penal statutes. These things were bitterly resented. The Upper House took the royal message into consideration, and for three whole sittings debated the unaccustomed title of Protector and Supreme Head without coming to any agreement. The judges and councillors sent to them said they had no commission to conclude about the general pardon for the *præmunire* till the title was acknowledged; but the intimation produced no effect. The king then sent them by Anne Boleyn's brother, Viscount Rochford, another message allowing them to modify the title by the insertion of the words *post Deum* after *Supremum Caput*, and refusing to discuss the matter further. Even this form, however, was not accepted, but in place of it Archbishop Warham, on February 11, suggested the words–"of the Church and clergy of England, whose especial Protector, single and supreme lord, and as far as the law of Christ allows, even Supreme

Head we acknowledge his Majesty to be." And when this was proposed not a word seems to have been said to second it. The situation was evidently growing painful, but the archbishop found a way out of it. "Whoever is silent," he said, "seems to consent." "Then we are all silent," one voice replied; and thus the clause passed the Upper House, and was agreed to by the Lower. With this the king had to be content, . . . Convocation modified other articles also, correcting, among other things, the statement that the cure of the souls of his subjects was committed to his Majesty. . . .

The Convocation of York was then asked to follow the example of the southern province, and ultimately did so; but not without a protest from Tunstall, now Bishop of Durham, against the title as admitted by the southern clergy. . . . The York Convocation also bought their pardon from the *præmunire* for the sum of £18,840 0s. 10d. But protests were sent to the king from both Convocations in May against the new kind of sovereignty he was endeavouring to establish over them.[1]

Parliament confirmed the pardon for the province of Canterbury, and later for that of York. And the Commons themselves becoming alarmed because they had received no pardon, persuaded the King to grant them one under his own seal.

On March 30th, the day before its prorogation, More was commanded by the King, along with twelve other members of the House of Lords, spiritual and temporal, to visit the House of Commons and inform them that the Bishop of London would lay before them the opinion of the Universities collected on the matter of the King's marriage with Katherine of Aragon; and in the discussion that followed, being asked his own opinion, he replied that he had often expressed it to the King himself.

On February 24th, 1532, Warham, as Archbishop of Canterbury, made a formal protest to the newly assembled Parliament against all its previous enactments in derogation of the Pope's authority and the spiritual prerogatives of the province of Canterbury. Chapuys, the imperial ambassador, believed that even at that time they were discussing measures subversive of episcopal authority altogether; and in March, on the initiative of the Court rather than of their own, they made a Supplication to the King against the bishops, in which it was asserted that much discord and ill-will had lately arisen between the King's subjects, spiritual and temporal, owing, on the one hand, to the new and fantastic opinions, and, on the other, to the severity and unkind

---

[1] Gairdner, *A History of the English Church in the Sixteenth Century*, pp. 107-9.

behaviour "of divers ordinaries, their commisaries and substitutes", in their examination of errors and heretical opinions. At the same time a work written by Christopher St. German, a lawyer, "Concerning the division between the spiritualty and the temporalty", emphasises the same contention, though More denied it in his *Apology* written in 1533. Gairdner writes on this Supplication: "that some of the grievances were plausible, and some perhaps not altogether theoretical, may be assumed almost as a matter of course; but the main object of the Supplication was to suggest that there were matters connected with the spiritual administration in which the clergy could not be trusted, as they hitherto had been, to reform themselves, and which, therefore, the King must take into his own hands."[1] Convocation was, in fact, at this time shaping measures of correction for a large number of abuses; but by this very Bill its action was altogether paralysed.

The Supplication having been approved by the Commons, it was agreed to present it to the King; and on March 18th the presentation was made by the Speaker and a deputation of members to Henry himself. At the same time, because of the great cost and inconvenience of their long attendance in this Parliament, they prayed for a dissolution, in order that they might return to their own homes in the country, a request that made the whole thing seem very unreal. The King, however, seeing that their Bill contained such weighty matter, said that they must stay and hear what the clergy had to say for themselves. At the same time he also sent them a Bill, the object of which was to guard the Crown against a great loss of feudal dues on the succession of heirs; and this they refused to pass.

Parliament, however, adjourned for Easter until April 10th; but in the meantime it passed, seemingly much against its will, an Act against the payment of *annates* (or first-fruits on benefices) to Rome. Even in the House of Lords it met with opposition from other besides bishops and abbots; and the Commons could only be persuaded to pass it on the condition that it was not to take effect for a year.

Yet the Pope's nuncio, then in England, was told by the Duke of Norfolk that the King had been obliged to pass it in order to satisfy the Commons, who had proposed other measures against the Holy See, and that it was still in the King's power to secure payment to the Pope of his old accustomed dues if he and his Holiness could come to a proper understanding with each other.[2]

---

[1] *History of the English Church in the Sixteenth Century*, p. 115. [2] *Ib.*, p. 116.

On the reassembling of Parliament, More, as Lord Chancellor, with other peers, again visited the Commons, this time to ask for money in order to defend the Scotch border. The Commons were not at all agreeable to this demand; and one member, named Temse, was bold enough to say that there was no danger to be feared from the Scots, and that the King should be petitioned to take back his wife (Katherine) and treat her well, as her nephew, Charles V, could do them greater mischief than any other power. Temse's motion was seconded and carried with general applause; so the question of the money for the Scotch border was for the time deferred.

On April 12th the Archbishop laid the Supplication of the Commons before Convocation; and a reply to it, in the name of the ordinaries, was made with unmistakable clearness. They denied that they were wanting in charity towards the laity; and, as to heretics, they had only done their duty in punishing them.

The power of making laws for themselves could not be a grievance to the community, for it was founded "upon the Scripture of God and the determination of Holy Church"–the principles by which all laws, spiritual and temporal, must be tested–and they were always ready to reform such statutes as did not agree with them. In fulfilment of a high trust committed to them by God, they were not at liberty to submit their canons to the king's assent; but they humbly besought him from henceforth to declare to them his mind on any subject, and they promised to do their best to follow it if it pleased God so to inspire them. The king, they were sure, would acquit them of encroaching on his prerogative, whatever less learned persons might say.[1]

This "Answer of the Ordinaries" was presented to the King; and on April 30th he sent for the Speaker, Audeley, and a deputation of the Commons, and delivered it to them for their consideration. "We think", he said, "their answer will smally please you, for it seemeth to us very slender. You be a great sort of wise men, and we will be indifferent between you." The Commons quite understood what the King's "indifference" meant, since, before dismissing the deputation, he wished them to know that he was surprised to hear that the Commons had ventured to speak of his having parted from the Queen. He would have them know that questions of matrimony were not for them; and what he had done was purely for conscientious reasons, after consulting "the doctors of the universities". Furthermore, he was forty-one years

---

[1] *History of the English Church in the Sixteenth Century*, pp. 117–18.

old, and was not likely at that age to be moved to such things by mere lust. So the Speaker departed, and conveyed the King's observations to the House.

Henry was not one to be moved by such evidences of his unpopularity, as, even before this, he had received a plainer indication of it. On Easter Day, March 31st, William Peto, the provincial of the Friars Observant at Greenwich, had spoken in a sermon, preached before the King, of the danger which princes stood from evil counsellors. After the sermon Henry summoned Peto to a private interview; but the intrepid friar warned the King more severely of his ill conduct towards Katherine, and said that by it he was endangering not only his popularity, but his crown as well. Henry then ordered one of his own chaplains, Dr. Richard Curwen, to preach in the same place and contradict what Peto had said; upon which Henry Elstowe, the warden of Peto's convent, denounced Curwen as a lying prophet; and when one of the courtiers threatened Elstowe, saying that he ought to be put in a sack and drowned in the Thames, he replied, "These threats are for courtiers; the way to heaven is open as well by water as by land."

The King, not being satisfied with the reply of the ordinaries, induced Convocation to make a further reply. As he had taken exception to the right they claimed of making laws for themselves without the royal assent, they said that it rested upon the determination of the Church, accepted throughout all Christendom, that the prelates, having a spiritual jurisdiction, had power to make laws without the consent of any temporal power, and showed that hitherto Christian princes had agreed thereto. Indeed, it was founded upon Scripture, and had been defended by the King himself in his book against Luther. Nevertheless, considering the King's wisdom, learning and goodness, they were willing to forbear from further legislation without his consent, unless it were for the maintenance of the faith. As to past laws, if there were any not in use and not affecting the faith or the correction of sin, they were ready to revoke them when they should be pointed out.[1]

But even this was not enough to satisfy the King; a more complete submission must be made. On May 10th, 1532, Foxe brought in to the Convocation a set of three articles proposed by Henry himself for their acceptance, which required them to forgo their right to make ordinances for themselves; and on the day following he again sent for the

---

[1] *History of the English Church in the Sixteenth Century*, p. 119.

Speaker and twelve other members, whom he is reported to have addressed as follows:

Well-beloved subjects, we thought that the clergy of our realm had been our subjects wholly; but now we have well perceived that they be but half our subjects—yea, and scarce our subjects. For all the prelates at their consecration make an oath to the Pope clean contrary to the oath they make to us, so that they seem his subjects and not ours.

On May 13th the three articles were admitted with some limitation; after which the Convocation adjourned until the 15th. On that day the Archbishop received a writ from the King to prorogue their deliberations until November 5th. Finally, certain bishops brought in and read a communication from the King which the bishops were asked to agree to without any limitation. All agreed except Clerk, Bishop of Bath, and it was sent down to the Lower House for its assent. The writ of prorogation was then read, and the next day, May 16th, the Archbishop delivered to the King the formal document known as "The Submission of the Clergy".

And a submission it was; for by it they promised to enact no new canons, constitutions provincial, or ordinances provincial or synodal without the King's licence; to submit it to the examination of the King and of thirty-two persons, half lay and half ecclesiastical, all to be chosen by the King, whether any of their past constitutions and ordinances were against God's laws and those of the realm, and if found so by the majority, that they should be abolished; and lastly, that the laws which that majority approved should receive the King's assent and continue in full force. Though it was a surrender against their will, they threw the responsibility upon the broad shoulders of Henry VIII, "a really wise and learned king", perhaps with the vain hope that in future reigns they would recover what they had lost.[1]

On the same day, May 16th, 1532, More surrendered the great seal, feeling, no doubt, that as Lord Chancellor he would now be abetting rather than helping to restrain the King in his anti-Catholic policy, which had of late become so very pronounced.

---

[1] Cf. *History of the English Church in the Sixteenth Century*, pp. 120–2.

11

Tyndale at Antwerp

N ow NO longer burdened with the cares of high office, More set
himself whole-heartedly to the task of confuting heresy by
argument rather, he hoped, than by force. In the July of 1532
Tyndale published his *Answer to Sir Thomas More's Dialogue*, and by
September of the same year More had issued the first part of his
immense *Confutation of Tyndale's Answer*. He writes to Erasmus on
June 14th, 1533, mentioning his resignation, and continues:

I am good for nothing when I am ill. We are not all Erasmuses!
Here are you in a condition which would break the spirit of a vigorous
man, still bringing out book after book, for the instruction and admira-
tion of the world. What matter these attacks upon you? No great
writer ever escaped malignity. But the stone which these slanderers
have been rolling so many years is like the stone of Sisyphus, and will
recoil on their own heads, and you will stand out more grandly than
ever. You allow frankly that if you could have foreseen these pestilent
heresies you would have been less outspoken on certain points. Doubt-
less the Fathers, had they expected such times as ours, would have been
more cautious in their utterances. They had their own disorders to
attend to, and did not think of the future. . . . The bishops and the king
try to check these new doctrines but they spread wonderfully. The
teachers of them retreat into the Low Countries, as into a safe harbour,
and send over their works written in English. Our people read them,
partly in thoughtlessness, partly from a malicious disposition. They
enjoy them, not because they think them true, but because they wish
them to be true. Such persons are past mending, but I try to help those
who do not go wrong from bad will, but are led astray by clever rogues.[1]

In another letter to Erasmus in the same year More also writes:

As touching heretics, I hate that vice of theirs, and not their persons,
and very fain would I that the one were destroyed and the other be
saved.

And again:

I so entirely detest that race of men that there is none to which I

[1] Q.*v.* E. M. C. Routh, *Sir Thomas More and his Friends*, p. 187.

would be more hostile–unless they amend. For every day more and more, I find them to be of such sort that I greatly fear for what they are bringing upon the world. As to what I wrote in my letter that I gave trouble to heretics, I took pride in writing this.[1]

There is a saying of More's which like a golden thread guides us through all the twists and dark turnings of heretical teaching: "Remember now, good reader," he writes, "that Christ's Church can be but one. Whereupon it must needs follow, that there can be none go out of it to begin any new church of Christ. But those therefore that go out thereof, must needs be churches of heretics."[2]

But before considering in detail Tyndale's *Answer* and More's *Confutation*, it would be well for us to take up the thread of Tyndale's life from the point at which we left it.[3]

From 1529 onwards, being still in exile, he made his headquarters in the neighbourhood of Antwerp, a city that for him was very convenient, though not without danger. Living there, he was within easy reach of England, and could quickly transport his books to English soil. He could also welcome unorthodox refugees fleeing from the home country.

We know from Chapuys, the ambassador of Charles V, that Tyndale's *Practice of Prelates* had been condemned by royal proclamation; but suddenly we hear, on the same authority, that the King, unwilling that so able a man should write against him, at the instance of Cromwell, withdrew his censure with the hope of persuading him to support the royal cause. Tyndale, however, was unamenable to such persuasion.

Having translated the New Testament, he now turned his attention to the Old; but in order to do this he had first to learn Hebrew–and it took him two years to master the elements of that difficult language. He then translated the Pentateuch, which was published in 1530, Jonah, which appeared about May 1531, and at the end of a new edition of his New Testament, a translation of those passages which were read instead of Epistles at Mass.

And then, as we gather on good authority, though there are those who question it, he undertook the translation of the later historical books, Joshua to II Chronicles, which he left at his death and which were included in the so-called Matthew's Bible of 1537. This is borne out by internal evidence as adduced by Mr. Mozley. He first of all gives

---

[1] Q.v. Bridgett, *Sir Thomas More*, p. 250.
[2] *E.W.*, *The Confutation*, p. 628 A, B.   [3] See p. 123.

us examples from Tyndale's known work, comparing them with the more ordinary renderings of the Authorised and Revised versions, which are given in brackets:

Genesis iii. 4. Then said the serpent unto the woman: *Tush, ye shall not* die.

Genesis xxx. 29. Thou knowest what service I have done thee, and *in what taking* thy cattle have been under me.

Genesis xxxix. 2. And the Lord was with Joseph, and he was a *lucky fellow*.

Exodus xv. 4. His [Pharaoh's] *jolly* captains are drowned in the Red Sea.

Numbers xi. 4. And the *rascal people* that were among them fell alusting.

Deut. xxxiv. 7. And yet his eyes were not dim, nor his *cheeks* abated. (The Vulgate renders it, His teeth had not fallen out.)

Mr. Mozley now gives us renderings from Joshua to II Chronicles:

Joshua v. 1. To the *seaward* (*westward*) implying knowledge of the Hebrew.

Ruth iii. 11. For all the *gates* of my people knoweth thou art a woman of virtue.

II Samuel xxii. 17. Plucked me out of *mighty* waters.

I Kings xxii. 34. And certain men drew a bow *ignorantly*, and smote the king between *the ribs of his harness*. (A.V. and R.V. *lung and stomach*.)

II Kings iv. 35. And then the lad *neesed* seven times (*yawned, gaped*).

II Kings xii. 4. All the silver that is dedicate and brought to the house of the Lord *in current money* (*according to the assessment*, R.V.).

So far we seem to trace Tyndale's hand. . . . But the strongest proof is still to come. A rendering of a difficult phrase, or a rendering that is in any way remarkable in itself, might be imitated by a disciple, who, mistrusting his own competence for the work of translation, thought it safer to follow Tyndale. But in these unnamed books we find also the little peculiarities, the unusual habits, the tricks and inconsistencies, which we have learnt to know in Tyndale's New Testament and Pentateuch. No one could imitate these, or could succeed if he tried to do so. Thus we find once more the roundabout imperative, the needless inversion of two nouns, the use of *what* for *who*, and *as soon as* for *when*, the repetition of nouns to make the meaning clearer, and so on. These devices are not constantly used, but only when he has a mind.

Above all, the extravagant love of variation is here. Thus a *covenant* between God and man is frequently rendered by *appointment* and *testament*, and in other connections it becomes a *bond, league* or *con-federation*. The phrase *it came to pass*, when not omitted, is rendered by *chanced, fortuned* and *happened*. . . . Tyndale finds many opportunities of introducing variety. *Rest* can become *remnant*; *acts* are also *deeds*, the book of the Chronicles becomes also *book of the histories, book of deeds* (or *acts*) *done in the days*, or simply *stories*. . . . He can hardly have twice given the formula in the same way. . . .

There are the same bold touches, the same quaint turns of phrase, which though sometimes rather free of the Hebrew, always awake our interest and pleasure. Thus he gives:

Judges iv. 15. But the Lord *trounced* Sisera (*discomfited*, A.V.).
Judges xiii. 5. The lad shall be an *abstainer* (*Nazarite*).
I Samuel vi. 6. When he [God] had *played his pageants with them* (*wrought wonderfully among them*).
II Samuel xiii. 28. (Absolom to his young men). *Be bold therefore and play the lusty bloods* (be courageous and be valiant).
II Kings ix. 20. For he driveth *as he were mad* (*furiously*).
II Kings xix. 27. *How thou settest up thy bristles* (*thy rage*) against me.

Or if we test the version in large, our conclusion is the same. There is the same firm hand, the same simple and direct style, the same wonderful rhythm, the same noble dignity that rises with its theme. All bears the stamp of Tyndale.[1]

When the King, at the instance of Cromwell, changed his mind about Tyndale and suddenly decided to invite him back to England, hoping, no doubt, to enlist his services as a royal pamphleteer, he chose as his agent a certain Stephen Vaughan, a close friend of Cromwell's, a Catholic, anti-papal, but not, it would seem, inclined to Lutheran Protestantism,[2] and now a merchant adventurer at Antwerp. From his letters to Cromwell and to the King we get a good deal of information about Tyndale, and, indeed, the first for some considerable time. On January 26th, 1531, he reports to the King what little progress he had so far been able to make.

My mind continually labouring and thirsting . . . to attain the know-ledge of such things as your Majesty commanded me to learn and practise in these parts and thereof to advertise you from time to time as the case should require. . . . Of late I have written three sundry letters

---

[1] J. F. Mozley, *William Tyndale*, pp. 177–85 *passim*. But see the whole of Chapter VIII, a most satisfying piece of critical attribution for which I am indebted to the author.
[2] Cf. a letter from Vaughan to Cromwell expressing his indignation of the appoint-ment of Rowland Lee to the see of Lichfield, "You have lately holpen an earthly beast, a mole, and an enemy of all godly learning, into the office of his damnation, *a papist*, an Idolater, and a fleshly priest." Ellis, *Original Letters*, 3rd series, vol. ii, p. 285.

unto William Tyndale, and the same sent, for the more surety, to three sundry places, to Frankfort, Hamburg, and Marburg: I then, not assured in which of the same he was. As I had heard say in England, that he would, upon the promise of your majesty and of your most gracious safe conduct, be content to repair and come into England, I made him the offer, using certain other persuasions to move him, and above all promising him that "whatsoever surety he would reasonably desire for his safe coming in and going out of your realm, my friends [Cromwell] should labour to have the same granted by your majesty." I had great hopes of success, but "the bruit and fame of such things as, since my writing to him, hath chanced within your realm," has led him not only to refuse, but to suspect a trap to bring him into peril. Were he but in your gracious presence, he would soon perceive how needless are his fears: for you are ever so benign and merciful to your subjects, who "knowledging their offences," humbly ask your pardon. In reply to my offer he sent me a "letter written with his own hand," and also the copy of another letter of his, answering some other person, whom your majesty perhaps had commanded to persuade by like means: . . . which letters, like as together I received from the party, so send I herewith enclosed to your highness. I informed you in a previous letter that Tyndale's answer to my lord chancellor's book is finished. I have searched for a copy to send your majesty, and indeed I was doing so, even before the treasurer of your household gave me the instruction, but I have failed to find one; nor can I even discover whether it be yet printed: but as soon as it is, I will send it without fail.[1]

Vaughan sent a copy of this letter to Cromwell, and also Tyndale's answer to himself, asking Cromwell to show the former to His Majesty at the opportune moment, but concludes, for the reason given by Tyndale himself, that it is unlikely to get him to return to England: and adds, "After this book answering my lord Chancellor's book . . . I think he will write no more. The man is of greater knowledge than the king's highness doth take him for; which well appeareth by his works. Would God he were in England!"

On March 25th Vaughan writes to Cromwell that he has obtained a manuscript copy of the third part of Tyndale's book, so rudely scribbled, however, that he is copying it out, and meanwhile will do all he can to get hold of the rest of it, which he will also copy and send the completed transcription to the King. He then continues:

Sir, he hath made in the beginning of the same a pistle to the king's highness, as I am informed, which as yet is not come into my hands.

---

[1] Q.v. Mozley, *William Tyndale*, pp. 186–7.

I would gladly have your advice, whether it is best that I shall put it to his book, as he putteth it, or otherwise, I am in doubt whether the king's highness will be pleased to receive any such epistle from him or not; I pray you let me have herein your advice, as soon as is possible. I promise you, he maketh my lord chancellor such an answer, as I am loth to praise or dispraise. No work that ever he made is written in so gentle a style. Sir, this work will he not put in print, till he know how the king's highness will accept and take it. Howbeit, whether he come or not come into England, he will make no more works after this. He will no doubt come into England, and submit him to the king's highness, if he has any sure hope of his gracious favour. I can little or nothing profit with him by my letters, for so much as the man hath me greatly suspected.

In three weeks' time Vaughan had completed his fair copy, and on April 18th he sends it with a letter to the King, saying that this is a third part of the *Answer*, and that he will likewise copy what remains and let His Majesty have it as soon as he can. He then tells the King that unexpectedly he has managed to get an interview with Tyndale himself:

The day before the date hereof I spake with Tyndale without the town of Antwerp, and by this means. He sent a certain person to seek me, whom he advised to say that a certain friend of mine, unknown to the messenger, was very desirous to speak with me; praying me to take pains to go unto him, to such place as he should bring me. . . . Thus doubtful what this matter meant, I concluded to go with him, and followed him till he brought me without the gates of Antwerp, into a field lying nigh unto the same; where was abiding me this said Tyndale.

At our meeting, "Do you not know me?" said this Tyndale. "I do not well remember you," said I to him. "My name," said he, "is Tyndale." "But Tyndale," said I, "fortunate be our meeting." Then Tyndale, "Sir, I have been exceeding desirous to speak with you." "And I with you; what is your mind?" "Sir," said he, "I am informed that the king's grace taketh great displeasure with me for putting forth of certain books, which I lately made in these parts; but specially for the book named *The Practice of Prelates*; whereof I have no little marvel, considering that in it I did but warn his grace of the subtle demeanour of the clergy of his realm towards his person, and of the shameful abusions by them practised, not a little threatening the displeasure of his grace and weal of his realm: in which doing I showed and declared the heart of a true subject, which sought the safeguard of his royal person and weal of his commons, to the intent that his grace, thereof warned, might in due time prepare his remedies against their subtle dreams. If for my pains therein taken, if for my poverty, if for mine exile out of my natural country, and bitter absence from my friends, if for my hunger, my thirst, my cold, the great danger wherewith I am everywhere encompassed, and finally if for innumerable other hard and sharp fightings which I endure, not yet feeling their asperity by reason I hoped with my labours to do honour to God, true service to my prince, and pleasure to his commons; how is it that his grace, this considering, may either by himself think, or by the persuasions of other be brought to think, that in this doing I should not show a pure mind, a true and incorrupt zeal and affection to his grace? . . .

After more in the same strain, Vaughan continues:

Thus after a long conversation had between us, for my part making answer as my wit would serve me, which were too long to write, I assayed him with gentle persuasions, to know whether he would come into England; ascertaining him that means should be made, if he thereto were minded, without his peril or danger, that he might so do; and that what surety he would devise for the same purpose, should, by labour of friends, be obtained of your majesty. *But to this he answered, that he neither would nor durst come into England, albeit your grace would promise never so much surety*; fearing lest, as he hath before written, your promise made should shortly be broken, by the persuasion of the clergy, which would affirm that promises made with heretics ought not to be kept.

After this, he told me how he had finished a work against my lord chancellor's book, and would not put it in print till such time as your grace had seen it; because he apperceiveth your displeasure towards him, for hasty putting forth of his other work, and because it should appear that he is not of so obstinate mind, as he thinks he is reported unto your grace. This is the substance of his conversation had with me, which, as he spake, I have written to your grace word for word, as near as I could by any possible means bring to remembrance. My trust therefore is, that your grace will not but take my labours in the best part, I thought necessary to be written unto your grace. After these words, he [Tyndale] then, being something fearful of me, lest I should have pursued him, and drawing also towards night, he took his leave of me, and departed from the town, and I toward the town, saying I should shortly, peradventure, see him again, or if not, hear from him. Howbeit I suppose he afterward returned to the town by another way; for there is no likelihood that he should lodge without the town. Hasty to pursue him I was not, because I had some likelihood to speak shortly again with him; and in pursuing him I might perchance have failed of my purpose, and put myself in danger.

To declare to your majesty what, in my poor judgment, I think of the man, I ascertain your grace, I have not communed with a man . . .[1]

[1] *Q.v.* Mozley, *William Tyndale*, pp. 193–5.

But here Vaughan's despatch breaks off; and it is said that the King was so displeased with it that he tore it across, even as King Jehoiakim cut and burnt the roll of Jeremiah.

Cromwell made the following reply to Vaughan's letter, which reached him on May 18th, 1531:

I have received your letters, dated at Antwerp the 18th day of April, with also that part of Tyndale's book inclosed in leather, which ye with your letters directed to the king's highness. These I took to the court and presented to the king, who answered that he would read them at his leisure. On my next visit to court he called for me, and communicated to me the contents of both letter and book. I could see that he is pleased with your pains and trouble, "yet his highness nothing liked the said book, being filled with seditions, slanderous lies, and fantastical opinions, shewing therein neither learning nor truth." I could see also that he thought that ye bare much affection towards the said Tyndale; whom in his manners and knowledge in worldly things ye undoubtedly in your letters do much allow and commend; whose works, being replete with so abominable slanders and lies, imagined only and feigned to infect the people, doth declare him both to lack grace, virtue, learning, discretion, and all other good qualities, nothing else pretending in all his works, but to seduce, deceive and sow sedition among the people of this realm. The king's highness therefore hath commanded me to advertise you, that ye should desist and leave any further to persuade or attempt the said Tyndale to come into this realm; alleging that he, perceiving the malicious, perverse, uncharitable, and indurate mind of the said Tyndale, is in manner without hope of reconciliation in him, and is very joyous to have his realm destitute of such a person, than that he should return into the same, there to manifest his errors and seditious opinions, which, being out of the realm, by his most uncharitable, venemous and pestilent books, crafty and false persuasions he hath partly done already. For his highness right prudently considereth, if he were present, by all likelihood he would shortly (which God defend) do as much as in him were to infect and corrupt the whole realm, to the great inquietation and hurt of the commonwealth of the same.

Wherefore, Stephen, I heartily pray you, in all your doing, providing, and writing to the king's highness, ye do justly, truly and unfeignedly, without dissimulation shew yourself his true, loving and obedient subject; bearing no manner favor, love or affection to the said Tyndale, nor to his works, in any manner wise, but utterly to contemn and abhor the same. Otherwise you will anger the king, check your own advancement, and disappoint the hopes of myself and your other friends.

As touching Frith, mentioned in your said letter [a lost one], the king hears good reports of his learning, and laments that he should mis-use it in furthering the "venemous and pestiferous works, erroneous and seditious opinions of the said Tyndale and the other." He hopes, however, that he is not "so far yet inrooted" in such evil doctrines, but that he may be recalled to the right way; and he instructs you to speak with Frith if you are able, and to urge him to leave his wilful opinions, and like a good Christian to return to his native country, where he assuredly shall find the king's highness most merciful, and benignly, upon his conversion, disposed to accept him to his grace and mercy. Wherefore eftsoons I exhort you, for the love of God, not only utterly to forsake, leave, and withdraw your affection from the said Tyndale and his sort, but also to endeavour to win over Frith and other here-tical persons in those parts. So you will win merit with God, and thanks from the king.[1]

Cromwell himself, while writing as the King wished, really hoped to bring about a reconciliation between Tyndale and his master, as is indicated by a postscript to the above letter, of which we first learn from Vaughan's reply to His Majesty sent from Bergen on May 20th, 1531, in which a most interesting record of his second interview with Tyn-dale is given. After saying that he will do all he can to bring Frith back to the paths of orthodoxy, he goes on:

I have again been in hand to persuade Tyndale; and to draw him the rather to favour my persuasions, and not to think the same feigned, I showed him a clause contained in Master Cromwell's letter, containing these words following: "And notwithstanding other premises in this my letter contained, if it were possible, by good and wholesome exhortations, to reconcile and convert the said Tyndale from the train and affection which he now is in, and to excerpt and take away the opinions and fantasies sorely rooted in him, I doubt not but the King's highness would be much joyous of his conversion and amendment; and so being converted, if then he would return into his realm, undoubtedly the King's Royal Majesty is so inclined to mercy, pity, and com-passion, that he refuseth none which he seeth to submit themselves to the obedience and good order of the world."

In these words I thought to be such sweetness and virtue as were able to pierce the hardest heart of the world; and as I thought, so it came to pass. For after sight thereof I perceived the man to be exceedingly altered, and to take the same very near unto his heart, in such wise that water stood in his eyes, and answered, *"What gracious words are these! I assure,"* said he, *"if it would stand with the king's most gracious pleasure to grant only a bare text of the Scripture to be put forth among his people,*

---

[1] *Op. cit.*, pp. 196-7.

like as it is put forth among the subjects of the Emperor in these parts, and of other Christian princes, be it of the translation of what person soever shall please his Majesty, I shall immediately make faithful promise never to write more, nor abide two days in these parts after the same; but immediately to repair into his realm, and there most humbly submit myself at the feet of his Royal Majesty, offering my body to suffer what pain or torture, yea, what death his Grace will, so that this be obtained. And until that time I will abide the asperity of all chances, whatsoever shall come, and endure my life in as much pains as it is able to bear and suffer. And as concerning my reconciliation, his Grace may be assured that, whatsoever I have said or written in all my life against the honour of God's Word, and [it be] so proved, the same shall I before his Majesty and all the world [utterly] renounce and forsake, and with most humble and meek mind [embrace] the truth, abhorring all error, sooner at the most gracious and benign [request] of his Royal Majesty (of whose wisdom, prudence, and learning I [hear] so great praise and commendation), than of any other creature living. But if those things which I have written be true and stand with God's Word, why should his Majesty, having so excellent [gift] of knowledge in the Scriptures, move me to do anything against my conscience?" with many other words which were too long to write.

Finally [continues Vaughan], I have some good hope in the man, and would not doubt to bring [him] to some good point, were it that some thing now and then might proceed from your Majesty towards me, whereby the man might take the better comfort of my persuasions. I advertised the same Tyndale that he should not put forth the same book, till your most gracious pleasure was known: whereunto he answered, mine advertisement came too late, for he feared lest one that had his copy would put it shortly in print, which he would let [prevent] if he could; if not, there is no remedy. As yet it is not come forth, nor will not in a while, by that I perceive. Luther hath lately put forth a work against the Emperor, in the German tongue, which I would cause to be translated into Latin and send it to your Majesty if I knew your gracious pleasure. In it are many things to be seen.[1]

Though not as yet successful, both Cromwell and Vaughan were willing to try once more to persuade Tyndale to return to England; and of this effort Vaughan writes to Cromwell as follows:

I have spoken with Tyndale, and shewed him as you wrote me what the King's royal pleasure was, but I find him always singing one note [about not returning to England]. You wrote that the *Answer* which he made to the Chancellor was unclerkly done: and so seem all his works to eloquent men, because he useth so rude and simple style, nothing

---

[1] Ellis, *Original Letters*, 3rd series, vol. ii, pp. 200–3.

like any vain praise and commendation. If the King's royal pleasure had been to have looked thereupon, he should then have better judged it than upon the sight of another man. The prophets Esay and Jonas are put forth in the English tongue, and it passeth any man's power to stop them coming forth.[1]

The correspondence now ceased for a time, as Vaughan had returned to England; but what was happening there is enough to show that Tyndale's fears and suspicions were justified. In the next two years six heretics were burnt, while Foxe, the "martyrologist", gives a list of sixty persons in the London diocese who were compelled to abjure their heresies between 1528 and 1532. In the August of 1531 Bilney perished in the flames at Norwich; Richard Bayfield and a leather-seller named Tewkesbury suffered the same fate in December: George Constantine disclosed, under examination by More, the names of certain of his friends, including Robert Necton and Stephen Vaughan, of whom we have just been speaking. Vaughan indignantly denied the charge of heresy, and in a long letter proclaiming his orthodox position he courageously attributes the spread of heresy itself to the cruel measures adopted by the authorities of whom he makes More the most responsible.

On November 14th, 1531, he writes to Cromwell:

I am informed that George Constantine hath of late declared certain things against me before my lord Chancellor. If it be true, I pray you let me know what things they be. Be you hereof assured, he can declare nothing against me, that is truth, to hurt me. Peradventure he hath declared that I spake with Tyndale. If so he have done, what hath he herein declared, that I myself have not signified to the king's highness? Peradventure he hath also declared that I labored Tyndale, upon the king's safe conduct, to come into England. This also I have signified to his highness. What other thing soever he have declared against me, being true, I care not for it; if otherwise, *veritas liberabit*.

This and another letter of Vaughan's seem to have crossed one from Cromwell, telling him that Constantine was likely to accuse him of Lutheranism, and urging him to be more circumspect. On December 9th, three days after Constantine had arrived in Antwerp, he writes as follows:

If Constantine have accused me to be of the Lutheran sect, a fautor and setter forth of erroneous and suspect works, I do not threat mar-

---

[1] Ellis, *Original Letters*, 3rd series, vol. ii, pp. 207–8.

vel, for two causes specially. One is, for that my lord chancellor, in his examination of the said George, and of all other men, as I am credibly informed, being brought before him for cases of heresy, doth deeply inquire to know what may be said of me; and in the examination there-of sheweth evident and clear desire in his countenance and haviour to hear something of me, whereby an occasion of evil might be fastened against me. . . . The other is, for that George, besides the imminent peril and danger wherein he was, abiding prisoner in my lord's house, was vehemently stirred and provoked, what with the remembrance of his poor wife, remaining here desperate, bewashed with continual tears and pinched with hourly sorrow, sighs and mourning . . . likely to be brought into an extreme danger of poverty. . . . Will not these perils, fears, punishments, make a son forget the father which gat him, and the mother that bare him and fed him with her breasts? If they will, who should wonder though he would accuse me, a thousand times less dear unto him than either father or mother, to rid him out of the same?

Stephen Vaughan utters, too, in this letter, a noble protest against cruel persecution as a likely way of stamping out heresy:

Would God it might please the king's majesty to look into these kinds of punishment; which in my poor opinion threateneth a more hurt to his realm than those, that be his ministers to execute the same tortures and punishments, do think or conject; and by this reason only. It shall constrain his subjects in great number to forsake his realm, and to inhabit strange regions and countries, where they shall not practise little hurt to the same. Yea, and whereas they think that tortures, punishments and death shall be a mean to rid the realm of erroneous opinions, and bring men in such fear that they shall not once be so hardy to speak or look; be you assured, and let the king's grace be thereof advertised of my mouth, that his highness shall duly approve [make proof] that in the end it shall cause the sect to wax greater, and those errors to be more plenteously sowed in the realm than ever afore. . . . Counsel you the king's highness, as his true subject, to look upon this matter, and no more to trust other men's policies, which threateneth in mine opinion the weal of his realm; and let me no longer be blamed nor suspected for my true saying. That I write, I know to be true, and daily do see the experience of that I now write, though per-adventure you have little regarded it. But tarry awhile, and you shall be learned by experience. I see it begin already.

I write not thus because, as they suppose, I belong to the sect and desire them to go unpunished. Nay, truly; but I would have evildoers charitably punished, and if possible won over thereby.

Vaughan then gives his own view as to the main cause of the spread of heresy:

And let his majesty be further assured that he shall with no policy, nor with no threatenings of tortures and punishments, take away the opinions of his people, till his grace shall fatherly and lovingly reform the clergy of his realm. For *there* springeth the opinion. From *thence* riseth the grudge of the people; out of *that* take and find men occasions to complain. If I say truth, let it be for such received. If otherwise, I protest before God and the world that whatsoever I here write I mean therein nothing but the honour, glory, and surety of my only Prince and Sovereign, and the public weal of his realm.

Then speaking of himself, he says:

And as to myself and the fame and opinion of [by] some men had of me, let all men know, whatsoever the world babble of me, that I am neither Lutheran nor Tyndalian; nor have them or any other or esteem them any other for my gods, nor for the persons in whom or in whose learning I have any trust; nor yet do trust in the doctrine and learning of any earthly creature: for all men be liars, *in quantum homines*, as Scripture saith; and again *maledictus qui confidit in homine. Christ's Church hath admitted me a learning sufficient and infallible, and by Christ taught, which is the Holy Scripture*; let the world brawl, I am sure to have none other. I find not myself deceived, nor I trust shall be. As the world goeth, men's learnings are not to be trusted; God's learning cannot deceive [me if] that I embrace it humbly and with reverence. His learning is the only truth in the world; and among men, besides that, is there found no truth, but contrary, sin, untruth, corruption, and wretchedness.

This passage in the mouth of a good Catholic and with the interpretation indicated by the words of St. Augustine, "For my part, I should not believe the gospel except as moved by the authority of the Catholic Church,"[1] would be unexceptionable; but as expressed by Stephen Vaughan it may have been otherwise.

He then declares his loyalty to Henry VIII:

And as to my truth to my Prince and Sovereign, and my service towards his Grace, be not afraid [this is to Cromwell, of course], nor think that any worldly thing can corrupt my mind or move my body or any member thereof, once to think or do any manner of thing that shall not become a Christian man and also a true and faithful subject to his Prince. . . . I am unkindly handled to have such sharp inquisition made of me in mine absence; I am unkindly handled for my service.

[1] *"Ego vero Evangelio non crederem nisi me Catholicae Ecclisiae commoveret auctoritas"* St. Augustine, *Contra Ep. Manichaei*, 6.

Such stripes and bitter rewards would [make] faint and weak the heart of some men towards their Prince: but I am the stronger because I know my truth, and am at defiance with all men pretending the contrary. What, should I be longer in declaring my mind? Receive you the sum thereof in short words. I will not be untrue to my Prince, though he were the odiablest [most odious] person of his realm, though his governance were such as should offend both heaven and [earth]. As his Grace is the very contrary, most noble, gracious, benign . . . am I not commanded by God to be obedient to my Prince. . . . I can no longer forbear, but show you my mind; it pierceth my heart with a deadly wound when I hear that I am otherwise meant. I had much rather forsake my natural country, my most dear friends and family, and wander into some strange region and country, there to lead the rest of my short life than thus to be handled for my true service and good mind; considering that truth hath no better estimation, is so much . . . standeth in such danger, and is so vilely reputed. . . .

He is grieved that Cromwell, his friend, should take the same view of him as that taken by the Lord Chancellor–namely, that he has deceived them both. Also that Cromwell has excused himself to the King for having recommended Vaughan for the service abroad he has done his best to perform.

But whatsoever you have said, or shall say, have done, or shall do, it cannot yet turn my heart from you, of whom I have received far greater pleasures than these displeasures. . . . But I declare, by this my writing unto you, the earnest meaning of my heart, and that thereunto (I speak not feignedly) your exceeding merits have before drawn me, *nolens volens*. Here leave I to write any farther of this matter, till I hear either from you or some other my friends.

And then as a postscript he adds some other business which need not concern us, except that:

George Constantine [who had reported of him to More] came to Antwerp after his breaking from my Lord Chancellor, the sixth day of December [1531]. With him nor with none other such, will I meddle or have to do, considering that I am beaten with mine own labours. . . .
I would that they all, which so greedily examine, did know that I am no heretic, nor for them all will be made one.[1]

Meanwhile, Tyndale did his best to evade notice, and writing in 1533, More speaks of him in a letter to Erasmus as *hereticus noster, qui et ubique exsulat*, our heretic who is in exile and seems to be everywhere and

[1] Cotton MSS., *Galba*, B. x, pp. 21 *et seq.*, quoted from Demaus, *William Tyndale*, pp. 309–17. Vaughan seems to have lived until 1549.

nowhere. Stephen Vaughan's efforts, not I think altogether whole-hearted, had failed; and we must leave him; but not without a tribute to his candour and genuine kindliness of heart.

The case of Stephen Vaughan is, I think, worthy of our serious consideration, because his religious position, at a time so soon after the royal break with the Holy See, seems to have been that of other of his fellow-countrymen. They, like himself, were by no means Protestants, but victims rather of an intemperate loyalty to Henry VIII. St. Thomas More was just as loyal; but his deep religious sense kept him, as the King himself had commanded him, to be loyal to God first.

But we must return to Tyndale's *Answer to Sir Thomas More*.

Having laid it down in the preface that "the love of God and of his neighbour . . . is the spirit and life of all laws", Tyndale asks his reader to judge "whether the pope, with his, be the church; whether their authority be above scripture; whether all they teach without scripture be equal with the scripture; and whether they have erred, and not only whether they can".

Judge [he continues] whether it be possible that any good should come out of their dumb ceremonies and sacraments unto thy soul. Judge their penances, pilgrimages, pardons, purgatory, praying to posts, dumb blessings, dumb absolutions, their dumb pattering and howling, their dumb strange holy gestures, with all their dumb disguisings [in vestments], their satisfactions and justifyings. And because thou findest them false in so many things, trust them in nothing.[1]

He goes on to discuss the various meanings of the word Church.

First, it signifieth a place or house whither Christian people were wont in old time to resort at times convenient for to hear the word of doctrine, the law of God, and the faith of our Saviour Jesus Christ, and how and what to pray, and whence to ask power and strength to live godly. For the officer thereto appointed preached the pure word of God only, and prayed in a tongue that all men understood: and the people harkened unto his prayers, and said thereto, Amen; and prayed with him in their hearts, and of him learned to pray at home and everywhere, and to instruct every man his household.

Now [he continues] we hear but voices without significations, and buzzings, howlings and cryings, as it were the hallooing of foxes, or baiting of bears; and wonder at the disguisings and toys [that is, the vestments and the whole beautiful, severe and reverent ceremonial of the Mass] whereof we know no meaning. . . . And of the law of God

[1] Tyndale, *Works*, vol. iii, pp. 8–9.

we think as do the Turks . . . and of prayer . . . that no man pray but at church; and that it is nothing else but to say *pater noster* unto a post.

In another signification [the word church] is abused and mistaken for a multitude of shaven, shorn and oiled: which we now call the spiritualty and clergy.

It hath yet, or should have (as Tyndale considers) another signification little known among the common people now-a-days. That is, to wit, it signifieth *a congregation*; a multitude or a company gathered together in one, of all degrees of people. As a man should say, "the church of London", meaning not the spiritualty only . . . but the whole body of the city, of all kinds, conditions and degrees: and "the church of Bristow", all that pertain unto that town generally. And in this third signification is the church of God, or Christ, taken in scripture; even for the whole multitude of all them that receive the name of Christ to believe in him, and not only for the clergy only. . . .

Notwithstanding yet it is sometimes taken generally for all them that embrace the name of Christ, though their faith be naught, or though they have no faith at all.

And sometimes it is taken specially for the elect only; in whose hearts God hath written his law with his Holy Spirit, and given them *a feeling faith* of the mercy that is in Christ Jesu our Lord.[1]

We may notice this expression "a feeling faith", for it is a token phrase, which Tyndale borrowed from Melanchthon, and characteristic of English Protestantism from Tyndale's day unto our own. In another place he makes a distinction between it and "historical faith".

There are two manner faiths [he writes], *an historical faith*, and *a feeling faith*. The historical faith hangeth of the truth and honesty of the teller, or of the common fame and consent of many; as if one told me that the Turk had won a city, and I believed it, moved with the honesty of the man; now if there came another that seemeth more honest, or that hath better persuasions that it is not so, I think immediately that he lied, and lose my faith again. And a feeling faith is as if a man were there present when it was won, and there were wounded, and had there lost all he had, and were taken prisoner there also: that man should so believe, that all the world could not turn him from his faith.

Of a feeling faith it is written (John vi) "They shall all be taught of God". That is, God shall write it in their hearts with his Holy Spirit. And Paul also testifieth (Rom. viii) "The Spirit beareth record unto our spirit, that we be the sons of God". And this faith is none opinion; but a sure feeling, and therefore ever fruitful.

Of this we have an ensample (John iv) of the Samaritanish wife, which left her pitcher, and went into the city, and said, "Come, and see

[1] Tyndale, *Works*, vol. iii, pp. 11-13.

a man that hath told me all that ever I did. Is not he the Christ?" And
many of the Samaritans believed, because of the saying of the woman,
how that he had told her all that ever she did; and went out unto him,
and desired him to come in. Which faith was but an opinion; and no
faith that could have lasted, or have brought out fruit. But when they
had heard Christ, the Spirit wrought, and made them feel. Whereupon
they came unto the woman, and said: "We believe not now because
of thy saying, but because we have heard ourselves, and know that he is
Christ, the Saviour of the world." For Christ's preaching was with
power and spirit, that maketh a man feel and know, and work too; and
not as the Scribes and Pharisees preached.[1]

Tyndale concedes that "images, relics, ornaments, signs or sacraments, holy days, ceremonies or sacrifices" have a religious use.

If [he says] I take a piece of the cross of Christ, and make a little cross
thereof, and bear it about me, to look thereon with a repenting heart
... then it serveth me, and not I it; and doth me the same service as if I
read the testament in a book, or as if a preacher preached it to me.
And so, if I make an image ... and if I take the true life of a saint,
and cause it to be painted or carved, to put me in remembrance of the
saint's life ... and to see the saint's love to his neighbour ... then doth
the image serve me, and not I it.

And again:

... To speak of pilgrimages, I say, that a Christian man, so that he
leave nothing undone at home that he is bound to do, is free to go
whither he will. ... If he go to this place or that place, to hear a sermon, or because his mind is not quiet at home; or if, because his heart
is too much occupied in his worldly business ... it is well done ....
God is a spirit, and will be worshipped in the spirit; that is, though
He be present everywhere, yet He dwelleth lively and gloriously in the
minds of angels only, and hearts of men that love His laws and trust His
promises. And wheresoever God findeth such a heart, there He heareth
prayer, in all places and times indifferently. So that the outward place
neither helpeth or hindereth, except (as I said) that a man's mind be
more quiet and still from the rage of worldly businesses, or that some
thing stir up the word of God and example of our Saviour in one place
than another.[2]

Here, too, he admits that "all sacraments, ceremonies, or signs ... so
long as it is understood what is meant by them ... do not hurt the
people greatly".

[1] Tyndale, *Works*, vol. iii, pp. 50–2.
[2] *Ib.*, pp. 59–64 *passim*. But later he seems to have withheld this concession to church
customs and ceremonials.

The first section of the book ends with a protest against what Tyndale calls *pope-holy works* whereby the prelates crept into men's consciences and "robbed them of the knowledge of our Saviour Christ, making them to think that there were none other way to heaven but to build abbeys, cloisters, chauntries, and cathedral churches with high steeples, striving and envying one another who should do most. And as for the deeds that pertain unto our neighbours and the commonwealth, they have not regarded them at all, as things which seemed no holy works or such as God would not at once look upon."

Surely if, as Tyndale here asserts, the prelates had robbed men of the knowledge of our Saviour Christ, lay-folk would hardly have devoted their means so generously to build Him "abbeys, cloisters, chauntries and cathedral churches with high steeples"?

Later in the book he speaks of what our Lord is to those who love Him much in the way that St. Bernard did:

All is Christ with him; and Christ is his, and he is Christ's. All that he receiveth, he receiveth of Christ, and all that he doth, he doth to Christ. Father, mother, master, lord, and prince, are Christ unto him; and as Christ he serveth them with all love. . . . And his neighbour he serveth as Christ, in all his need, of such things as God hath lent; because that all degrees are bought, as he is, with Christ's blood. And he will not be saved for serving his brethren; neither promiseth his brethren heaven for serving him. But heaven, justifying, forgiveness, all gifts of grace, and all that is promised them, they receive of Christ, and by his merits freely, as one hand doth the other; seeking for their service no more than one hand doth of another, each other's health, wealth, help, aid, succour, and to assist one another in the way of Christ. And God they serve in spirit only, in love, hope, fear and dread.[1]

But even in this otherwise edifying passage, Tyndale denies the merit of all good deeds; and a little further on he openly preaches heresy.

Whereas the elect, having the law written in their breasts, and loving it in their spirits, sin there never; but without in the flesh. Against which sin they fight continually, and minish it daily with the help of the Spirit, through prayer, fasting, serving their neighbours lovingly with all manner service, out of the law that is written in their hearts. And their hope of forgiveness is in Christ only, through his blood, and not in ceremonies.[2]

He objects at length to all intercession to or by means of saints, but seems to allow the possibility of certain miracles done to "stablish the

[1] Tyndale, *Works*, vol. iii, p. 109.   [2] *Ib.*, p. 114.

faith of Christ's death" or, for instance, that of the woman who was healed by "touching Christ's coat", which miracle "was showed to provoke to the worshipping of the preaching, and not of the coat: though to keep the coat reverently in the memorial of the deed, to provoke unto the faith of Christ, were not evil in itself".[1]

In another place he writes:

It is an article of my belief that Christ's elect church is holy and pure without sin, and every member of the same [even in this life] through faith in Christ, and that they be in full favour of God.[2]

His references to More are both prejudiced and misinformed; for he seems certain that More was ambitious for place and power and wealth, and that to obtain them he was ready even to sell his soul. The known facts of More's life and death are sufficient to disprove this; but Tyndale could never forgive More for his attack on his translation of the New Testament, nor the important part he had taken in having it condemned "in order to get honour, promotion, dignity and money, by help of our mitred monsters". "Covetousness maketh many", he also writes, "whom truth pleaseth at the beginning the cruel enemies thereof, after the ensample of Sir Thomas More, knight, which knew the truth, and for covetousness forsook it again. . . . Covetousness blinded the eyes of that gleering fox more and more, and hardened his heart against truth, with the confidence of his painted poetry, babbling eloquence and juggling arguments ground on his 'unwritten verities', as true and authentic as his story of *Utopia*."[3]

On this point [writes Mr. Mozley] Tyndale does his enemy a serious injustice. . . . More was not venal, as his after history proved. . . . In the summer of 1532 the news reached Antwerp (where Tyndale then was) that the clergy had collected the big sum of £4000 or £5000 to present to More, on his resignation from the chancellorship, in gratitude for his championship of the church, this—even though More refused the gift, saying that he would sooner throw it in the Thames—would be likely to confirm rather than allay [Tyndale's] suspicions, since it at least proved the eagerness of the bishops to reward their defender with money.[4]

Tyndale's *Answer* got into More's hands in the summer of 1531, and while still Lord Chancellor he began his lengthy reply to it in the first three books of his immensely long *Confutation*.

[1] Tyndale, *Works*, vol. iii, p. 124. [2] *Ib.*, p. 142.
[3] *Ib.*, vol. ii, p. 100. [4] *William Tyndale*, pp. 220-1.

12

More's Supposed Cruelty to Heretics and His
Confutation

As LORD CHANCELLOR between October 25th, 1529, and May 30th, 1532, More was officially concerned with the suppression of heresy, but it was rather by his controversial writings against Tyndale and others than by more forcible legal measures that he hoped to be able to fulfil his bounden duty. It was Foxe, I suppose, who, in his *Book of Martyrs*,[1] first popularised the charge of cruelty against More; and Foxe was followed by Burnet,[2] who again was followed by James Anthony Froude and others. Froude, for instance, writes that "no sooner had the seals changed hands [from Wolsey to More] than the Smith-field fires recommenced . . . encouraged by the Chancellor",[3] and yet another popular historian records that More's Chancellorship was "*chiefly* notable for his persecution of heretics . . . burnings at Smithfield became numerous".

Perhaps the cause of these mistakes made by modern writers may have been an ignorance or misunderstanding of Canon law which exactly defines the position of the clergy with regard to the capital punishments of heretics:

Canon law has always forbidden clerics to shed human blood and therefore capital punishment has always been the work of officials of the State and not of the Church. Even in the case of heresy . . . the function of ecclesiastics was restricted invariably to ascertaining *the fact of heresy*. The punishment, whether capital or other, was prescribed and inflicted by civil government.[4]

The charge of persecution is based on a passage in More's *Apology* which, until 1930, had never been reprinted since 1557, in the collected edition of More's *English Works*. In this passage it is asserted that More

[1] Foxe, *Acts and Monuments*, ed. of 1563, Cattley, vol. i, p. 698.
[2] Burnet, *History of the Reformation*, vol. i, pp. 270-1.
[3] Froude, *History of England*, vol. i, p. 559.
[4] *The Catholic Encyclopædia*, vol. xii, p. 567. It should be noted that More, as Chancellor, presided over a court of equity and not a criminal court. *Ib.*, vol. ix, p. 70.

admits that he had twice flogged for heresy. But this is not exactly true.

Let us listen to what he has to say in his own defence.

The first case is that of a child from an heretical home whom he had received into his own household. "He once ordered this child to be flogged–not for holding heretical dogmas, but for teaching them to another child in the house."[1] In More's time the houses of the great fulfilled, and perhaps more than fulfilled, the social functions of a public school; but it was not unreasonable that in a Catholic household Catholic doctrines and practices would be taken for granted. When More found that other children in the house were being taught unorthodox doctrines by this new-comer, it was to be expected that rightful and customary punishment would follow; and so it did. Boys are still birched for serious disobedience.

The second case, as reported on two occasions in nineteenth-century accounts, does seem at first sight both callous and cruel; for More undoubtedly caused a half-witted heretic to be flogged–but not for heresy. The man was flogged for making indecent attacks upon women, and that in church at the time of the Elevation. For in accounts already spoken of the relevant passage has been expurgated in the interests of morality, but for justice sake it must be put in its proper place:

And if he [the man in question] spied any woman kneeling at a form, if her head hung anything low in her meditations, then would he steal behind her, and if he were not letted, would labour to lift up all her clothes and cast them quite over her head.[2]

The flogging evidently did the man good; for More writes later, "I hear none harm of him now".

Then there is the legend of the tree or of the two trees in More's garden, at which More himself was accused of flogging heretics. More's own words prove this to be untrue.

"One Segar, a bookseller of Cambridge, which was in mine house about four or five days, and never had either bodily harm done him, or foul word spoken him while he was in mine house, hath reported since, as I hear say, to divers that he was bounden to a tree in my garden, and thereto so piteously beaten, and yet beside that bounden about the head with a cord and wrungen, that he fell down dead in a swoon. And this tale of his beating did Tyndale tell to an old acquaintance of

[1] R. W. Chambers, *Thomas More*, p. 275, following Fr. Bridgett, has shown in detail how unreliable are Foxe's charges against More.
[2] *Apology*, c. 36, *E. W.*, p. 901 G, H.

O

his own, and to a good lover of mine, with one piece farther yet, that while the man was in beating, I spied a little purse of his hanging at his doublet, wherein the poor man had (as he said) five marks, and that caught I quickly to me and pulled it from his doublet and put it in my bosom, and that Segar never saw it after. And therein, I trow, no more did Segar himself neither, in good faith.[1]

Finally, there are More's own solemn words of denial of this charge of cruelty to heretics.

And of all that ever came in my hand for heresy, as help me God, saving as I said, the sure keeping of them (and yet not so sure neither, but that George Constantine could steal away) else had never any of them any stripe or stroke given them, so much as a fillip on the forehead.[2]

We may now turn once again to More's controversial efforts against Tyndale and other heretics. Tyndale has replied to More's *Dialogue* with his *Answer to Sir Thomas More*, and More wrote, as a rejoinder, the first part of his *Confutation*, running to some 300,000 words, while he was still Lord Chancellor. But in 1533, the year following his resignation, he added five more books to those already written, bringing it to a total of over 457,000 words. There is no need just here to give a detailed account of this immense treatise, as one hopes to do in the next two volumes of More's *English Works*. But a few characteristic quotations from it will give the main points made by St. Thomas More against Tyndale's *Answer*.

SELECTIONS FROM THE CONFUTATION
1. TRUTHS NOT TO BE FOUND IN SCRIPTURE

Now have ye heard, as far as I can find, all that ever Tyndale either hath said or can say in this matter, either himself or any man else, for the proof of his own part, or for the disproof of ours. And thereby see ye well that he neither hath proved, nor never shall he prove while he liveth, neither himself nor no man else, the thing that he so boldly saith that all thing necessary for salvation is written in scripture. . . .

Ye shall well find also that notwithstanding all that hath ever been written since, either by the prophets, Evangelists or any other Apostle, yet will it never appear that all is written that was taught by mouth, but that the Church of Christ hath taught unto them by the Spirit of

---

[1] *E.W., Apology*, p. 902 C, D.   [2] *Ib.*, p. 901 H, 992 A.

God divers truths which no good man can doubt in whereof the scripture nothing determineth, and which therefore false heretics bring in question, and let not to say the contrary, as in the common examples of our Lady's perpetual virginity, of the assumption of her blessed body, which God would else have had found in earth, and honoured as well as the bodies of any other saint, of whom Himself hath caused by special revelation divers to be sought out and found, to be worshipped here in earth for his sake, and confirmed it by many manifest miracles, as we find in authentic stories.

By these traditions have we also the praying to saints and the knowledge that they pray for us, albeit in the book of Machabees yet the thing well appeareth.

By these traditions have we the holy Lenten fast which these idle fellows so boldly take upon them to break, and as Lollards to eat flesh, and which holy fast these fools in their writing call the foolish fast. By these have we also the Saturday changed into Sunday, which they care not to turn into Friday now.

By these have we the hallowing of chalices, vestments, paschal taper, and holy water, with divers other things.

By these traditions of that Holy Spirit hath the Church also the knowledge how to consecrate, how to say Mass, and what things to pray for, and to desire therein.

By this have we also the knowledge to do reverence to the images of holy saints, and of our Saviour, and to creep to His cross, and to do divine honour unto the Blessed Sacrament of the altar, to which yet to say the truth tradition needed. For since the scripture is plain that it is Christ's own precious Body, which is not dead but quick, with that blessed Soul and with them the Godhead unseparably joined; what frantic fool could doubt but it should be with divine honour worshipped through neither God nor man beside that knowledge, had given knowledge thereof.

But yet is Tyndale so far beside himself that he believeth not the scripture of God nor the word spoken by God's own mouth when He said that it is His own Body, and is so blasphemous against God that he calleth it a great sin to do to the blessed Body of Christ in the sacrament, he saith, any honour at all because it is not commanded . . . in scripture.

By this may ye good Christian readers see to what point at last this heresy bringeth this folk. For when they first fall to the point that they regard not God's word but if He give it them in writing, within a while after fall they down so far that they neither regard His word nor His writing, not yet Himself neither.

E.W. 513–14, *passim.*

2. THE KNOWN CHURCH THE SURETY OF FAITH

It must needs be that there is by God provided and left some surety as may bring us out of all perplexity. And that is . . . His Holy Spirit sent and left perpetually with His Church, to lead it so by His own promise ever into all necessary truth, that whoso hear and believe His Church may be sure that he cannot be deceived, but that if a false teacher would lead men out of the right faith the Church of Christ shall reprove him and put the people in certainty. For which cause Saint Paul saith that the Church is the firm establishment and the pillar of truth for the inviolable surety of doctrine.

And therefore that can never be no Church but a known Church.

The true Church of Christ . . . is the common known Church of all Christian people not gone out nor cast out. This whole body both of good and bad is the Catholic Church of Christ, which is in this world very sickly, and hath many sore members, as hath sometime the natural body of a man . . .

This Catholic known Church is that mystical body, be it never so sick, whereof the principal head is Christ. Of which body, whether the successor of Saint Peter be his vicar general and head under him, as all Christian nations have now long taken him, is no part of this question. For to this matter it is enough that this body mystical of Christ, this Catholic Church, is that body that is animated, hath life spiritual, and is inspired with the Holy Spirit of God that maketh them of one faith in the House of God, by leading them into the consent of every necessary truth of revealed faith, be they in conditions and manner never so sick, as long as they be conformable and content in unity of faith to cleave unto the body. Of this Church can we not be deceived, nor of the right faith can we not be deceived while we cleave to this Church, since this Church is it into which God hath given His Spirit of faith, and in this Church both good and bad profess one faith. For if any profess the contrary faith, be it any one man or any one country, they be controlled, noted, and reproved by the whole body and soon known from the body. Now if it happen any privy heretics to lurk in this body, yet all the while they agree with the body in open profession of faith, and teach nothing contrary, they cannot beguile us though they may by secret heresies of their hearts sinfully deceive themselves. And when they teach the contrary, then are they, as I say, reproved openly by the body and either reformed and cured, or else cut off from the body and cast out thereof. So that this Church is known well enough, and therefore may be well used as a sure judge for to discern between the true doctrine and the false, and the true preacher and false, concerning the right faith, and discerning of the true word of God, written or unwritten, from the counterfeit word of man, and in the discerning of the right understanding of the scripture of God, as far forth as of necessity pertaineth unto salvation.

And this advantage that I speak of, have we by that this Church is known, whereas Tyndale's chosen church of repenting sinners we can never know them but if we see them walk in our Church in procession with a candle before the Cross, or stand before the pulpit with a faggot on their necks.

E. W. 527–528

3. THE NATURE OF TRUE FAITH

If all the faith of such truths as are taught were in such wise inspired into every man's heart that is a faithful man, as he by that inward inspiration had such a full, perfect and clear perceiving thereof in the inward sight of the understanding as the bodily eye hath of the thing that it plainly seeth and looketh upon, or as the sight of the soul hath in such evident and open conclusions as it doth plainly and openly behold, such I mean, as are the general petitions in the first book of Euclid's geometry, as that every whole thing is more than its own half, or such other like; then would I well agree with Tyndale that when the thing were so showed unto my wit, I could not but agree thereto with my will. But I say that albeit God is able in such wise to inspire and infound the faith, if that him list, yet I say that ordinarily into his faithful folk ... he giveth not the belief or faith on that fashion. For if he did, then were it not faith nor belief, but very sight and knowledge. And such kind of so certain and open revelation were unto the man occasion of belief and credence necessarily, surely and inevitable, but therefore, as it seemeth, neither thankworthy nor rewardable. ...

Now doth God, with his Christian folks, ordinarily take that way in the giving them their belief and faith, that though they do not merit with any foregoing good deeds, nor deserve the gift of believing, yet may they with good endeavour and obedient conformity, deserve and merit in the believing.

And therefore since God will for that cause bind us to the belief, because he will that we merit and be rewarded for our belief, the reason of which desert and merit on our part standeth in the respect and regard that God hath to our obedience, by which we willingly submit ourselves to the credence of God's word, unwritten or written, telling us anything against our own reason telling us the contrary, then if our belief lost its merit (as that holy Pope Gregory saith it should) if reason plainly proved us the thing that we believe, so were the merit of our belief lost in likewise, if the thing were in such wise given us, as we more perfectly perceived it than we perceive any such, as reason may most perfectly prove us.

And therefore I say, that God doth not ordinarily give unto men the faith in such manner, because he will not utterly take away the merit from man, for as much as he hath ordained him to joy by the mean of some merit, some conflict, passion or pain upon his own part, though not sufficient and worthy (for as Saint Paul saith, all the passions and sufferances of this world be not worthy the glory that is to come that shall be revealed in us) yet such at the leastwise as his high goodness accepteth and rewardeth for worthy, through the force and strength of those merits that are indeed sufficient and worthy (the merits, I mean, of the bitter pain and passion of his alone only begotten and tenderly beloved son), then say I now, that since the faith is not ordinarily with such, open, inevitable, and invincible lightsomeness inspired into the soul, that the man must of necessity and very fine force clearly perceive and agree with it, but by God provided so sufficiently to be showed and taught, as he that will be conformable and walk with God's grace, may find good cause enough to captive his reason to the belief, and yet not so great and urgent causes, but that he, which will be ill willed and froward, may let grace go, and find himself cavillations proudly to rest upon his own reason against the word of God, either saying that his reason seeth it not sufficiently proved for God's word (as Tyndale saith in all God's word unwritten) or else that God's word is not so meant as all Christ's Church understandeth them (as Tyndale saith touching the plain scriptures against the marriages made between friars and nuns) the points of the faith are not, I say, in such wise showed, nor the wit in them so thoroughly and so clearly instructed, but that *the thing which in the wit lacketh and remaineth imperfect, may by the will be perfected and made up*, and, instead of sure and certain sight, be from distrust or doubtful opinion brought, by God's working with man's will, into sure faith and undoubted belief. And this I say for the time of this present life, and, in the life to come, then turned into full sight and inevitable contemplation.

And that this is the ordinary manner of the faith given by God into the soul, with the pliable and conformable will of man, and not an inevitable sight of the truth inspired into the man whether he will or not, in such manner wise, that he cannot choose but believe it, the scriptures be plain and evident.

Doth not Saint Paul unto the Hebrews in the definition of faith, openly and clearly declare that the faith is an argument or matter of things that appear not. Now if the resurrection of our own body were in this world in such manner appearing unto us, as it shall after the resurrection when we be in heaven, it were now no faith at all, but a sure knowledge. And therefore saith Saint Paul also that we see now as it were but in a glass, and behold but as it were in a dark riddle, but, in the other world, shall we see face to face.

To show also that God giveth not ordinarily the faith to folk but with some manner of towardness and conformity of their own good will, our Lord saith himself unto the city that he so sore longed to convert, "Jerusalem, Jerusalem, how oft have I willed to gather thy children together, as an hen gathereth together her chickens, and thou wouldest not."

No man here doubteth but that our Lord, if he would have used some ways as he could, it was in his power to inspire the knowledge of himself into their hearts, and of all thing that he would have them believe, and that, in such wise, that they should not choose but believe, for they should not choose but know it, and that in such wise they could not have thought the contrary. But God had determined to bring man to salvation, not in such inevitable wise, nor without some willing conversion and turning of man toward him, though man cannot turn unto him without prevention and concurrent help of God's especial grace. But since *the goodness of God provideth that his grace is ever ready to him that will use it*, therefore, though the will of man may nothing do without grace, yet without any speaking of grace, we commonly let not to say, man may do this, and man may do that, as believe, and hope, and love, and live chaste, and do alms, and fast, and many such other things, not meaning, though we make no mention of grace, that man can therefore do them without grace. Like as we say that a man may see to thread a needle and speak nothing of the light, and yet mean we not that he can thread it in the dark.

And *therefore let not Tyndale look to* bring us in darkness, and because man's will can nothing do without grace, therefore *tell us that man's will can nothing do, nor tell us neither than man's will hath no part in belief in faith*, and make us ween it were so because the will cannot (as he saith) go before the wit, whereof experience proveth many times the contrary, and sometime with Tyndale too. But though a man cannot have any will at all in that thing whereof he hath utterly nothing known nor heard tell of, nor had imagination in his mind, nor anything thought upon, yet when the mind with divers reasons and arguments is once moved of a matter, the will as it happeth of other occasions at the time to be well or evil affectionate, so may give itself in to the consent and agreement of the one side or of the other, yea, and that sometime on the side for affection, upon which side he seeth least part of his wit and reason. And therefore it is not alway true that Tyndale saith in these words.

E.W. 582–584

4. WHERE CAN WE FIND TYNDALE'S CHURCH?

(Tyndale) hath nothing proved which is the Church, though we would yet of our courtesy further grant him, that all his whole heresies were the very faith; and that the very "elects" were only those in whose hearts the devil hath written his law, or else (which were yet far worse) that the very elects were only those in whose holy hearts God had himself so written his will with his Holy Spirit that they should thereby feel that spiritual folk should please God with waxing fleshly, and friars with wedding nuns, and that if they would be saved they should have therein no respect unto good works, but think that only faith in the promise, and bare repentance without shrift or penance, shall sufficiently save them, so that they believe sure that all the seven sacraments serve nothing, but be but bare signs and tokens, and utterly as graceless as themselves are witless; and specially, so that they believe that the blessed body nor blood of Christ be not in the sacrament of the altar, nor that they do none other honour in no wise thereto, but only believe and remember that there is nothing but a memorial of his Passion in a cup of wine and a gobbet of cake bread, and yet in doubt or question whether it be bread or starch.

And then, that with this godly belief, they see surely to themselves that they serve no saints, but rail upon their relics, and despise their images, and therewith the crucifix too, and the holy cross itself also, and then lest they might hap to lose a whole day in God's service, keep themselves well and warily from all holy days, and specially (for so these heretics in their books call it) from the foolish fast of Lent.

And thus living, and therewith believing these aforesaid heresies so firmly, that they think verily they feel their false faith with their very fingers' ends, be bold then hardly and believe verily that their feeling faith shall never fail them, but at all times so preserve them, that they cannot only never be damned, but over that can never do no deadly sin, though they do never so many devilish deeds, but for all their falsehood, theft, adultery, vow breaking, treason, murder, incest and perjury, shall for their only feeling faith be good and faithful false faithless wretches, and therefore God Almighty his own minions still.

And thus good Christian readers, since ye now plainly perceive that Tyndale hath here for his own part nothing proved us that his false framed elects, nor yet that only the very true elects be the Church of Christ in earth, nor hath nothing showed us which is, and therefore only with all his long process, uttered and taught his errors and his heresies, and left the matter not unproved only, but untouched too, which he took upon him and professed to prove, that is to wit which is the Church, but as though he had well and plainly proved it which he hath not so much almost as spoken, leaveth off his own part now, and turneth him to impugn ours, I shall leave him, for his part, awhile in the mire, in which himself hath overthrown his matter, and shall show you shortly how angrily he riseth up and royally arrayed in dirt, because he cannot prove the Church of Christ here in earth to be a congregation unknown, layeth his miry hands upon the known Catholic Church of Christ, and fain would pull that down too, and so leave no Church at all.

E.W. 613–614

5. TYNDALE'S UNKNOWN CHURCH

Ye have already, good Christian readers, well seen and perceived that Tyndale hath in a long process laboured to prove you that the Church of Christ is another company than the known Catholic company of all Christian regions, that is, to wit, *a certain secret scattered congregation unknown to all the world beside, and to their own fellows too, and every man by his inward feeling not only known only to himself, but also so well and surely known unto himself for a virtuous, good and faithful final elect of God, that he is in himself very certain and sure that he cannot but be saved,* and that he so hath the spirit of God imprisoned in his breast, and so fast fettered in his holy heart, whereof himself hath lost the key, that neither the spirit can creep out, nor himself let him out by no manner mean, but there must the spirit abide and so preserve and keep that special chosen creature, that he suffer him to do many great abominable, horrible, devilish deeds, but yet never suffer him in no wise to do any deadly sin.

This, I say, ye have already seen, that Tyndale hath by a long process laboured much to prove us, and hath in conclusion not only nothing proved thereof, but hath instead of feeling, faithful folk, brought us forth such a sort, as never was there pudding stuffed so full of forcing, as his holy, feeling faithful folk are forced full of heresies.

E.W. 614

6. TYNDALE ATTACKS THE POPES

Surely the things for the teaching whereof Tyndale rebuketh here the Pope, hath ever been the doctrine of Popes, Patriarchs, Prophets, Apostles, and our Saviour Himself and all.

For, first, he proveth that the Pope believeth not to be saved through Christ, because he teacheth to trust in holy works for remission of sins and salvation. Is not here a perilous lesson, trow ye, namely so taught as the Church teacheth it, that no good work can be done without help of God's grace, nor no good work of man worthy the reward of heaven but by the liberal goodness of God, nor yet should have a price set upon it, save through the merits of Christ's bitter passion, and that yet in all our deeds we be so unperfect that each man hath good cause to fear for his own part lest his best be bad. I would ween that good works were not so deadly poison, but taking not too much at once, for cloying of the stomach, no more at once lo than I see the world wont to do many drachms of such treacle mixed with one scruple of dread, were able enough, for ought that I can see, so to preserve the soul from presumption, that one spoonful of good works should no more kill the soul than a potager of good worts should kill and destroy the body.

The scripture biddeth us watch and fast and pray, and give alms, and forgive our neighbour; and we poor men that lack the high spiritual sight that Tyndale hath, and his holy elects, take these things for good works. And God saith in his holy writ that he will forgive our sins the rather for them and will reward us for them, and through the scripture this cryeth God in our ears, and faithfully promiseth almost in every leaf. And now ye see Tyndale that preacheth so fast of the faith and trust of God's promises, would have us in these promises trust God nothing at all.

But herein is great peril, specially to hope and trust to get any good at God's hand for the works of penance enjoined. For the sacrament of penance is to Tyndale a great abomination, and therein indeed he saith somewhat. For well ye wot, even of natural reason, a wise man will soon see that since the punishment that a man wilfully taketh for the sin that he hath done, cometh of an anger and displeasure that he beareth toward himself for the displeasure that his sin hath done to God, and that his willing submitting of himself to the correction of his ghostly father, cometh of great humility given by God, and taught by all good men. God must needs therefore, perdy, both be angry and abhor all them that for the fruits of these good affections can hope for any favour, grace or pardon at his merciful hand.

If Tyndale list to look in Saint Austin in his book of penance, he shall there find that holy doctor and saint bid every man put himself whole in his confessor's hand, and humbly receive and fulfil such penance as he shall enjoin him.

. . . Then doth Tyndale specially touch that the Church teacheth to put trust in vows and in chastity, for that is the thing, in the ears of Luther's elects, of all things the most abominable. But the Church teacheth none other trust therein than the scripture doth itself, and our blessed Saviour himself.

They teach (saith Tyndale) to trust other men's prayers and holy living, in friars and friars' coats. Is not here an abominable sin, that any man should have so little pride in himself that he should think other men much better than himself, and therefore desire them to pray for him too, beside himself? In how many places doth the scripture exhort each of us to pray for other? And when the scripture saith that the diligent prayer of a just man is much worth, should we then trust nothing therein, but think that it were right nought worth at all? Or because the scripture so commendeth the prayer of a good man, should we like his prayer the less for his holy living, and bid him pray not for us, but if he live nought? . . . Then goeth he from good livers in earth unto saints in heaven, and findeth yet more fault, in that men are taught to go in any pilgrimage, or do any worship there to them, or to think that their good living was so pleasant unto God, while they lived here in earth, that he will therefore vouchsafe to do anything at their request for any lover of theirs, while they be with him in heaven. Howbeit in this point I dare be bold to say for Tyndale myself that he is not so foolish but that he seeth well enough that if I may well pray my neighbour to pray for me, that is here with me in earth, I may much better pray the saints pray for me that are with God in heaven, saving that he believeth that they be not there, nor neither hear us nor see us, but lie still as Luther saith asleep.

He blameth us and belieth us as though we took their dead images for quick. But himself seemeth yet much worse indeed, that taketh God's quick saints for dead, against Christ's own words. . . .

Then cometh Tyndale in at the last with the ceremonies of the Church and the sacraments, against which prick he specially spurneth with his kybed[1] heel. But it will not help him. The gentleman is so proud that the holy sacraments must be his waiting servants. For now he saith that they are but superstitious and serve for nought, but be set instead of Christ, and are (as they be taught) the denying of Christ's blood. How should they now be the denying of Christ's blood when the Church teacheth us, as God hath taught it, that they all have their strength by Christ's blood, and that in the one of them is Christ's very own blood and his blessed body both. . . .

And now that ye see good Christian readers for what doctrine Tyndale rebuketh the common Catholic Church, ye cannot but thereby perceive what doctrine he would have them teach, that is to wit that we should have no respect to good works, use no shrift nor penance, beware of chastity and bless us well therefrom, let no good man pray for us, nor none that use holy living, nor Franciscan friar bid any bead for us in his Friar's coat, till he off his grey garments and clothe himself comely in gay kendal green, set saints at nought, and all holy ceremonies used in God's service and also the seven sacraments too, make mocks at the mass and at Christ's body, and take it for nothing but cake bread or starch. And when the clergy teacheth this once, then shall they be the Church. But for lack of this doctrine they be no part thereof. For Tyndale telleth us that, till they teach us thus, they can never believe to be saved through Christ. And I say, as I be saved through Christ, if Tyndale lay mad in the midst of Bedlam, he could not to good Christian men tell a more frantic tale.

E. W. 617–618

---

[1] kybe–chilblain.

7. TYNDALE AND PERMISSION FOR CONCUBINAGE

TYNDALE

Another reason is, whosoever believeth in Christ, consenteth that God's law is good. The Pope consenteth not that God's law is good, for he hath forbidden lawful wedlock unto all his [clergy], over whom he reigneth, as a temporal tyrant with laws of his own making, and not as a brother exhorteth them to keep Christ's.

And he hath granted unlawful whoredom unto as many as bring money. As through all Dutchland every priest, paying a gylden unto the Archdeacon, shall freely and quietly have his whore, and put her away at his pleasure and take another at his own lust, as they do in Wales, in Ireland, Scotland, France and Spain. And in England thereto they be not few which have license to keep whores, some of the Pope, and some of their ordinaries. And when the Parishes go to law with them to put away their whores, the Bishop's officers mock them, pole them, and make them spend their thrifts, and the priests keep their whores still. Howbeit in very deed since they were rebuked by the preaching of Wyclif, our English spiritualty have so laid their snares unto men's wives to cover their abomination, though they bide not always secret.

MORE

Here Tyndale proveth us that no Pope believeth in God. For none of them confesseth that God's law is good. He proveth that they consent not that God's law is good because they make (he saith) laws of their own beside, and therefore he saith that they not only consent not that God's law is good, but also that they reign over Christian people like temporal tyrants.

Whereby, Tyndale teacheth us that every temporal prince making any law beside the law of God, consenteth not that God's law is good nor useth not himself as a lawful Prince, but as an unlawful tyrant, because he doth not only as a brother exhort Christ's law, but also like a tyrant compelleth them to keep his own.

Now this glance that Tyndale in railing upon Popes maketh by the way at all temporal Princes and laws is (if they plainly durst speak it out) the very principal point of all his whole purpose, and his master Martin Luther's too, and all the serpentine seed that is descended of them. For Luther saith that we need no more laws, but only the gospel, well and truly preached after his own false fashion. And he babbleth also in his *Babylonica* that neither man nor angel hath any power or authority to make any law, or any one syllable of a law upon any Christian man, without his own agreement given thereunto. And by Friar Barnes's heresy a man may without deadly sin break all the laws that are made by men.

And thus ye may see that the shrewd sort of all *this sect would not only have Popes and Popes' laws gone and taken away, but kings and kings' laws too*, if their purpose might prosper and make all people lawless, because all laws are lets, as they take them, to their evangelical liberty, by which they claim to be bound or compelled to nothing, but *exhorted only to live every man after the gospel by every man expounded after his own mind*, which manner of exhorting amounteth unto as much as to let all run at riot without any bond or bridle, and then exhort every man to live as he list himself.

But now is it good to see what law so especially lieth in Tyndale's eye, for which he generally raiseth upon all the remnant. That is for that, he saith, that the Pope hath forbidden lawful wedlock.

In this he meaneth two things, with which two Luther and Wyclif were evil content, before. One, that there is marriage now forbidden between brother's and sister's children that was not before forbidden by the scripture. For which cause Wyclif saith that such marriages are forbidden without any foundation or ground. . . .

The other law that he layeth so sore against the Pope is that priests, friars, canons, monks, and nuns may not be suffered to be wedded contrary to their own vows and promises made unto God, which no man compelled them to make. Is not this a great fault that Friar Tuck may not marry Maid Marion?

. . . But Tyndale letteth not to lie out aloud, and say that the Pope hath himself granted unlawful whoredom to as many as bring money, and in another place of his book, he saith that the Pope hath in Rome set up a stew of boys.

We have had many pardons come hither, and many dispensations and many licenses too, but yet I thank our Lord I never knew one such, nor I trust never shall, nor Tyndale I trow neither, but that he listeth loud to lie.

And as for his licenses customably given by the ordinaries, I trust he lieth in other countries, for as for England I am sure he lieth. . . .

E. W. 618–620

8. TYNDALE'S OMISSION

to answer More's *Dialogue*, Bk. 2, c. 2, to which he never refers.

(In my *Dialogue*) I had proved, first, that the Church of Christ here in earth shall ever endure and continue as long as the world shall last. Which thing is, I doubt not, in such wise proved there that Tyndale dare not himself deny it here. I, then, in the second book did after prove that the known Catholic Church is that same Church and none of all the sects of heretics, because they be come out of it, and that therefore all they be but branches cut off or broken off from this vine of Christ's mystical Body, the known Catholic Church, and that since they be from that stock they therefore dry up and wither away and wax worth nothing, nor meet for nothing but worthy for the fire. . . .

Now cometh Tyndale and barely rehearseth my reason, dissimuling after his accustomed fashion all that ever I laid forth for the proof. Of all which things neither in his answer here, which he calleth his solution, nor afterward when he cometh to the place in his particular answer unto every chapter [in the *Dialogue*] in order, he never maketh any manner mention, but when he cometh to my second book, *goeth from the first chapter to the third, as though the printer had left the second unprinted.*

Is not this fashion a plain confession of his ignorance, and that he was at his wit's end and saw not what to say to it?

E. W. 627 E, G

9. CONTRAST BETWEEN MORE AND TYNDALE

Now consider . . . good Christian reader, how like these two reasons are together, Tyndale's, I mean, and mine, which Tyndale saith be not only like but also be both one, Christ and his apostles and St. John the Baptist went out of the Church or synagogue of the Jews, because the time was come in which by God's own ordinance the Jew's Church or synagogue should have an end. And therefore Luther, Tyndale, Huskin, and Zwinglius be gone out of the Catholic Church of Christ, which, while the world endureth, is ordained of God to have none end.

Also Christ and his apostles went as God had ordained out of the old Church to begin a new, because the old must by God's ordinance be left off and changed. And therefore, Luther, Tyndale, Huskin and Zwinglius be gone out of the old Church to begin a new because the old Church, by God's ordinance, shall never be left off in earth, nor never no new begun.

Also Christ and his apostles went out of the old Church to begin one new Church of all people agreeing in one faith, either with other, and therefore Luther, Tyndale, Huskin and Zwinglius be gone out of the old Church to begin a great many new, divers Churches, of which never one should agree with other, nor almost in any of them, any one man with other.

Finally, Christ went with his apostles out of the old Church to begin a new that was prophesied to be a perpetual church without end, against which the gates of hell should never prevail. And Luther, Tyndale, Huskin and Zwinglius be gone out of the old Church to begin a great many new, which are all prophesied by Christ and his apostles to be stark heretics, and that none of them should endure and last, no more than hath done the Churches of Arius, Helvidius, Pelagius or Manichaeus, with forty such sects more. All whom the very gates of hell prevailed against.

E. W. 629 D, G

10. THE SCOURGE OF A MERCIFUL FATHER SHALL NOT LAST

God hath not done. But what harm soever such heretics, as God's scourge, be suffered to work for the while, His mercy shall not fail in conclusion both to provide for the perpetual safeguard of his Catholic Church (which He hath promised never to forsake, but though he visit their iniquities with the rod of correction, yet His grace and good will He hath warranted never to take from them) and also shall His goodness turn again from their errors some such as those arch-heretics deceive, and them whose malice He shall find incurable, He shall, as an old naughty rod, before the face of His faithful children of His Catholic Church, when He hath beaten and corrected them therewith, so, as a tender mother doth, break the rod in pieces and cast it in the fire.

E.W. 630 C, D

11. HOW HERESY BEGETS ANARCHY

MORE

Ye may see that Tyndale affirmeth now not only those abominable heresies that be taught before, but all those also that Anabaptists have added unto them since. And so now be the true Church with him and agree with scripture and with the law of God, all those that say the baptizing of children is void, and they that say that there ought to be no rulers at all in Christendom, neither spiritual nor temporal, and that no man should have anything proper to his own, but that all women ought to be common to all men . . . and then, finally, that our Blessed Lord was but only man and not God at all.

And in good faith I never thought other yet from soon after the beginning, but that when this folk fell once to these horrible heresies which Tyndale in his book hath taught us, they should not fail to fall soon after unto those other two of which the very worst is not worse yet than divers of those that Tyndale taught us before, nor lightly can there be none worse, except only one, that were to say there is no God at all. And, as help me God, I verily fear they shall fall into at last. And then reckoning neither upon God nor devil, nor immortality of their own souls . . . thus reckoning upon nothing but only upon this world, and therefore reckoning for nothing but only for the body.

E.W. 656–657

12. LEARNED OR UNLEARNED

MORE

Now when he (Tyndale) saith: "Thou shalt always know them by their faith examined by scripture, and by their profession and consent to live after the law of God". I would fain wit which "Thou" he meaneth, thou learned or thou unlearned? Well, yet wot that among the learned the very sense is in question, and upon debating thereof ariseth all variance. Which "thou" meaneth he then? Thou that art unlearned, thou that canst scantly read it, or thou that canst not read it at all? When they that are learned cannot perceive it, then thou, perdy, that art unlearned, shall perceive it anon, and examine and judge by the scripture which of them say best for their faith of whom thou understandest neither one nor the other, but the longer thou hearest them dispute upon the scripture, but if (unless) thou bring the true faith thither, the less shalt thou perceive.... And, therefore, for every man learned and unlearned, for so far toucheth the necessary doctrine of true faith and living, and exposition of scripture that appertaineth thereto, the very fastness and surety is to rest unto the Church, which is, as St. Paul saith, the pillar and ground of truth. And that can be none unknown Church, which can neither learn nor teach.

E.W. 658 F–H

13. HERETICS GO OUT FROM THE CHURCH BUT THE CHURCH REMAINS

For as that glorious martyr holy Saint Cyprian saith: *Out of us be they all gone, and not we out of them,* but ever from the beginning as heretics or schismatics have risen, either have they by profession departed out, or the Church has cast them out, and the Church evermore hath as the very flock continued still and remained, and the branches so cut off, have first or last withered away. And so shall all these at length, when the Catholic Church shall abide, and remain and stand fast with God and God with it, according to God's promise, till the world take an end, and ever miracles in it, and in only it, to declare and make open that the very faith, the very hope, the very charity still continueth therein, and that how sick so ever it be, and how much dead flesh soever be found in the sick and sore parts of the same, yet alive is ever the body of this Church, for in it is the soul and the spirit, and out of the body of this known, continued Catholic Church, there is in the body of any other Church gone out or cast out of this for their contrary belief and faith, or for their rebellious behaviour, there neither is, I say, nor can be among them all, as all the old holy doctors and saints fully record and testify, neither health, life, head, nor spirit.

E.W. 659 C–E

14. LUTHER HIMSELF ALLOWS THAT THE CHURCH CAN DISCERN THE WORDS OF GOD FROM THE WORDS OF MEN

Luther himself confesseth that God hath given the Church that gift of God, that it can discern the words of God from the words of men. And wherefore hath He given the Church that gift but because He will not suffer His Church to fall into such a perilous error as to take the words of men for the words of God, whereby men might fall to some evil opinions as well in faith as other virtues.

E. W. 662 H

15. WHETHER WOMEN MAY SAY MASS

The Anglican Church has talked of reconsidering the question as to whether women should say Mass. This question was raised by William Tyndale and dealt with by St. Thomas More in a very simple and direct way in his *Confutation* as follows:

TYNDALE

They will haply demand where it is written that women should baptise. Verily in this commandment, Love thy neighbour as thyself, it is written that they may and ought to minister not only baptism but all other sacraments also in time of need, if they be so necessary as they preach them.

MORE

Lo, sir, here ye see that if the Mass be so necessary as the Church teacheth, which saith and hath ordered that it is necessary to be said unto the parish at the leastwise every Sunday; if the priest be not at home, then some good wife may for a need step to the altar and say Mass in his stead, because the scripture saith, Love thy neighbour as thyself.

What is there that these folk (the reformers) may not prove by scripture, if they may deduce it thus, and have their deduction allowed. Osa made as good a deduction as this and yet had thanks. For he thought that because of the commandment, Thou shalt honour thy Lord God, he might and was bound to set his hand unto the staying and keeping the ark of the covenant that was about to fall. But God taught other men by that man's sudden death that he was too malapert to meddle with that kind of God's honour that was not meet for him. And Tyndale, because a woman must love her neighbour as herself, will have her not touch the ark but the Blessed Body of God and boldly consecrate it herself, which neither the blessed mother of Christ, nor the

P

highest angel in heaven, durst ever presume to think because God had not appointed him to that office. Such deductions upon scripture made they of likelihood that took upon them in the Old Testament more than their part came to, as Chore and Abiron and the King Osias, that would needs play the priest and incense God Himself; for which honourable service our Lord sent him shame and sorrow.

Now if Tyndale ask me why a woman may christen and not consecrate since both are sacraments, I can answer him the common answer that though both be necessary, yet both be not like great nor like necessary. For both is there greater reverence to be had for the Sacrament of Christ's Body than the other, since for fault of baptism salvation faileth and not for fault of housel. But, as for my part, I will give him none answer to the question other than the ordinance of God's Spirit, which I see that God hath taught His Church; and else would he not suffer them to believe that it were well done, whereof no man is bound to give a precise cause. But it were overmuch boldness to think that we could precisely tell the cause of eveything that it pleaseth God to devise, though Tyndale and his spiritual sort will not obey God's bidding till themselves, as he saith, have ensearched and found the full cause why.

E. W. 462 C–H

More confessed after finishing his *Confutation* that the writing of it had been "some pain and labour. . . . But, so help me God," he continues, "I find all my labour not half so grievous to me as the tedious reading of blasphemous heresies, that would to God, after my labours done, so that the remembrance of their pestilent errors were erased out of Englishmen's hearts, and their abominable books burnt up, mine own walked with them, and the name of these matters utterly put in oblivion."[1]

[1] *E. W.* 375 D, G.

13

Erasmus and Luther

WE LEFT Erasmus in 1516, settled at Basle and at the height of his fame, having recently published his *Novum Instrumentum*, the great edition of St. Jerome in which he had a determining part, and his *Institutio Principis Christiani*, dedicated to the young King Charles of Castile, later to become the Emperor Charles V. He writes to a friend of his, in a sanguine mood, about the maintenance of peace and the progress of learning.

It is no part of my nature to be excessively fond of life: whether it is that I have, to my own mind, lived nearly long enough, having entered into my fifty-first year, or that I see nothing in this life so splendid or delightful, that it should be desired by any one who is convinced of the Christian faith that a happier life awaits those who in this world earnestly attach themselves to piety. But at the present moment I could almost wish to be young again for no other reason than this, that I anticipate the near approach of a golden age; so clearly do we see the minds of princes, as if changed by inspiration, devoting all their energies to the pursuit of peace. . . Therefore when I see that the highest sovereigns of Europe, Francis of France, Charles the King, Henry of England, and the Emperor Maximilian, have set all their warlike preparations aside, and established peace upon solid, and as I trust, adamantine foundations, I am led to a confident hope that not only morality and Christian piety but also a genuine and purer literature may come to renewed life or greater splendour.[1]

But Erasmus's hopes for peace were hardly to be realised; for, as he tells us somewhat later:

. . . Certain persons, who get nothing by peace and a great deal by war, threw obstacles in the way which prevented this truly kingly purpose from being carried into execution. After this great disappointment, I sat down and wrote by desire of John le Sauvage (Chancellor of Burgundy) my *Querela Pacis* (1517): but, since that period, things have been growing worse and worse; and I believe, I must soon compose the

[1] F. M. Nichols, *The Epistles of Erasmus*, vol. ii, pp. 505–6 (1517).

epitaph instead of the complaint of Peace, as she seems to be dead and buried and not likely to be revived.[1]

There can be no doubt that the *Complaint of Peace*, or, to give it the original title, *Querela Pacis undique gentium ejectae profligataeque*, gives utterance to the deepest convictions of Erasmus upon the two things dearest to his heart–the cause of peace and the cause of learning.

Where can peace be found [he asks] in these times of war and religious dissension? Nation contends with nation and school with school, the logician is at war with the rhetorician, the lawyer with the divine, even "religious" quarrel among themselves, Dominicans with Franciscans, Benedictines with Cistercians; and yet nothing can be more at variance with the temper, the teaching, and the example of our Lord Himself.[2]

In our day, Erasmus would be called a pacifist, for he scarcely permitted the justice even of a defensive war, except indeed against the incursions of the Turks, then a very real and terrible menace to western civilisation.

The treatise concludes with an earnest appeal to kings, bishops, and all in authority to follow the things that make for peace, pointing out that the greatest sovereigns of the day, Francis, Charles, Maximilian, and Henry, and above all the Pope himself, are in its favour, and urging that thus, the empire of kings will be more august, when they shall rule over a pious and prosperous people, the priests will have more time for the performance of their sacred duties, the Christian name will be more formidable to the enemies of the Cross; while, above all, they will gain the favour of Christ, to please whom is the sum of all human happiness.

Erasmus now occupied himself with editions of Suetonius and Quintus Curtius, and a valuable contribution to Greek learning by his translation of the Greek Grammar of Theodore Gaza, the best that had so far been printed. Before he returned to Basle in the beginning of 1518, Froben had brought out a collection of his *Letters* enlarged from one published at Louvain in the preceding year, and a second volume followed it before he left Basle in the autumn. Thus his many readers were put in possession of a series of letters "the most entertaining that has ever been given to the world, unsurpassed for their flowing style, their biting satire, their graphic powers of description, their wit, elo-

[1] *Catalogue of Lucubrations,* 1524.
[2] An English translation of the *Complaint of Peace,* a reprint of the issue of 1802, was published in 1917, to celebrate the fourth centenary of its first appearance.

quence, and learning, and constituting now, with the additions that were subsequently made, one of the most interesting and delightful autobiographical sketches that it would be possible to name. . . . These letters were read with delight and eagerness at the time of their first appearance, and they will continue to be read as long as any interest is felt in the great men and great events of the time to which they belong."[1] And, in our time, no better beginning could be made with their perusal than in the three volumes translated by the late Mr. F. M. Nichols, enriched as they are by his learned and happy personal comments.[2]

While at Louvain, Erasmus wrote a *Paraphrase of the Epistle to the Romans*, which he dedicated to his old friend Cardinal Domenico Grimani, and published in 1517, followed, after about a year and a half, by the two Epistles to the Corinthians, and the Galatians. Then came the two Epistles of St. Peter, which he dedicated to Cardinal Wolsey. All these were received with universal favour and entirely escaped censure; and, as we know, they were so highly appreciated in England that in later years they were translated as part of a paraphrase of the New Testament and placed in every parish church.[3]

For many years Erasmus had been doing his unwearying best to help on the reformation of the Church *from within*, and already, as Lord Acton has said, had succeeded in diverting the current of Renaissance pagan learning into Christian channels.[4] But now the immense shadow of Luther looms large across his path, and almost at once he recognises it as a menace to his own lifework. He had hoped that by the advancement of learning and the diffusion of the Scriptures the Church might at one and the same time be purified, while her integrity and the unity of Christendom, under the visible headship of the Roman pontiff, might remain unimpaired.[5] At first his relations with Luther had been not unfriendly, but he makes his own position unmistakably clear. "If Luther stand by the Church, I will gladly join him," he writes. Soon however, he perceived that Luther's methods of reform were hasty and impatient, quite the opposite of everything that he himself desired and

[1] R. B. Drummond, *Erasmus*, vol. ii, pp. 402-5.
[2] F. M. Nichols, *The Epistles of Erasmus*, 3 vols. (Longmans, Green & Co.). See also the great edition of the late Dr. P. S. Allen, published by the Clarendon Press, Oxford, in their original Latin, and in eleven volumes.
[3] It should be noticed, however, that Erasmus own paraphrases were somewhat revised by Anglican editors.
[4] Acton, *The Study of History*, p. 8.
[5] R. B. Drummond, *Erasmus*, vol. ii, pp. 1-2.

had worked for so long. Without going into particular and unnecessary details, their differences came to a head over the Lutheran doctrine of Justification by Faith alone. Luther was a man of a strongly passionate nature, and being also scrupulous and religious-minded, he found, perhaps, in his doctrine of justification, a justification for his own and other people's all-too-human weaknesses. The Catholic doctrine, on the other hand, supplied a practical incentive to virtuous habits, and so far appealed to the commonsense of mankind. As St. Thomas More pointed out, the Lutheran theory destroyed human responsibility, and necessarily had a bad effect on private morals:

And this they call the liberty of the gospel, to be discharged of all order and all laws, and do what they list, which be it good or bad, be, as they say, nothing but the works of God wrought in them. But they hope by this means God shall for the while work in them many merry pastimes. Wherein, if their heresy were once received and the world changed thereby, they should find themself sore deceived. For the laws and orders among men, with fear of punishment taken away, there were no man so strong that could keep his pleasure long but that he should find a stronger take it from him. But after it were once come to that point, and the world once ruffled and fallen into wildness, how long would it be, and what heaps of heavy mischiefs would there fall, ere the way were found to set the world in order and peace again?[1]

Erasmus's friend, Cuthbert Tunstall, Bishop of London, writes to him in the summer of 1523 saying that the whole Church expected him to take up the cudgels against Luther on this very question of free-will and justification. And so, much against his will, Erasmus wrote his *De Libro Arbitrio*, which may be summed up in the concluding words of this very effective little treatise, "I approve of those who ascribe something to free-will, but rely most upon grace."

It may be imagined that Luther was not well pleased with this work and, after a year, wrote his reply, *Man's Will not Free*. Erasmus answered it in his *Hyperaspites*, published in two books in 1526-7. Luther wrote again describing one whom he had once called "my dearest brother" as "that enraged viper, Erasmus of Rotterdam, the vainest creature in the world".

After this disagreement with Luther, Erasmus seems to have gone through a period when he was unable to please anybody, a fate that often overtakes men as moderate as himself; but we may omit further

[1] *E.W., Dialogue*, bk. iv, c. 12, p. 274 F, G.

reference to his controversial warfare and follow him rather in his quiet, unceasing and learned labours at Basle. "During these stormy times, he kept pretty much at home, pursuing his studies in his own room, or perhaps wandering as far as Froben's garden, where on fine days he often spent his afternoons, walking up and down, or writing in the summer-house. Nor, while the peasant war lasted, would it have been very safe to have ventured far beyond the walls of the city. 'Every day,' he writes to Polydore Vergil, in the autumn of 1525, 'there are bloody conflicts between the nobles and the peasants so near us that we can hear the firing, and almost the groans of the wounded.' And in another letter he estimates the number of slain peasants at far more than a hundred thousand, 'and every day,' he adds, 'priests are imprisoned, tortured, hanged, decapitated, or burned.' "[1]

Meanwhile, in spite of the delayed allowances from the Emperor, Erasmus must have been pretty well off. Besides the pensions he received from his English friends, like Warham and Mountjoy, there were many wealthy and powerful people anxious to do him honour; and now that he had declared himself so definitely against Luther, Catholics on all sides began to look upon him one of the ablest defenders of the faith. But he is continually afflicted by his old enemy, the stone, and it is sad to think that modern remedies for that most painful complaint were not at his disposal. He, too, like ourselves, utters "a plague on those wars which take tithes of us so often". But his pleasant humour breaks through, and his witticisms have not yet lost their salt, which he rather enjoys rubbing into the wounds he has already inflicted upon his enemies. "The reformers", he writes, "have only two objects, a wife and a fortune." Or again, "Œcolampadius has lately married. His bride is not bad-looking. He wants, I suppose, to mortify the flesh. Some talk of the Lutheran tragedy; I think it's a comedy, for it always ends in a marriage." He had some consolation too in the passing away of some of his bitterest opponents. "I hear," writes his friend, Gattinara, the Chancellor of Charles V, "that two of your enemies are dead; thus does God favour His own." One of these was Egmund, the Carmelite, who for years had been the bane of his life; and the other, a Dominican friar, who, with three others, had written a scurrilous book against him, of which he often speaks in his letters.[2]

But the greatest grief which overtook him while at Basle was the death in 1527 of his dear and devoted friend, John Froben, his printer

[1] Drummond, *Erasmus*, vol. ii, p. 267.   [2] *Ib.*, p. 272.

and publisher. "I cannot endure the loss of Froben," he wrote, "he was a true friend, so simple and sincere that even if he had wished to conceal anything, it was so repugnant to his nature that he would have found it impossible. . . . To me his kindness was unbounded."[1]

Apart from his work of editing the Fathers, Erasmus wrote several devotional books, one on confession, another on prayer, a sermon on the boundless mercy of God, a Litany in praise of the Virgin of Laurentum, and a prayer to our Lady in adversity. He also wrote an exposition of the Lord's Prayer, arranged for each day of the week; and in his comparison of the Virgin and the Martyr, says that "to a virgin who loves her spouse the convent is not a prison, as some falsely say, but a paradise".

In 1526 he wrote the *Institution of Christian Matrimony* at the request of Lord Mountjoy, and dedicated it to Queen Katharine. He also wrote the "Ciceronian", turning into ridicule those who slavishly tried to write like Cicero. It even provoked the famous scholar, Scaliger, to make an abusive attack upon him; but Erasmus wisely refused to be drawn into a controversy with so powerful an opponent. During his last year at Basle he published a new edition of Seneca, as a previous one had been printed in his absence full of mistakes, so much so that he offended his old friend Bishop Tunstall by sending him one. Seneca had always been a favourite of his, the more so because St. Jerome had included him in his catalogue of saints. But Erasmus warns his readers that if they read him as a Christian, he wrote like a pagan; but if they read him as a pagan, he wrote like a Christian.

In 1529 he reluctantly made up his mind to leave Basle, having finished his new edition of Seneca and completed his labours on a critical edition of St. Augustine in ten volumes, incorporating therewith the work of his friend Vives on the *De Civitate Dei*. The state of religious opinion in Basle had sadly changed since his first arrival there fifteen years before. And he was particularly troubled by the attempt of the Protestant party in the city to compel him to write against the Catholic doctrine of transubstantiation.

It would appear, too, that Conrad Pellican, a Franciscan, who in 1526 had joined the reformers and married, had published it abroad in 1525 that Erasmus agreed with him in his heretical opinions about the Holy Eucharist. Erasmus writes to him in great indignation repudiating these false rumours.

---

[1] See p. 69 for a further description of John Froben.

. . . You privately instilled into the ear of an excellent young man that I held the same views about the Eucharist that you held . . . and whereas you now openly profess that opinion, you are giving it out and saying that I hold it along with you. . . . To bring my mind to do that I have ever declared it impossible, seeing especially that the texts of the Gospel and the Apostle speak so plainly of "the body which is given" and "the blood which is shed", and that it is marvellously consonant with God's unspeakable love to the human race that those whom He has redeemed, by the blood and body of His Son, He should be willing in some ineffable manner to nourish with the flesh and blood of His same Son, and, by this hidden presence of His Son, comfort them as with a pledge, until He return in his glory to be openly seen by all. . . .

It is my way with learned friends . . . to discourse about all manner of things. . . . But I will confess to the crime of parricide if any mortal man has heard from me, in earnest or jest, this statement that in the Eucharist there is nothing but bread and wine or that there is not there the body and blood of the Lord. . . .

I know what slight value you attach to the authority of Councils. But for my part, I do not despise the Roman Church herself and much less when she has all the churches in agreement with her. . . . The Church has taught me to believe the Gospel. Hitherto with all Christians I have adored Christ, crucified (*passum*) for me, in the Eucharist, and I still see no reason why I should go back upon that opinion. No human reasons avail to withdraw me from the consentient belief of the Christian world. . . .

If your mind wavers, it is the consensus of the Catholic Church that has hitherto kept my mind steady. If *you* are convinced that in the celebration of the Eucharist there is nothing else but bread and wine, *I* would rather be torn limb from limb than profess what you profess. . . . I will endure that you blurt out to all the world whatever else I have said; I will not endure that you make me either the author or abettor of this doctrine. So may I never be estranged from Christ. Amen.[1]

Another saying of Erasmus's may seem apposite in this connection: "Better unity with some hardship, than to hold one's own at the cost of discord". And finally a sentence from Sir Richard Jebb, a great and disinterested scholar: "Erasmus never departed an inch from his allegiance to Rome".[2]

A letter of his to his friend Pirckheimer well indicates the sad state of religious affairs at Basle and the urgent need for him to find shelter elsewhere. It is dated May 9th, 1529, and was written after his departure.

---

[1] P. S. Allen, *Erasmi Epistolae*, tom. iii, 950.   [2] *Essays and Addresses*, p. 353.

While the rabble were in arms in the market-place, where they had their guns regularly arranged, everybody who had anything to lose at home, was in terror. For sometime it looked as if there would be an armed encounter. The better part supported the cause of the Church, but they were numerically weaker, for the others had many strangers among them, besides a number of acknowledged ruffians whose only object was destruction. They began this tragedy close upon winter, when it was not easy either to take flight or to send for assistance. The Church party, finding that conventicles were held contrary to the order of the Council and the prescribed oath, took up arms, and soon the others followed their example, even bringing guns and other engines into the market. By the authority of the Council, the Church party were made to lay down their arms, which the others also did reluctantly. . . . On the order being issued for the destruction of images, they assembled in the market, got their engines into order, built an immense pyre, and passed some nights in the open air, amid the universal alarm of the citizens; however they broke into no house, nor did they attack any person, though the chief magistrate, my next-door neighbour, a good speaker, and, as was proved on many occasions, an excellent public servant, was obliged to fly by night in a boat, and would have been killed had he not done so. Many others also fled for fear, who, however were recalled by the Council if they wished to enjoy their rights as citizens, but all who favoured the old religion were removed from the Council, so as to put an end to disunion there. So far the Council had kept the mob under control, and everything that was allowed to be removed from the churches was removed by the smiths and workmen employed for the purpose; but they heaped such insults on the images of the saints, and the crucifix itself, that it is quite surprising there was no miracle, seeing how many there used to be whenever the saints were even slightly offended. Not a statue was left either in the churches, or the vestibules, or the porches, or the monasteries. The frescoes were obliterated by means of a coating of lime; whatever would burn was thrown into the fire, and the rest pounded into fragments. Nothing was spared for love or money. Before long the mass was totally abolished, so that it was forbidden either to celebrate it in one's own house or to attend it in the neighbouring villages. When I no longer feared the worst and there seemed reason to hope that no one's life or property would be attacked, this merciful course being recommended by Œcolampadius, notwithstanding new decrees continued to be issued every day by their synods, and so I began to think of moving, but without letting my purpose be known. I would have done so before Easter, but a violent stomach attack prevented me. Moreover I felt anxious lest changing my residence should be bad for my health; I was rather afraid too that they would try to stop me on my departure, and accordingly I obtained from King Ferdinand two certificates, one inviting me to his court, and the other securing my safe passage through his own and the Emperor's dominions. First of all I sent secretly my money, my rings, and my silver plate, and whatever is most liable to be stolen. Some time afterwards I loaded two waggons with my books and papers, quite openly, and on this account Œcolampadius and the preachers are said to be incensed against me. . . .

As I was about to get on board the boat, they raised some difficulty about the baggage of my servant-maid. In order to escape being stared at by the mob, I desired my boatman to loose from some retired place, but this the Council decidedly forbade. . . . I submitted, and loosed from the bridge, accompanied by some friends. No one said a word to me.

This change of residence (to Freiburg) has turned out better than I expected. The magistrates of this city offered me a hearty welcome of their own accord, before they saw King Ferdinand's letters of recommendation, and they have given me a royal palace to live in, one which was built for Maximilian but not finished.[1]

Erasmus had been apprehensive about the effects of the change of residence upon his health; but, contrary to his expectations, he seemed to be all the better for it, and to have recovered a great deal of his youthful energy. His chief literary effort of this year was the publication of his great edition of St. Augustine; but it was followed in the autumn by an illness which prevented any further work for some time.

In 1530 his complete *St. Chrysostom* appeared with a Latin translation and a life of the saint. In 1531 his *Apophthegms of the Ancients* was printed in six volumes, to which two more were added subsequently. In 1532 followed the works of St. Basil, of special interest as being the first work, other than the New Testament, issued in Greek from a German press.

Meanwhile he had been living at Freiburg in the unfinished palace spoken of before; but difficulties with a fellow-occupant led him to buy a house of his own of which he writes in an amusing way.

If any one were to tell you that Erasmus, who is now nearly seventy, had married, would you not make the sign of the cross at least half-a-dozen times? I am sure you would; and yet I have done a thing which has brought me no less annoyance and trouble and which is equally strange to my habits and pursuits. I have bought a house, a very nice-looking one, but it has cost me dear. Who need now despair of rivers returning to their sources when Erasmus, after giving up everything all

---

[1] Drummond, *Erasmus*, vol. ii, pp. 314–17; P. S. Allen, *Erasmi Epistolae*, tom. viii, pp. 161–4.

his life to the pursuits of literature, has become a bargainer, a buyer, a stipulator, a cautioner, and must exchange the society of the Muses for that of carpenters, smiths, masons and glaziers. These troubles, for which I never had the slightest taste, have all but finished me. I am still, however, a stranger in my own house, which, though roomy enough has not a corner where I can lie down in safety. I have had one room made with a chimney and wooden rafters and with a tiled floor, but I cannot yet venture to trust myself in it, on account of the strong smell of lime. However I take possession in a short time, and I hope the change may turn out well: which has not hitherto been the case.[1]

On August 22nd, 1533, Erasmus lost one of his most valued friends and supporters, William Warham, Archbishop of Canterbury, whose worn and weary countenance as perpetuated by Holbein tells us something of the spiritual strain of those difficult times. Erasmus wrote a beautiful eulogy of him, which appeared in the preface to the third edition of his St. Jerome, published after his death. He describes him as a man of most frugal tastes, who, amid the splendours of a sumptuous table, kept for his many guests, lived himself on the plainest fare, and was so liberal that when he died he only left enough money to pay for his own funeral, "enough," as he hoped, "to carry him to heaven." And often would he say, when on his death-bed, "How I wish I might once more see Erasmus and clasp him to my arms before I leave this world. I would never let him be parted from me." But Erasmus was very differently moved by the death of two other men, enemies of the Catholic faith who died about the same time. "It is a good thing", he said, "that two of the Protestant leaders have perished, Zwinglius, on the field of battle, and Œcolampadius shortly after a fever and an abscess."

The house in which Erasmus lodged at Freiburg was next to a Franciscan convent, and he liked to listen to the friars as they sang their office, which he could join in without leaving his own room. But he was obliged to change his residence, and from the end of February to September 1533 fell into a state of some depression, owing perhaps to a lack of wine which he could never do without. On the accession of Paul III in 1534 it was thought he might become a Cardinal, but, as always, he was averse to official positions, however exalted, and in a letter to a friend, he said that it would be like "putting a cat into petticoats".

[1] Drummond, *Erasmus*, vol. ii, p. 327.

14

More's Last Controversial Works

IN THE years between his resignation of the Great Seal and his committal to the Tower of London, More finished his *Confutation* and wrote his last controversial works–The *Letter against Frith*, his *Apology*, the *Debellacyon* of *Salem and Bizance*, and his *Answer to the Supper of the Lord*.

The *Letter against Frith* is quite short–about a dozen folio pages–and its tone affectionately compassionate towards this very likeable and brilliant young canon of Christ Church who had written a treatise against "the most august of Catholic mysteries".

More's next work was his *Apology*, written in 1533, in which he meets the objections that have been raised against his controversial writings, especially their great length.

It is a shorter thing and sooner done to write heresies than to answer them [he replies], but greatly can I not marvel, though these evangelical brethren think my works too long. For everything think they too long that aught is. Our Lady's Psalter think they too long by all the Ave Marias and some good piece of the Creed too. Then the Mass think they too long by the secrets, and the canon, and all the collects wherein mention is made either of saints or souls. Instead of a long porteous [breviary], a short primer shall serve them; and yet the primer think they too long by all our Lady's matins. And the seven [penitential] psalms think they long enough without the litany; and as for *dirige* [the Office of the Dead] or commemoration for their friends' souls, all that service think they too long altogether.[1]

But the main purpose of the *Apology* was to confute a book, written by the lawyer Saint German, *Concerning the Division between the Spiritualty and the Temporalty*, a division at that time hardly pronounced, but which St. German's work did a great deal to exacerbate. St. German, writing anonymously, called himself the Pacifier, and, writing in an apparently suave and non-committal style, nevertheless calls continual attention to the failings of the clergy. Compared to this manner

[1] *E.W.*, *Apology*, p. 848 B, C.

of controversy, More's own style might even be called rough and opprobious; but More says in self-defence that he is a plain man who can but speak plainly, calling a traitor a traitor, a fool a fool, and a heretic a heretic.[1]

The Pacifier, though he calls himself a Catholic, lays great stress upon the written, or rather one might now say, printed word, being the *only* "Word of God". But More reminds him that "the word of God unwritten is of as great authority as is the word of God written".

The Church was gathered, and the faith believed, before any part of the New Testament was put in writing. And which writing was or is the true scripture, neither Luther nor Tyndale knoweth but by the credence that they give to the Church. And therefore since the word of God written Tyndale cannot tell but by the Church, which hath the assistance of the spirit of God therein, the gift of discretion to know it, and since that gift is given (as saint Austen saith, and Luther himself confesseth) to this common known Catholic Church: why should not Luther and Tyndale as well believe the Church in that it telleth them, This thing did Christ and his apostles *say*, as they must believe the Church (or else believe nothing) in that it telleth them, This thing did Christ's evangelists and apostles *write*?[2]

More repeats what he had previously said in his *Dialogue*, "that the Church was before the gospel was written; and that the faith was taught, and men were baptised and masses said, and the other sacraments ministered among Christian people before any part of the New Testament was put in writing; and that this was done by the word of God unwritten".[3] "And there is like surety and like certain knowledge of the word of God unwritten, as there is of the word of God written, since ye know neither the one nor the tother to be the word of God but by the tradition of the Church."[4]

Then, as to the interpretation of the Scripture, we have to make our choice between the Church and such fathers as St. Austen, St. Jerome, St. Ambrose, St. Cyprian, St. Chrysostom, St. Basil, St. Cyril, with all the other old holy doctors of the faithful doctrine on one side, or else the tother side, lewd Luther, and Lambert and Barnes, Huskin and Zwinglius and young father Frith.[5]

Reference is made to the distinction between "historical faith" and "feeling faith" which Tyndale had borrowed from Melanchthon.

If his distinction be true [writes More], yet upon God's gracious pre-

[1] *E.W.*, p. 864.   [2] *Ib.*, p. 852 F, G.
[3] *Ib.*, p. 853 G.   [4] *Ib.*, p. 853 K.   [5] *Ib.*, pp. 857-8.

vention and first calling upon, I say (and in my *Confutation* prove) that the willing endeavour of man in following, helpeth to the attaining of every manner kind of faith, and procureth the progress and increase of grace to the perfecting of that virtue in man, and with man, which God first began in man by God's own prevention (previous intervention) without man, but when man refuseth (except he mend and turn) else God leaveth his own good work begun unfinished. And therefore saith saint Austin to every man that hath use of reason: "He that hath created thee without thee, doth not justify thee without thee."

Another charge made much of by his opponents is that More received money from the clergy for his controversial writings, which accounted for his over-partiality towards them. "Men", retorts More, "were wont to call those folks suspect that were suspect of heresy. And this is now a new kind of suspects, if men be now suspected of the Catholic faith. Howbeit in that suspicion I am glad to be fallen, and purpose never to purge it."

"Now touching partiality upon my part towards the spiritualty, I marvel whereof they gather it." As to the receiving of money from them he writes:

All the lands and fees that I have in all England, besides such lands and fees as I have of the gift of the king's most noble grace, is not this day . . . worth yearly to my living, the sum of full fifty pounds. And thereof have I some by my wife, and some by my father (whose soul God assoil) and some have I also purchased myself, and some fees have I of some temporal men. And then may every man guess that I have no very great part of my living by the clergy, to make me partial to them.

And over that, this shall I truly say, that of all the yearly living that I have of the king's gracious gift, *I have not one groat by means of any spiritual man*, but far above my deserving have had it only of his singular bounty and goodness and special favour towards me.[1]

More then makes reference to the fact which no doubt brought him into suspicion that a great collection *was made* by the clergy in order to reward him for his labours in defence of the Church, amounting to four or five thousand pounds—that is, £70,000 of our money. But he refused to accept it, thinking it unfitting that he should receive any monetary rewards for these spiritual labours of his.

"Not so, my Lords," he made reply to them, "I had liefer see it cast into the Thames, than I or any of mine, should have thereof the worth of one penny."[2]

[1] *E.W.*, p. 867 A, B.   [2] Roper, *Life of Sir Thomas More*, p. 48.

He also added, "And would I . . . upon condition that all heresies were suppressed, that all my books were burned and my labour utterly lost." And in another place he says that he wished people neither to read these heretics' books nor his, but occupy their minds better with such English books as most nourish and increase devotion, mentioning as his favourites Hilton's *Scale of Perfection*, a translation of St. Bonaventure's *Life of Christ*, and the *Imitation of Christ* by Thomas à Kempis. All he had written or done or wished to do was to confirm and strengthen the Catholic faith of his fellow-countrymen, of which he writes in the strength of his own splendid faith:

As the sea shall never surround and overwhelm the land, and yet it hath eaten many places in, and swallowed whole countries up, and made places now sea that sometime were well-inhabitd lands, and hath lost part of his own possession in other parts again; so though the faith of Christ shall never be overflowen with heresies, nor the gates of hell prevail against Christ's Church, yet in some places it winneth in a new people, so may there in some places by negligence be lost the old.[1]

More then emphasises his loyalty "toward those two eminent orders that God hath here ordained in earth, the two great orders, I mean, of special consecrated persons, the sacred princes and priests". He writes:

I cannot see what need there were that I should rail upon the clergy, and reckon up all their faults. For that part hath Tyndale played, and frere Barnes both already, and left nothing for me to say therein, not though my mind were sore set thereon. They have with truth and lies, together, laid the living of bad to bad and good both in such vile villainous fashion, that it would make a good stomach to vomit to hear their ribaldrous railing. And yet not against sacred persons only, but against the blessed sacraments also. . . . And herein fare they much alike, as if there were a sort of villain wretched heretics, that meeting the priests and clerks, religious, and other, going with banners, copes, crosses, and censers, and the sacrament borne about with them upon a Corpus Christi day, would pick quarrels with them, and first call them all that could come in their vilainous mouths, and haply say true by some, and then catch them all by the heads, and throw them in the mire, surplices, copes, censers, crosses, relics, sacrament and all. And then if any man rebuked their vilainous dealing, and would step unto the priests, and would pull them up, and help to wipe the copes, and reverently take up the crosses, the relics and the blessed sacrament: were it not now well and wisely spoken if one would reprove him that thus did?[2]

It is interesting to hear More's opinion of the spiritual state of the country at a time so close to the religious changes that were so soon to come about.

I have not letted furthermore to say the thing which I take also for very true, that as this realm of England hath had hitherto, God be thanked, as good and as laudable a temporalty, number for number, as hath had any other Christian region of the quantity, so hath it also number for number, compared with any realm Christened of no greater quantity, as good and as commendable a clergy.[1]

But More thinks it strange that Saint German in his treatise should go about to emphasise and exaggerate the division and differences between the laity and the clergy with the intention, as he says, to pacify and appease both laity and clergy alike, whereas, so far from doing this, the effect of the Pacifier's treatise is to bring unfair and groundless charges against the clergy, and by his "soft and smotherly spoken" advocacy to create and incense public opinion against them on the vague authority of his "Some-say", or "They say", or "Folk say". As More justly concludes, the author, Christopher Saint German, deserves the rebuke of that good woman who, when a tale-bearer denounced her husband for his various infidelities, said to him, "I pray you, good man 'Some-say', get you shortly hence. For my husband and I shall agree the much sooner if no such brother 'Some-say' come within our doors."[2]

Christopher Saint German replies with his dialogue between two Englishmen, one named Salem, and the other Bizance, to which, again, More retorted in the same year, 1533, with his *Debellacyon of Salem and Bizance,* and so ended the controversy, giving further occasion for More's quaint flashes of humour at the expense of "Simken-Salem and Brother Bizance".

In the same year, too, More wrote his last controversial treatise, most fittingly in defence of the Catholic faith in the Blessed Sacrament of the Altar, in reply to a book called the *Supper of the Lord,* and now known to have been written by Tyndale.[3] He intended it to be in two parts, but the second part was never written owing to the troubles that overtook him in 1534.

---

[1] *E. W.,* p. 870.   [2] *Ib.,* p. 873.
[3] See *Notes and Queries,* Nov. 21st, 1942, art. "Tyndale's *Supper of the Lord,*" by Rev. J. F. Mozley.

15

The Oath of Supremacy

EARLY IN 1533 Anne Boleyn was secretly married to Henry VIII. Cranmer, who had succeeded Warham as Archbishop of Canterbury, pronounced the King's marriage with Katherine of Aragon null and void; and in June the new Queen was crowned with great magnificence at Westminster Abbey. Some of More's friends–Bishops Tunstall, Gardiner and Clarke–tried to persuade him to attend the ceremony, and made him a present of twenty pounds to buy himself a gown for the occasion. But More, while keeping the gift, absented himself from the ceremony, remarking playfully, when next he met them, that, having granted one of their requests, he thought he might be the bolder to deny the other. But his absence brought upon him the undying hatred of Anne Boleyn.

In 1534 the succession to the crown was vested in the heirs of Henry and Anne; and in the preamble to the Act of Succession it was stated that the King's marriage with Katherine was invalid, while his marriage with Anne was a valid one, Katherine being henceforth designated as princess-dowager to Prince Arthur. It was then decreed that not only Parliament but all the King's subjects should swear before the Royal Commissioners that they would "observe and maintain" the Act. Cranmer, Audley, Norfolk, and Suffolk were appointed as the first Commissioners, and the oath was taken by the members of both houses of Parliament on March 30th.

This oath was made the test of loyalty and approval of all that the King had done and chose to do. Cromwell was instructed to see that it was duly administered to all the King's subjects; and it amounted to nothing less than a final repudiation of papal authority.

More now knew himself to be in the greatest danger. Early in 1534 he was charged with writing a pamphlet against a proclamation justifying the King's marriage with Anne; but he cleared himself easily of this charge. Other charges were then sought for. As Lord Chancellor, it was said, he had received bribes. He admitted that he had been offered "a fair gilt cup" by a lady, which he had accepted. Lord Wiltshire, Anne Boleyn's father, cried out in joy at this discovery, "Lo, my lords, did I not tell you that you would find this matter true?" But More answered that after pledging the lady's health he had returned the cup to her again.

An attempt was then made to implicate him in the affair of the "Holy Maid of Kent". His name, with that of Bishop Fisher, was included in a bill of attainder on the charge of misprision of treason. William Roper was examined by Cromwell, who hoped thereby to incriminate More himself; but More had carefully refused to hear anything from her concerning the King.

Friendly persuasion having failed to move More in favour of the divorce, the Councillors tried what their threats might do. "My lords," quoth he, "these terrors be arguments for children, and not for me." After this examination he returned by river to Chelsea, and after they had landed, Roper questioned him anxiously of the result:

I trust, sir, that all is well, because that you be so merry.
It is so, indeed, son Roper, quoth he.
Are you then put out of the Parliament bill? quoth I.
By my troth, son Roper, quoth he, I never remembered it.
Never remembered it, sir, said I, a case that toucheth yourself so near, and us all for your sake! I am sorry to hear it, for verily I trusted, when I saw you so merry, that all had been well.
Then said he, Wilt thou know, son Roper, why I am so merry?
That would I gladly, sir, quoth I.
In good faith, I rejoiced son, quoth he, that I had given the devil a foul fall, that that with those lords I had gone so far as without great shame I could never go back again.
At which words, waxed I very sad, for though himself liked it well, yet liked it me but little.[1]

More was now in peril of his life. On Sunday, April 12th, 1534, he went with William Roper to hear the sermon at St. Paul's, and afterwards to his old house at Bucklersbury, where John and Margaret Clement then lived. One of the King's officers followed him there and cited him to appear on the following morning before the Commissioners of the Archbishop at Lambeth in order to take the oath. He went home at once, and the same evening bade farewell to his family, whom he hardly expected to see again after he had refused to take the oath. The next morning he went to an early Mass, made his confession and

---

[1] Roper, *Life of Sir Thomas More*, ed. Hitchcock, pp. 67–70.

received Holy Communion, as was his custom before any important happening of his life.

And [writes Roper] whereas he evermore used before his departure from his wife and children, whom he tenderly loved, to have them bring him to his boat, and there to kiss them all and bid them farewell, then, would he suffer none of them forth of the gate; and with a heavy heart, as by his countenance it appeared, with me and our four servants there took he his boat towards Lambeth. Wherein sitting still sadly awhile, at the last he suddenly rounded me in the ear, and said: "Son Roper, I thank our Lord the field is won."[1]

On his coming to Lambeth, on that morning of April 13th, he found himself in the presence of Archbishop Cranmer, the Lord Chancellor Audley, the Abbot of Westminster, and Thomas Cromwell, the Commissioners appointed to administer the oath. More asked to see both the Act of Succession and the oath, and declared that while he was willing to be sworn to the Succession, he could not in conscience assent to the clauses which implied a repudiation of the Pope's spiritual authority in England and also asserted the invalidity of the King's marriage with Katherine of Aragon. For the four days after his refusal of the oath he was kept in the custody of the Abbot of Westminster, "during which time the King consulted his Council what order it were meet to be taken with him. And albeit in the beginning they were resolved that with an oath, not to be known whether he had to the supremacy been sworn, or what he thought thereof, he should be discharged, yet did Queen Anne, by her importunate clamour, so exasperate the King against him, that contrary to his former resolution, he caused the said oath of the Supremacy to be administered to him. Who, albeit he made a discreet qualified answer, nevertheless was forthwith committed to the Tower."[2] This was on Friday, April 17th, 1534.

[1] Roper, *Life of Sir Thomas More*, ed. Hitchcock, pp. 72–3.   [2] *Ib.*, p. 74.

16

Imprisonment in the Tower

WHAT ROPER writes about More's imprisonment in the Tower is so simple and so moving that it would be well to follow his narrative as closely as may be.

Now when he had remained in the Tower a little more than a month, my wife (Margaret Roper), longing to see her father, by her earnest suit at length got leave to go to him. At whose coming, after the seven psalms and litany said (which, whensoever she came to him, ere he fell in talk of any worldly matters, he used accustomably to say with her) among other communication he said unto her: "I believe, Meg, that they that have put me here ween they have done me a high displeasure. But I assure thee, on my faith, good daughter, if it had not been for my wife and you that be my children, whom I account the chief part of my charge, I would not have failed long ere this to have closed myself in as strait a room, and straiter too. But since I am come hither without mine own desert, I trust that God in his goodness will discharge me of my care and with his gracious help supply my lack among you. I find no cause, I thank God, Meg, to reckon myself in a worse case here than in my own house. For methinketh God maketh me a wanton, and setteth me on his lap and dandleth me." Thus by his gracious demeanour in tribulation appeared it that all the troubles that ever chanced unto him by his patient sufferance thereof, were to him no painful punishments, but of his patience profitable exercises.[1]

A little while after her father's imprisonment, Margaret Roper wrote to him a letter, "wherein she seemed somewhat to labour to persuade him to take the oath (though she nothing so thought) to win thereby credence with Master Thomas Cromwell, that she might the rather get liberty to have free resort unto her father: unto which letter her father wrote an answer. The copy whereof here followeth.

Our Lord Bless you

If I had not been my dearly beloved daughter at a firm and fast point, I trust in God's great mercy this good great while before your lamentable letter had not a little abashed me surely far above all other things, of which I hear divers times not a few terrible toward me. Surely they

[1] Roper, *Life of Sir Thomas More*, pp. 75–6.

all touched me never so near, nor were so grievous unto me, as to see you, my well beloved child, in such vehement piteous manner labour to persuade unto me that thing wherein I have of pure necessity, for respect unto mine own soul, so often given you so precise answer before. Wherein as touching the points of your letter, I can make none answer. For I doubt not but you well remember that the matters which moved my conscience (without declaration whereof I can nothing touch the points) I have sundry times showed you that I will disclose them to no man. And therefore, daughter Margaret, I can in this thing no further, but like as you labour me again to follow your mind, to desire and pray you again, to leave of such labour, and with my former answers to hold yourself content . . .[1]

Margaret Roper writes in reply:

Mine own good father, it is to me no little comfort, since I cannot talk with you by such means as I would, at the least way to delight myself among, in this bitter time of your absence, by such means as I may, by as often writing to you as shall be expedient, and by reading again and again your most fruitful and delectable letter, a very faithful messenger of your very virtuous and ghostly mind, rid from all corrupt love of worldly things, and fast knit only in the love of God, and desire of heaven, as becometh a very true worshipper and a faithful servant of God, which I doubt not good father holdeth his holy hand over you, and shall (as he hath) preserve you both body and soul and namely now when you have abjected all earthly consolations, and resigned yourself willingly, gladly and fully, for his love, to his holy protection. Father, what think you hath been our comfort since your departing from us? Surely the experience we have had of your life past, and godly conversation, and wholesome counsel, and virtuous example, and a surety not only of the continuance of the same, but also of great increase by the goodness of our Lord, to the great rest and gladness of your heart devoid of all earthly dregs, and garnished with the noble vesture of heavenly virtue, a pleasant palace for the holy spirit of God to rest in, who defend you (as I doubt not, good father, but of his goodness he will) from all trouble of mind and body . . . that we may in conclusion meet with you mine own dear father in the bliss of heaven to which our most merciful Lord hath brought us with his precious blood. . . .[2]

Within a while Margaret Roper obtained permission to resort unto her father in the Tower, whereupon More himself addressed this short letter:

To all my loving friends

Forasmuch as being in prison, I cannot tell what need I may have, or what necessity I may have to stand in, I heartily beseech you all that if

[1] *E.W.*, p. 1431, D, G.   [2] *Ib.*, p. 1432.

my well beloved daughter Margaret Roper (which only of all my
friends hath, by the King's favour, license to resort unto me) do anything desire of any of you of such thing as I shall hap to need, that it may
like you no less to regard and tender it than if I moved unto you and
required it of you personally present myself. And I beseech you all to
pray for me, and I shall pray for you.

your faithful lover and poor bedesman
Thomas More, knight, prisoner.[1]

The following letter gives an account of the meeting between More
and his daughter in the Tower, of which Father Bridgett wrote, "I
doubt whether in the *Acts of the Martyrs* there is a nobler scene than
this." It is addressed to Lady Alington, More's stepdaughter, who had
written to Margaret Roper telling her that Audley, the Lord Chancellor,
considered her father "so obstinate in his own conceit in that everybody
went forth withal (to take the oath) save only the blind bishop (Fisher)
and he."

Margaret Roper to Lady Alington

When I came next unto my father . . . methought it both convenient
and necessary to show him your letter. Convenient, that he might thereby see your loving labour taken for him, necessary, that since he might
perceive thereby that if he stand still in this scruple of conscience (as it
is at the leastwise called by many that are his friends and wise) all his
friends that seem most able to do him good, either shall finally forsake
him, or peradventure not be able indeed to do him any good at all. And
for these causes at my next being with him after your letter received,
when I had awhile talked with him, first of his diseases both in his
breast of old and his reins now, by reason of gravel and stone, and of the
cramp also at divers nights (that) grippeth him in his legs, and that I
found by his words there were not much increased, but continued after
this manner that they did before, sometime very sore, and sometime
little grief, and that at that time I found him out of pain, as one in his
case might, meetly well-minded, after our vii. Psalms and the litany
said, to sit and talk and be merry, beginning first with other things . . .
I added, "I pray God, father, that their prayers (of his family) and ours,
and your own therewith, may purchase of God the grace that you may
in this great matter (for which you stand in this trouble, and for your
trouble all we also that love you) take such a way by time, as standing
with the pleasure of God, may content and please the King, whom ye
have always found so singularly gracious unto you, that if ye should
stiffly refuse to do the thing that were his pleasure, which God not
displeased you might do (as many great wise and well learned men say

[1] *E.W.*, p. 1432 G.

that in this thing you may) it would be both a great blot in your worship in every wise man's opinion, and as myself have heard some say (such as yourself have alway taken for well learned and good) of peril unto your soul also.

But as for that point will I not be bold to dispute upon, since I trust God and your good mind that ye will look surely thereto. And your learning I know for such, that I wot well you can. . . .

It can hardly be doubted that by these words Margaret was moved to press her father even to the point of submission to the King's will.[1]

With this my father smiled upon me and said: "What mistress Eve! (as I called you when you came first) hath my daughter Alington played the serpent with you, and with a letter set you awork to come tempt your father again, and for the favour that you bear him labour to make him swear against his conscience, and send him to the devil?"

And after that, he looked sadly again and earnestly said unto me: "Daughter Margaret, we two have talked this thing ofter than twice or thrice. And the same tale in effect that you tell me now therein, and the same fear too, have you twice told me before, and I have twice answered you too, that in this matter if it were possible for me to do the thing that might content the King's grace, and God therewith not offended, there hath no man taken this oath already more gladly than I would do: As he that reckoneth himself more deeply bounden unto the King's highness, for his most singular bounty many ways showed and declared than any of them all beside.

"But since standing [by] my conscience I can in no wise do it; and that for the instruction of my conscience in the matter, I have not flightily looked, but by many years studied and advisedly considered, and never could yet see nor hear the thing, nor I think I never shall, that could induce my own mind to think otherwise than I do. I have no manner remedy, but God hath given me to that strait, that either I must deadly displease him, or abide any worldly harm that he shall for mine other sins, under name of this thing suffer to fall upon me. Whereof (as I before this have told you too) I have ere I came here, not left unbethought nor unconsidered the very worst and the uttermost that can by possibility fall. And albeit that I know mine own frailty full well, and the natural faintness of mine own heart, yet if I had not trusted that God should give me strength rather to endure all things than offend him by swearing ungodly against mine own conscience, you may be very sure I would not have come here. And since I look in this matter but only unto God, it maketh me little matter though all men call it, as it please them, and say it is no conscience but a foolish scruple."

[1] She had herself taken the oath "as far as it would stand with the law of God".

At this word, [said Margaret], I took good occasion, and said unto him thus:

"In good faith, father, for my part I neither do, nor it cannot become me, either to mistrust your good mind or your learning. But because you speak of that that some calleth but scruple, I assure you you shall see by my sister's [Lady Alington's] letter, that one of the greatest estates in this realm, and a man learned too and (as I dare say yourself shall think when you know him, and as you have already right effectually proved him) your tender friend and very special good lord for a right simple scruple.[1] And you may be sure he saith it of good mind, and lieth no little cause. For he saith that where you say your conscience moveth you to this, all the nobles of the realm and almost all other men too, go boldly forth with the contrary, and stick not thereat, save only yourself and one other man, whom, although he be right good and very well learned too, yet would I ween few that love you give you the counsel, against all other men, to lean to his mind alone."[2]

And with this word [writes Margaret to Lady Alington], I took your letter, that he might see my words were not feigned, but spoken of his mouth, whom he much loveth and esteemeth highly. Thereupon he read over your letter. And when he came to the end, he began it afresh and read it over again. And in the reading he made no manner haste, and pointed every word. And after that he paused, and then thus he said:

"Far forth daughter Margaret, I find my daughter Alington such as I have ever found her, and I trust ever shall, as naturally minding me as you that are mine own. Howbeit, her take I verily for mine own too, since I have married the mother and brought her up as a child as I have brought you up, in other things and in learning both, wherein I thank God she findeth now some fruit, and bringeth her own up very virtuously and well. . . . In this matter she hath used herself like herself, wisely and like a very daughter to me, and in the end of her letter, giveth as good counsel as any man the wit had would wish. God give me grace to follow it, and God reward her for it."[3]

In the course of this long letter More makes it clear to his daughter Margaret that though all men differed from him in the matter of the oath, and even were the Bishop of Rochester among them, he could see no reason to alter his decision. Yet he adds "in this matter that I was not led by him very well and plainly appeareth, both in that I refused the oath before it was offered to him, and in that also this his lordship was content to have sworn of that oath (as I perceived since by you when you moved me to the same) either somewhat more, or in some

---

[1] Audley, Lord Chancellor.   [2] St. John Fisher.   [3] E. W., 1435, G.

other manner than ever I minded to do. Verily daughter, I never intend (God being my good Lord) to pin my soul at another man's back, not even the best man that I know this day living; for I know not whither he may hap to carry it. There is no man living, of whom, while he liveth, I may make myself sure."

Then, with that play of humour like sunshine on the darkening waters, Margaret says, "Why should you refuse to swear, father? For I have sworn myself."

At this he laughed and said, "That word was like Eve, too; for she offered Adam no worse fruit than she had eaten herself."

But replied Margaret in effect, "Suppose at the very end, when it was too late, you should realise that you had been wrong in refusing the oath?"

Too late, daughter Margaret? I beseech our Lord that if ever I make such change, it may be too late indeed. For well I wot the change cannot be good for my soul, that change, I say, that should grow but by fear. And therefore I pray God that in this world I never have good of such change. For so much as I take harm here, I shall have at the leastwise the less therefore when I am hence. And if it so were that I wist well now that I should faint and fall, and for fear swear hereafter, yet would I wish to take harm by the refusing first: for so should I have better hope for grace to rise again. And albeit Margaret that I wot well my lewdness hath been such: that I know myself well worthy that God should let me slip, yet can I not but trust in his merciful goodness, that as his grace hath strengthened me hitherto, and made me content in my heart to to lose goods, land, and life too, rather than to swear against my conscience, and hath also put in the King toward me that good and gracious mind, that as yet he hath taken from me nothing but my liberty, wherewith, as help me God, his grace hath done me great good by the spiritual profit that I trust I take thereby, that among all his great benefits heaped upon me so thick, I reckon upon my faith, my prisonment even the very chief. I cannot, I say, therefore distrust the grace of God, but that either he shall conserve me and keep the King in that gracious mind still to do to me none hurt, or else, if his pleasure be, that for mine other sins I shall suffer in such a case in sight as I shall not deserve, his grace shall give me the strength to take it patiently, and peradventure somewhat gladly too, whereby his high goodness shall (by the merits of his bitter passion joined thereunto, and far surpassing in merit for me all that I can suffer myself) make it serve for release of my pain in Purgatory, and over that for increase of some reward in heaven. Mistrust him Meg, will I not, though I feel me faint. . . .

And finally, Margaret, this wot I well, that without my fault, he will not let me be lost. I shall therefore with good hope commit myself wholly to him. And if he suffer me, for my faults, to perish, yet shall I then serve for a praise of his justice. But in good faith, Meg, I trust that his tender pity shall keep my poor soul safe and make me commend his mercy. And therefore, mine own good daughter, never trouble thy mind for anything that ever shall hap me in this world. And I make me very sure that whatsoever that be, seem it never so bad, in sight, it shall indeed be the best.

And with this, my good child, I pray you heartily, be you and all your sisters and my sons too, comfortable and serviceable to your good mother, my wife. And of your good husbands minds I have no manner doubt. Commend me to them all, and to my good daughter Alington and to all my other friends, sisters, nieces, nephews, and allies, and unto all our servants, man, woman, and child, and all my good neighbours and our acquaintance abroad. And I right heartily pray, both for you and them, to serve God and be merry and rejoice in him. And if anything hap me that you would be loath, pray to God for me, but trouble not yourself: as I shall full heartily pray for us all, that we may meet together once in heaven, where we shall make merry for ever, and never have trouble after.[1]

Unconsciously, too, he gives us a picture of himself, alone in his cell in the Tower, as he faces the final sacrifice he feels himself called upon to make. It comes in the *History of the Passion*, which he wrote in the Tower and was unable to complete. He is speaking of the courage of the holy martyrs:

And what will you say if God . . . of his goodness giveth some men grace not to be afeared [of martyrdom] at all? Not for that he most liketh and rewardeth such men's boldness, but he knoweth them to be faint-hearted that they were else likely to give over for fear. For many of truth have there been that at the first brunt have fearfully shrunk and fainted, and yet afterward valiantly passed through all the pain that was put upon them.

Now albeit, I cannot deny but that the example of them that suffer death with a bold and hardy courage is a right expedient for a great many to hearten them to do the like; yet, on the other side, forasmuch as all the sort of us in effect be very timorous at the coming of death, who can tell how many take good by these folk too, which though they come to it, as we see, with much anguish and dread, do yet in conclusion manfully pass through those horrible strong stops of weariness, fear, and heaviness, and so, stoutly breaking all those violent lets [hindrances], do gloriously conquer death, and mightily get up into heaven. And do not these persons put other faint and feeble souls, such as I mean as they were themselves, in good courage and comfort, that in time of persecution, and although that feel themselves inwardly in never so sore trouble, dread and weariness, and horror of most cruel death, yet shall they not utterly yield and give over? . . . but master their own weariness, sorrow, and fear, three most violent affections and three most cruel enemies.[1]

All attempts to alter More's frame of mind in the matter of the oath having proved ineffectual, other means were adopted in order to break down his constancy–he was not allowed to hear Mass, or to see his spiritual director, and at the same time was deprived of the company of his wife and his other children; and there can be little doubt that Margaret Roper was only given access to her father in the hope that her tender appeals might soften him into compliance with the royal wishes.

In his talks with Margaret he did not speak much of the Court, but once the name of Anne Boleyn seems to have come up. "How say they that she is?" asked More. "In faith, father, never better," was the reply. "Alas Meg," quoth he, "it pitieth me to think into what misery that poor soul shall come, and that very shortly too."

It having been discovered that More was still writing to some of his friends, the newly-made king's solicitor, Sir Richard Southwell, and Palmer, a servant of Cromwell's, were sent to take from him his books, papers and writing material.

From now onwards More's only means of written communications were scraps of paper procured by chance, and his pen a piece of coal. Speaking of his daughter Margaret, to whom he thus wrote, he said "a whole peck of coal would not suffice me to do justice to her goodness".

Having passed through the winter months, we find this short note to Margaret.

Mine own good Daughter:–Our Lord be thanked, I am in good health of body, and in good quiet of mind, and of worldly things I no more desire than I have, I beseech him to make you all merry in the hope of heaven. As to such things as I somewhat longed to talk with you all, concerning the world to come, our Lord put them into your minds, as I trust he doth, and better too by his Holy Spirit. May he bless and preserve you all.

Written with a coal, by your tender loving father, who in his poor prayers forgetteth none of you all. . . . And thus fare ye heartily well for lack of paper,

Thomas More, Knight.

[1] *E.W.*, pp. 1368 G–1370 C.

On May 10th, John Houghton, prior of the Charterhouse, London, Augustine Webster, prior of Axeholme, and Robert Lawrence of Belleval, together with Reynolds, a monk of the monastery of Sion, suffered the barbarous sentence of the law at Tyburn; and More, together with Margaret Roper, who was with him in the Tower at the time, saw them led to their martyrdom. On July 1st, 1535, More himself was brought to trial.

17

Trial, Sentence and Death

IT BEING now the May of 1535, and Sir Thomas More still a prisoner in the Tower,[1]

...Whereas the oath confirming the supremacy and matrimony was by the first statute in few words comprised, the Lord Chancellor and master Secretary (Cromwell) did of their own heads add more words unto it, to make it appear unto the King's ears more pleasant and plausible. And that oath, so amplified, caused they to be administered to Sir Thomas More, and to all other throughout the realm. Which Sir Thomas More perceiving, said unto my wife: "I may tell thee, Meg, they that have committed me hither, for refusing of this oath not agreeable with the statute, are not by their own law able to justify my imprisonment. And surely, daughter, it is a great pity that any Christian prince should by a flexible Council ready to follow his affections, and by a weak clergy lacking grace constantly to stand to their learning, with flattery to be so shamefully abused." But at length the Lord Chancellor and master Secretary, espying their own oversight in that behalf, were fain afterwards to find the means that another statute should be made for the confirmation of the oath so amplified with their additions. . . .[2]

Not long after, there came to him the Lord Chancellor, the dukes of Norfolk and Suffolk with master Secretary (Cromwell) and certain other of the Privy Council, at two several times, by all the policies possible procuring him, either precisely to confess the supremacy, or precisely to deny it; whereunto it appeareth by his examination in the said great book, they could never bring him.

Shortly hereupon, master Rich, afterwards Lord Rich, then newly made the King's Solicitor, Sir Richard Southwell, and one master Palmer, servant to the Secretary, were sent to Sir Thomas More in the Tower, to fetch away his books from him. And while Sir Richard Southwell and master Palmer were busy in the trussing up of his books, master Rich, pretending friendly talk with him, among other things, of a set course, said unto him: Forasmuch as it is well known, master

---

[1] For a fuller account of More's last days in the Tower, see my *Last Letters of Sir Thomas More* (Manresa Press, 3s. 6d.).

[2] Roper, *Life of Sir Thomas More*, ed. Hitchcock, pp. 77-8.

More, that you are a man both wise and well learned as well in the laws of the realm as otherwise, I pray you therefore, Sir, let me be so bold as of good will to put unto you this case. Admit there were, Sir, quoth he, an act of parliament that all the realm should take me for king? Would not you, master More, take me for king?

Yes, Sir, quoth More, that would I.

I put case further, quoth master Rich, that there were an act of parliament that all the realm should take me for Pope. Would not you then, master More, take me for Pope?

For answer [Sir], quoth Sir Thomas More, to your first case: the parliament may well, master Rich, meddle with the state of temporal princes. But to make answer to your other case, I will put you this case: Suppose the parliament would make a law that God should not be God. Would you then, master Rich say that God were not God?

No, Sir, quoth he, that would I not since no parliament may make any such law.

No more, said Sir Thomas More, as master Rich reported of him, could parliament make the King supreme head of the Church.

Upon whose only report was Sir Thomas More indicted for treason upon the statute [whereby] it was made treason to deny the King to be supreme head of the Church. Into which indictment were put these heinous words–"maliciously, traitorously, and diabolically".[1]

On July 1st, 1535, More was brought from the Tower to Westminster Hall to answer the indictment, and at the King's Bench before the Judges thereupon arraigned.

And for proof to the jury that Sir Thomas More was guilty of this treason, master Rich was called forth to give evidence unto them upon his oath, as he did. Against whom [thus] sworn, Sir Thomas More began in this wise to say: "If I were a man, my lords, that did not regard an oath, I needed not, as it is well known in this place, at this time, not in this case, to stand [here] as an accused person. And if this [oath] of yours master Rich, be true, then pray I that I never see God in the face; which I would not say, were it otherwise, to win the whole world."

Then recited he to the court the discourse of all their communication in the Tower, according to the truth, and said, "In good faith, master Rich, I am sorrier for your perjury than for my own peril. And you shall understand that neither I, no, nor any man else, to my knowledge, ever took you to be a man of such credit as in any matter of importance I, or any other, would at any time communicate with you. And I, as you know, of no small while have been acquainted with you and your conversation, who have known you from your youth hitherto; for we long dwelled both in one parish together, where, as yourself can tell (I

---

[1] Roper, *Life of Sir Thomas More*, ed. Hitchcock, pp. 84–6.

am sorry you compel me to say) you were esteemed very light of your tongue, a great dicer, and of no commendable fame. And so in your house at the Temple, where hath been your chief bringing up, were you likewise accounted.

"Can it therefore seem likely unto your honourable Lordships that I would, in so weighty a cause, so inadvisedly over shoot myself as to trust master Rich, a man of me always reputed for one of so little truth, as your lordships have heard, or of any other noble Councillors, that I would unto him utter the secrets of my conscience, touching the King's supremacy? The special point and only mark at my hands so long sought for: A thing which I never did, nor never would, after the statute thereof made, reveal either to the King's highness himself, or to any of his honourable Councillors, as it is not unknown to your honours, at sundry several times sent from his grace's own person unto the Tower unto me for none other purpose? Can this in your judgments, my lords, seem likely to be true? And [yet], if [I] had so [done] indeed, my lords, as master Rich hath sworn, seeing it was spoken but in familiar secret talk, nothing affirming, and only in putting cases, without other displeasant circumstances, it cannot justly be taken to be spoken maliciously; and where there is no malice, there can be no offence. And over this I can never think, my lords, that so many [worthy] bishops, so many honourable personages, and [so] many other worshipful, virtuous, wise and well learned men as at the making of that law were in the parliament assembled, ever meant to have any man punished by death in whom there could be found no malice, taking 'malitia' [for] 'malevolentia'. For if 'malicia' be generally taken for 'sin', no man is there than that can thereof excuse himself: *Quia si dixerimus quod peccatum non habemus, nosmetipsos seducimus, et veritas in nobis non est.* And only this word 'maliciously' is in the statute material, as this term 'forcible' is in the statute of forcible entries. By which statute, if a man enter peaceably, and put not his adversary out forcibly, it is no offence. But if he put him out forcibly, then by that statute it is an offence, and so shall he be punished by this term 'forcibly'.

"Besides this, the manifold goodness of the King's highness himself, that hath been so many ways my singular good Lord and gracious sovereign, that hath so dearly loved and trusted me, even at my [very] first coming into his noble service with the dignity of his honourable privy Council vouchsafing to admit me, and to offices of great credit and worship most liberally advanced me, and finally with that weighty Room of his grace's high Chancellor (the like whereof he never did to temporal man before) next to his own royal person the highest officer in this noble realm, so far above my merits or qualities able and meet therefor, of his incomparable benignity honoured and exalted me, by the space of twenty years and more showing his continual favour towards me. And (until at my own poor suit, it pleased his highness, giving me license, with his majesty's favour, to bestow the residue of my life for the provision of my soul in the service of God, of his especial goodness thereof to discharge and unburden me) most benignly heaped honours continually more and more upon me. All this his highness's goodness, I say, [so long] thus [bountifully extended towards me], were, in my mind, my Lords, matter sufficient to convince this slanderous surmise by this man so wrongfullly imagined against me."

Master Rich, seeing himself so disproved, and his credit so foully defaced, caused Sir Richard Southwell and master Palmer, that at [the] time of their communication were in the chamber, to be sworn what words had passed between them. Whereupon master Palmer, upon his deposition, said that he was so busy about trussing up of Sir Thomas More's books in a sack, that he took no heed to their talk. Sir Richard Southwell likewise, upon his deposition, said that because he was appointed only to look unto the conveyance of his books, he gave no ear unto them.

After this were there many other reasons, not now in my remembrance, by Sir Thomas More in his own defence alleged, to the discredit of master Rich's aforesaid evidence, and proof of the clearness of his own conscience. All which notwithstanding, the jury found him guilty.[1]

Or as Cresacre More puts it, "The jury of twelve men . . . going together and staying scarce one quarter of an hour (for they knew what the King would have done in that case) returned with their verdict, Guilty."[2]

The Lord Chancellor Audley was then proceeding with unseemly haste to pronounce sentence upon More, when he, in a dignified and courteous manner, observed "that in his time, it was customary, in such a case, to ask the prisoner, before judgment, if he had aught to say why judgment should not proceed against him." The timeliness of this rebuke from the old Lord Chancellor to the new had its due effect; and Audley, "arresting his sentence, wherein he had already partly proceeded", demanded of Sir Thomas what he was able to say in this instance to the contrary, whereupon the prisoner spoke as follows:

"Forasmuch as, my Lord, this Indictment is grounded upon an act of parliament directly repugnant to the laws of God and his holy Church, the supreme government of which, or of any part whereof, may no temporal prince presume by any law to take upon him, as rightfully belonging to the See of Rome, a spiritual pre-eminence by the mouth of our Saviour himself, personally present upon earth, [only] to St.

[1] Roper, *Life of Sir Thomas More*, ed. Hitchcock, pp. 87–92.
[2] Cresacre More, *Life of Sir Thomas More*, p. 329.

R

Peter and his successors, Bishops of the same See, by special prerogative granted; It is therefore in law among Christian men insufficient to charge any Christian man. And for proof thereof, like as, among divers other reasons and authorities, he declared that this realm, being but one member and [small] part of the Church, might not make a particular law, disagreeable with the general law of Christ's universal Catholic Church, no more than the city of London, being but one poor member in respect of the whole realm, might make a law against an act of parliament to bind the whole realm; So farther showed he that it was contrary both to the laws and statutes of our own land yet unrepealed, as they might evidently perceive in *Magna charta*: *Quod ecclesia Anglicana libera sit, et habeat omnia jura sua integra et libertates suas illaesas*; And also contrary to that sacred oath which the King's highness himself and every other Christian prince always with great solemnity received at their coronation: Alleging moreover that no more might this realm of England refuse obedience to the See of Rome than might the child refuse obedience to his [own] natural father. For, as St. Paul said of the Corinthians: 'I have regenerated you, my children in Christ,' So might St. Gregory, Pope of Rome, of whom St. Austin, his messenger, we first received the Christian faith, of us Englishmen truly say: 'You are my children, because I have given to you everlasting salvation, a far [higher and] better inheritance than any carnal father can leave to his child, and by [re]generation made you my spiritual children in Christ.'

Then was it by the Lord Chancellor thereunto answered, that seeing all the bishops, universities, and best learned men of [this] realm had to this act agreed, it was much marvelled that he alone against them all would so stiffly stick [thereat], and so vehemently argue there against.

To this Sir Thomas More replied, saying: "If the number of bishops and universities be so material as your lordships seemeth to take it, then see I little cause, my lord, why that thing in my conscience should make any change. For I nothing doubt but that, though not in this realm, yet in Christendom about, of these well learned bishops and virtuous men that are yet alive, they be not the fewer part that be of my mind therein. But if I should speak of those which already be dead, of whom many be now holy saints in heaven, I am very sure it is the far greater part of them that, all the while [they] lived, thought in this case that way that I think now. And therefore am I not bound, my lord, to conform my conscience to the Council of one realm against the general council of Christendom."

Now when Sir Thomas More, for the avoiding of the indictment, had taken as many exceptions as he thought meet, and [many] more reasons than I can now remember alleged, the Lord Chancellor, loath to have the burden of that judgment, there openly asked the advice of the Lord FitzJames, then Lord Chief Justice of the King's Bench, and joined in commission with him, whether this indictment were sufficient or not. Who like a wise man, answered: "My lord all, by St. Julian" (that was ever his oath): "I must needs confess that if the act of parliament be not unlawful, then is not the indictment in my conscience insufficient."

Whereupon the Lord Chancellor said to the rest of the Lords: "Lo, my Lords, lo, you hear what my lord chief Justice saith," and so immediately gave he judgment against him. The sentence of the law against cases of treason was that of hanging, drawing and quartering; but this was commuted by the King's gracious pleasure to one of decapitation.

After which ended, the commissioners yet further courteously offered him if he had anything else to allege for his defence, to grant him favourable audience. Who answered: "More have I not to say, my Lords, but that like the blessed Apostle St. Paul, as we read in the Acts of the Apostles, was present and consented to the death of St. Stephen, and kept their clothes that stoned him to death, and yet be they [now] both twain holy saints in heaven, and shall continue there friends for ever. So I verily [trust], and shall therefore right heartily pray, that though your lordships have now [here] in earth been Judges to my condemnation, we may yet hereafter merrily all meet together, to our everlasting salvation."

Now after this arraignment, departed he from the bar to the Tower again, led by Sir William Kingston, a tall, strong, and comely knight, Constable of the Tower, and his very dear friend. Who, when he had brought him from Westminster to the Old Swan towards the Tower, there with a heavy heart, the tears running down his cheeks, bade him farewell.

Sir Thomas More, seeing him so sorrowful, comforted him with as good words as he could, saying, "Good master Kingston, trouble not your self, but be of good cheer; for I will pray for you, and my good Lady your wife, that we may meet in heaven together where we shall be merry for ever and ever."

Soon after, Sir William Kingston, talking with me of Sir Thomas More, said: "In good faith, master Roper, I was ashamed of myself, that, at my departing from your father, I found my heart so feeble, and his so strong, that he was fain to comfort me, which I should rather have comforted him."

When Sir Thomas More came from Westminster to the Tower-ward again, his daughter, my wife, desirous to see her father, whom she thought she should never see in this world after, and also to have his final blessing, gave attendance about the Tower wharf, where she knew he should pass by, before he could enter the Tower, there tarrying for his coming home. As soon as she saw him, after his blessing on her knees reverently received, she, hasting towards him, and, without consideration or care for herself, pressing in among [the midst of] the throng and company of the guard that with halberds and bills went round about him, hastily ran to him, took him about the neck, and kissed him.

Who, well liking her most natural and dear daughterly affection towards him, gave her his fatherly blessing and many [godly] words of comfort besides. From whom after she was departed, she, not satisfied with the former sight of him, and like one that had forgotten herself, being all ravished with the entire love of her dear father, having respect neither to herself, not to the press of the people and multitude that were there about him, suddenly turned back, ran to him as before, took him about the neck, and divers times together most lovingly kissed him; and at last, with a full heavy heart, was fain to depart from him: the beholding whereof was to many of them that were present thereat so lamentable that it made them for very sorrow thereof to mourn and weep.[1]

On the day next before his martyrdom—that is, on Monday, July 5th, 1535—St. Thomas More wrote, with a coal, a letter to Margaret Roper, and the last he ever wrote:

Our Lord bless you good daughter, and your good husband, and your little boy, and all yours, and all my children, and all my God-children, and all our friends. Recommend me when you may to my good daughter Cicily, whom I beseech our Lord to comfort. And I send her my blessing, and to all her children, and pray her to pray for me. I send her an handkerchief: and God comfort my good son her husband. My good daughter Daunce hath the picture in parchment, that you delivered me from my lady Coniers, the name is on the back. Show her that I, heartily pray her, that you may send it in my name to her again, for a token from me to pray for me. I like special well Dorothy Coly, I pray you be good unto her. I would wit whether this be she you wrote me of. If not, I pray you be good to the other, as you may in her affliction, and to my good daughter Joan Alleyn too. Give her I pray you some kind answer, for she sued hither to me this day to pray you be good to her.

I cumber you good Margaret much, but I would be sorry if it should be longer than to-morrow. For it is St. Thomas's even, and the octave of St. Peter: and therefore to-morrow long I to go to God: it were a day very meet and convenient to me. I never liked your manner toward me better than when you kissed me last. For I love when daughterly love and dear charity hath no leisure to look to worldly courtesy. Farewell my dear child, and pray for me, and I shall pray for you and all your friends, that we may merrily meet in heaven. . . .[2]

---

[1] Roper, *Life of Sir Thomas More,* ed. Hitchcock, pp. 97-9.   [2] *E. W.*, pp. 1457-8.

On Tuesday, July 6th–St. Thomas's Eve–1535, Sir Thomas Pope, More's "singular good friend", came to him with a message from the King and the Council, to say that he was to die before nine o'clock on the same morning.

When he was gone [writes Cresacre More], Sir Thomas, as one that had been invited to a solemn banquet, changed into his best apparel, and put on his silken camlet gown, which his "entire friend", Mr. Antony Bonvise, gave him whilst he was in the Tower, his beard long, which fashion he never had before used, his face pale and lean, carrying in his hand a reed Cross. . . .

Being now brought to the scaffold, whereon he was to be beheaded, it seemed to him so weak that it was ready to fall. Wherefore he said merrily to Mr. Lieutenant: I pray you, Sir, see me safe up, and for my coming down let me shift for myself. When he began to speak a little to the people, which were in great troops there to hear and see him, he was interrupted by the Sheriff. Wherefore briefly he desired all the people to pray for him, and to bear witness with him that he there died in and for the faith of the holy Catholic Church, a faithful servant of God and the King. Having spoken but this he kneeled down, and pronounced with great devotion the *Miserere* psalm; and the executioner asking him forgiveness, he kissed him saying: Thou wilt do me this day a greater benefit than ever any mortal man can be able to give me; pluck up thy spirit man, and be not afraid to do thy office; my neck is very short; take heed therefore that thou strike not awry, for saving thy honesty. When the executioner would have covered his eyes, he said: I will cover them myself; and presently he did so, with a cloth that he had brought with him for the purpose; then laying his head upon the block, he bade the executioner stay until he had removed his beard saying: that that had never committed any treason. So with great alacrity and spiritual joy, he received the fatal blow of the axe, which no sooner had severed the head from the body, but his soul was carried by angels into everlasting glory, where a crown of martyrdom was put upon him, which can never fade nor decay. . . .

When news of his death was brought to the King, who was at that time playing at tables, Anne Boleyn looking on, he cast his eye upon her and said: thou art the cause of this man's death; and presently leaving his play he betook himself into his chamber, and thereupon fell into a fit of melancholy.

Sir Thomas More's "head was put upon London Bridge, where as traitors' heads are set up upon poles; his body was buried in the Chapel of St. Peter, which is in the Tower".[1]

[1] Cresacre More, *The Life and Death of Sir Thomas More* (1642), pp. 349–57 *passim.*

18

More's Writings in the Tower

IT WAS during the earlier part of his imprisonment in the Tower that More wrote his *Dialogue of Comfort Against Tribulation*, his last considerable work, in order to comfort his family in their time of distress and fearful apprehension. As Monsignor Hallett remarks, "excepting his brief epitaph, it is the nearest approach to an autobiography that he ever wrote. It elaborates the sentiments and principles that guided him through life and steeled his face against martyrdom . . . a revelation of a martyr's inmost soul. With its beauty and elevation of sentiment, the pathos of its theme, and the tenderness of its devotion, it is worthy of a saint and a martyr."[1]

It is written in the form of a dialogue between Antony and his nephew Vincent, and reflects the general fear of an advance of the Turks into Western Europe after they had already conquered Greece and Syria and had taken Belgrade. The Great Turk of that time was Suleyman the Magnificent, who reigned from 1520 to 1566. But in fact it is but a thin disguise of a greater Turk at home, King Henry VIII, who was threatening the religious orders with the confiscation of their property and the very lives of those who remain faithful to the ancient faith. As More himself put the whole matter in a nutshell, "There is no born Turk so cruel as is the false Christian that falleth from the faith!"[2]

More uses the ninetieth psalm as the text upon which to found a great part of his argument. "Whensoever a man falleth into tribulation for the maintenance of justice, or for the defence of God's cause . . . So if he stand and persevere still in his confession of his faith, all his whole pain shall turn into glory".[3] This is the main theme of the dialogue.

And surely if he take hold of the grace that God therein offereth him,

---

[1] *Dialogue of Comfort Against Tribulation*, Introd., pp. vi, ix (Burns, Oates and Washbourne, 1937).

[2] It is of interest to note that only seven members of the House of Lords were in favour of the monastic confiscations. *Dial. of Comfort* (Everyman), p. 120.

[3] Everyman edition of *Utopia* and *A Dialogue of Comfort*, p. 147.

his tribulation is wholesome, and shall be full comfortable to remember, that God by this tribulation calleth him and biddeth him to come out of the country of sin that he was bred and brought up so long in, and come into the land of behest that floweth milk and honey.[1]

The round compassing pavice [shield] of God's truth shall in such wise defend us and keep us safe, that we shall dread none of them all [that tempt us].[2]

He comforts himself with the thought "that if a man had in his heart so deep a desire and love, longing to be with God in heaven, to have the fruition of his glorious face, as had these holy men that were martyrs in the old time, he would no more now stick at the pain that must pass between, than, at that time, the holy martyrs did."[3]

And in this dialogue he discourses at some length upon our natural love of private property in words that those who only read his *Utopia*, and misunderstand it, might well give serious attention to.[4]

In another passage the very land itself turns to rebuke its rich owner and all his pride:

Ah, thou pitiable poor soul, that weenest thou were half a god, and art amid thy glory but a man in a gay gown, I that am the ground here over whom thou art so proud, have had a hundred such owners of me, as thou callest thyself, more than ever thou hast heard the names of. And some of them that proudly went over my head, lie now in my belly, and my side lieth over them. And many one shall, as thou dost now, call himself owner after thee, that neither shall be sib to thy blood [related to thee] nor any word hear of thy name. Who owned your castle, cousin, three thousand year ago?[5]

Then follows a piece of sound common sense about the perishable goods of this life:

The more that a thing in its own nature giveth a man little surety and much fear of its continuance, the less cause we have to love it or to fear the loss thereof, or be loth to go therefrom.[6]

Turning to prayer as our sure refuge in tribulation, More draws a clear distinction between the spiritual value of prayer made in prosperity or in tribulation:

[1] Everyman edition of *Utopia* and *A Dialogue of Comfort*, p. 167.
[2] *Ib.*, p. 202.
[3] *Ib.*, pp. 273–4.
[4] More himself, as I have already shown, always believed in private property and was never a Communist, p. 93.
[5] *Ib.*, p. 276.
[6] *Ib.*, pp. 276–7.

Of all our Lord's holy prayers, the chief seemeth me those that he made in his great agony and pain of his bitter Passion. . . . In all these hideous pains, in all their cruel despites, yet two very devout and fervent prayers he made–the one for their pardon that so dispiteously put him to his pain, and the other about his own deliverance, commending his soul unto his holy Father in heaven. . . . And these prayers of our Saviour at his bitter Passion, and of his holy martyrs in the fervour of their torment, shall serve us to see that there is no prayer made at pleasure so strong and effectual as in tribulation.[1]

And a little further on he writes:

But I never found any place in scripture that I remember, in which though the wealthy man thank God for his gift, our Lord promised any reward in heaven, because the man took his ease and his pleasure here. And therefore since I speak but of such comfort as is very comfort indeed, by which a man hath hope in God's favour, and remission of his sins, with minishing of his pain in purgatory, or reward else in heaven. And such comfort cometh of tribulation well taken, but not for pleasure though it be well taken, therefore of your comfort that you double by prosperity you may, as I told you, cut very well away the half. . . .[2]

This I say yet again and again, that as for far the better thing in this world toward the getting of the very good that God giveth in the world to come, the Scripture undoubtedly so commendeth tribulation, that in respect and comparison thereof it discommendeth this worldly wretched wealth and discomfortable comfort utterly.[3]

And then, at the very last, we come to the discussion of the fear of bodily pain and death:

But surely, good uncle, says his nephew, when I bethink me farther on the grief and pain that may turn into thy flesh, here I find the fear that forceth mine heart to tremble.

Neither have I cause thereof to marvel, nor you cause to be dismayed therefore, replies his uncle. The great horror and fear that our Saviour had in his own flesh against his painful passion, maketh me little to marvel. And I may well make you take comfort too, that for such manner of grudging felt in your sensual parts, the flesh shrinking at the meditation of pain and death, your reason shall give over, but resist it, and manly master it. And though you would fain fly from the painful death and be loth to come thereto, yet may the meditation of his great grievous agony move you, and himself shall (if you desire him) not fail to work with you therein, and get and give you the grace that you

[1] Everyman edition of *Utopia* and *A Dialogue of Comfort*, p. 172.
[2] *Ib.*, p. 174.   [3] *Ib.*, p. 175.

shall submit and conform your will therein unto his, as he did unto his Father, and shall thereupon be so comforted with the secret inward inspiration of his Holy Spirit, as he was with the personal presence of that Angel that after his agony came and comforted him, that you shall as his true disciple follow him, and with good will without grudge do as he did, and take your cross upon your back and die for the truth with him, and thereby reign with him crowned in eternal glory.[1]

Here we are admitted, are we not, to the inmost thought of St. Thomas More, as, in the silence and solitude of his cell in the Tower, he contemplated the ultimate sacrifice that our Lord was asking of him?

And not only here, but also in that passage already quoted[2] from his *History of the Passion*, we come to an even closer intimacy with his own most intimate thought, witnessing, indeed, to his spiritual demeanour in those dreadful days as a wonderful proof of God's especial grace and assistance in his hour of need.

More also wrote while in the Tower his little *Treatise to Receive the Blessed Body of Our Lord*, this "precious marguerite, this pure pearl, the blessed body of our Saviour himself".[3]

We have also *Certain Devotions*[4] used by St. Thomas More while in the Tower, of which the first instruction reflects the holy mind he then entertained towards those who were persecuting him unto death:

Bear no malice nor evil will to no man living. For either that man is good or naught. If he be good, and I hate him, then am I naught. If he be naught, either he shall amend and die good and go to God, or abide naught and go to the devil. And then let me remember that if he shall be saved, he shall not fail (if I be saved too, as I trust to be) to love me very heartily, and I shall then in likewise love him.

And why should I now then, hate one for this while, which shall hereafter love me for evermore? And why should I be now then enemy to him with whom I shall in time coming, be coupled in eternal friendship? And on the other side, if he shall continue naught and be damned, then is there so outrageous eternal sorrow towards him, that I may well think myself a deadly cruel wretch, if I would not now rather pity his pain, than malign his person.

And More writes a little later:

But verily thus will I say, that I will give counsel to every good friend of mine, but if he be put in such room, as to punish an evil man lieth in his charge, by reason of his office, else leave the desire of punishing unto

---

[1] Everyman edition of *Utopia* and *A Dialogue of Comfort*, p. 304.
[2] See page 251.   [3] *E.W.*, p. 1264 C.
[4] Now printed as a leaflet by the Catholic Truth Society.

God and unto such other folk, as are so grown dead in charity, and so far cleave to God, that no secret, shrewd cruel affection, under the cloak of a just and a virtuous zeal, can creep in and undermine them. But let us that are no better than men of a mean sort, ever pray for such merciful amendment in other folk, as our own conscience showeth us that we have need in ourself.[1]

St. Thomas More has himself put these last thoughts of his into a very short form, which in itself seems to contain the whole matter of Christian perfection:[2]

Every man, as Æsop saith in a fable, carrieth a double wallet on his shoulder; and into the one that hangeth at his breast he putteth other folks' faults and therein he looketh and poreth often. In the other, he layeth all his own, and swingeth it at his back, which himself never listeth to look in; but other, that come after him, cast an eye in among.

And does it not seem from this simple spiritual truth that the way to become better oneself consists in turning the wallets round, so that we have our own faults under own gaze, and those of other people well behind us, though God may wish us to carry them nevertheless?

[1] *E. W.*, p. 1405 (misprinted 1425 in the *English Works*).
[2] *Dialogue Concerning Tyndale*, bk. iii, c. 11; *E. W.*, p. 225 D.

19

Tyndale – The Last Phase

As we have already seen,[1] Henry VIII, having tried unsuccessfully to capture Tyndale's controversial ability for his own cause, made up his mind to treat him as an enemy, and instructed his ambassador in the Netherlands to demand his delivery from the Emperor. But Charles V, being the nephew of Katherine of Aragon, was just then in no mood to oblige the King of England. Other expedients had therefore to be tried–Tyndale, in fact, was to be kidnapped and brought back to this country. It is not surprising under these circumstances that Tyndale did his best to elude arrest, hiding now in one place and now in another. But, unfortunately for himself, he was drawn very unwillingly into a controversy upon the Blessed Sacrament on behalf of John Frith, a brilliant young Oxford don, to whom he was much attached. St. Thomas More, too, was moved to do his utmost to save this attractive young man from the extreme penalties of heresy; and Tyndale, after having begged Frith in vain to keep his unorthodox views to himself, published anonymously his own treatise on *The Supper of the Lord*.[2] Even so, every opportunity seems to have been given to Frith to recant, and even to escape without doing so; but he refused to do either, and was burned at Smithfield on May 9th, 1532.

At this time Tyndale wrote his *Exposition upon the Fifth, Sixth and Seventh Chapters of Matthew*, wherein he makes it clear that he will obey no temporal ruler in spiritual matters:

> Though every man's body and goods be under the king, do he right or wrong, yet is the authority of God's word free and above the king. . . . The king is as deep under the spiritual officer, to hear out of God's word what he ought to believe and how to live, and how to rule, as is the poorest beggar in the realm.[3]

It is in these expositions that, wrongly informed, he accuses More of

[1] P. 264.
[2] For Mozley's proof of Tyndale's authorship, see *Notes and Queries*, November 21st, 1943.
[3] Tyndale, *Works*, vol. ii, p. 67.

the sin of covetousness which, he says, "blinded the eyes of that gleering fox more and more, and hardened his heart against the truth, with confidence of his painted poetry, babbling eloquence, and juggling arguments of subtle sophistry, grounded on his 'unwritten verities', as true and as authentic as his story of Utopia."[1]

Of Tyndale's doings during this year we know very little. He was approached by those against the King's divorce to revise a treatise that had been written against his recent marriage with Anne Boleyn; but he refused to meddle further in the prince's matter.

In the following year (1534) he brought out the second edition of Genesis and the New Testament with few changes; but the glosses in the first edition in which he had attacked the Pope were removed, showing him to be in a gentler frame of mind.

Meanwhile he had found a safe lodging in the English house of the Merchant Adventurers at Antwerp, his host being Thomas Poyntz, a member of the Grocers' Company and a distant kinsman of Lady Walsh of Little Sodbury in Gloucestershire, where, it will be remembered, he had lived in 1522. Here he dwelt for nine months revising his New Testament, which Bishop Westcott calls his "noblest monument". This edition is the text which Rogers used for his Matthew's Bible, and thus it became the foundation of the standard Authorised Version.

Thomas Poyntz provides us with an account of these last years which perhaps it would be fairer to give in his own words:

Tyndale was a man very frugal and spare of body, a great student, an earnest labourer in the setting forth of the scriptures of God. He reserved or hallowed to himself two days in the week, which he named his pastime, Monday and Saturday. On Monday he visited all such poor men and women as were fled out of England, by reason of persecution, into Antwerp; and these, once well understanding their good exercise and qualities, he did very liberally comfort and relieve; and in like manner provided for the sick and diseased persons. On Saturday he walked round about the town, seeking every corner and hole where he suspected any poor person to dwell; and where he found any to be well occupied, and yet over-burdened with children, or else were aged and weak, these also he plentifully relieved. And thus he spent his two days of pastime, as he called them. And truly his alms were very large, and so they might well be; for his exhibition [allowance] that he had yearly of the English merchants at Antwerp, when living there, was considerable; and that, for the most part, he bestowed upon the poor. The rest

[1] Tyndale, *Works*, vol. ii, p. 100.

of the days of the week he gave wholly to his book, wherein he most diligently travailed.

When the Sunday came, then went he to some merchant's chamber or other, whither came many other merchants, and unto them would he read some one parcel of scripture: the which proceeded so fruitfully, sweetly and gently from him, much like to the writing of John the Evangelist, that it was a heavenly comfort and joy to the audience to hear him read the scriptures; likewise, after dinner, he spent an hour in the same manner. He was a good man without any spot or blemish of rancour or malice, full of mercy and compassion, so that no man living was able to reprove him of any sin or crime; although his righteousness and justification depended not thereupon before God, but only upon the blood of Christ, and his faith upon the same.[1]

In addition to the revision of his New Testament, he was also translating a part of the Old Testament from Joshua to the Second Book of Chronicles, with the help, perhaps, of John Rogers, who became his literary executor.

But Tyndale's end was drawing near. A treacherous plan was devised for his capture. Pretending to sympathise with Tyndale's views, a certain Henry Phillips, a ne'er-do-well son of Richard Phillips, Collector of Customs at Poole, and grandfather of the builder of Montacute—a Catholic, too, be it said to his shame—went to Antwerp and gained the confidence and affection of the unsuspecting Tyndale; but never that of the shrewd Merchant Adventurer, Thomas Poyntz, in whose house Tyndale was lodged. One day, Poyntz himself being absent, Phillips invited Tyndale to dine with him.

No, said Master Tyndale; I go forth this day to dinner, and you shall go with me and be my guest, where you shall be welcome. So when it was dinner-time, Master Tyndale went forth with Phillips, and at the going out of Poyntz's house was a long narrow entry, so that two men could not go in a front. Master Tyndale would have put Phillips before him, but Phillips would in no wise, but put Master Tyndale afore, for that he pretended to show great humility. So Master Tyndale, being a man of no stature, went before, and Phillips, a tall comely person, followed after him; who had officers on either side of the door upon two seats, which being there, might see who came in the entry; and coming through the same entry, Phillips pointed with his finger over Master Tyndale's head down to him, that the officers which sat at the door might see that it was he whom they should take; as the officers that took Master Tyndale afterwards told Poyntz, and said to Poyntz, when they laid him in prison, that they pitied to see his simplicity when

[1] Greenslade, *The Work of William Tyndale*, pp. 15–16.

they took him. Then they took him and brought him to the Emperor's attorney or Procurer-General.[1]

This arrest was made on May 23rd, 1535, and Tyndale was immediately taken to the State prison of the Netherlands at Vilvorde, six miles from Brussels.

We know little of Tyndale's long imprisonment of a hundred and thirty-five days in the Castle of Vilvorde. Most of his property was confiscated; and a pathetic letter survives, asking for warmer clothes and Hebrew books. In the August of 1536 he was condemned and publicly degraded from the priesthood, "so that", as John Hutton wrote to Cromwell on August 12th, "he is like to suffer death this next week". But the execution was deferred, and it was not until October 6th (as tradition has it) that he "was brought forth to the place of execution, was there tied to the stake, and then strangled first by the hangman, and afterwards with fire consumed, in the morning at the town of Vilvorde, A.D. 1536; crying thus at the stake with a fervent zeal and a loud voice: Lord, open the King of England's eyes."[2]

---

[1] Mozley, *William Tyndale*, pp. 296–7, after Foxe.
[2] *Ib.*, p. 341, after Foxe.

20

Erasmus Dies at Basle

We left Erasmus living at Freiburg in 1535, and not in good health. But, on the death of Clement VII in 1534, Paul III became Pope, and elevated to the Sacred College such men of eminent learning and piety as Caraffa, Sadolet, Reginald Pole, and later Bembo, all of them personal friends of Erasmus. It was then hoped that he, too, would become a Cardinal, but the only difficulty seems to have arisen from his own unwillingness to accept the dignity. He wrote to Paul III, begging him to follow moderate counsels in dealing with the Reformation troubles and to devote all his energies to the strengthening of the faith and the pacification of the Church. The Pope's reply shows that he appreciated the advice, and himself determined to follow it. "Nor are we ignorant", he adds, "how much your extraordinary learning conjoined with an equal eloquence, can help us in rooting out these new errors from the minds of men." He begs him to lend his assistance in this holy work, and in defence of the Catholic faith, both before and after the Council which, with God's help, it is his intention to hold. Erasmus was also offered the provostship of Deventer, in itself a lucrative position, but this he refused, feeling that his strength might not be equal to it, and that he had sufficient means of his own to suffice for the rest of his days.

Meanwhile he went quietly on with his treatise on the art of preaching, which he had undertaken at the suggestion of his old friend, St. John Fisher. It was published at Basle in the following year under the title *Ecclesiastes, sive Concionator Evangelicus*, and was dedicated to the Bishop of Augsburg.

In the August of 1535 Erasmus went to Basle in order to put the finishing touches to this work now in the press. He had made up his mind to leave Freiburg, and, after returning to Basle for a short stay, to proceed down the Rhine to Brabant. His house at Freiburg was sold, and his furniture, chiefly consisting of books, brought to Basle, where he was hospitably entertained by Jerome Froben. Shortly after his arrival there he received the news of the martyrdom of St. John Fisher and of St. Thomas More. He was now suffering from the worst pains of arthritis, which kept him to his room and often to his bed. During these last months of his life he wrote *De Puritate Ecclesiae Christianae*, a commentary on the fourteenth Psalm. He also revised the text of Origen, and prepared a new and enlarged edition of his own *Letters*. In turning over these and seeing the names of so many of his friends now dead, he exclaimed, "If it shall please the Lord, I have no longer any desire to live." His last letter is dated June 28th, 1536, in which he expresses a wish to go to Besançon in order to improve his health. He was anxious, too, to get away from Basle, where there was so much opposition to the Catholic faith; but at Basle he died, in spite of his wish, during the night, between July 11th and July 12th, 1536. He was buried in the old Minster. It would seem that from September 1535 Erasmus was tenderly cared for by a young man named Lambertus Coomans, who had also been in the service of Cardinal van Enkevoirt in Rome. After Erasmus's death, thanks to the legacy Erasmus had left him for the purpose, he studied and became a priest, and finally was made a canon and dean in his native town of Turnhout. He proclaimed wherever he could that Erasmus had died in his arms as a devout Catholic, with an invocation to our Lady on his lips.[1]

In death as well as in life we are able to link the names of More and Erasmus as commemorated by Peter Nannius, one of the presidents of the *Collegium Trilingue* at Louvain:

De Moro et Erasmo

Vivebat in pectusculo Mori sui
Erasmus ille seculi nostri decus.
Vivebat in praecordiis Erasmicis
Morus, Britanniae unicum lumen suae.
Vitamque mutuabat alter alteri,
Aliena uterque non sua vixit anima
Mirum nihil si mortuo Moro, mori
Voluit Erasmus, nequit ultra vivere.[2]

And so died, within the short space of fifteen months, these three outstanding figures of the sixteenth century, so linked together in life, and

[1] A more detailed account of the death of Erasmus will be found in an appendix; and it may be of some interest in view of the different expressions of opinion upon it by differing writers on the subject.
[2] The great Erasmus, glory of our age, lived in the heart of More, his friend. More, the one great light of his own land of Britain, lived in the mind of Erasmus.
Lending life, the one to the other, each lived by a soul not his own. What wonder was it, therefore, that when More died, Erasmus wished to live no longer.

yet so different in disposition, in character and achievement, summing up in themselves the clashing convictions and events of that stormy Tudor period in which the masterful personality of Henry VIII played so determining a part.

Erasmus, anchored through life to the Catholic faith and devoted to the cause of sound learning, wandered over Europe, from the Netherlands to Paris, and from Paris to London, and from London to Florence and to Rome, and then back to England again, where at Cambridge he began, and for the most part completed, his *Novum Instrumentum* and his great edition of *St. Jerome*. After that he travelled through Germany to Basle and Freiburg, and then made one last visit to Basle, where, unexpectedly, he died, having previously heard of the martyrdom of his two best friends, St. John Fisher and St. Thomas More. No scholar of that time approached him in the greatness and range of his literary output or in his forward-looking vision of what was most necessary to Catholic apologetic, resting, as it must needs do, on the text of the inspired writings of the New Testament as interpreted by the "old holy Fathers" and the ever-living voice of the Catholic Church.

Dean Swift called More the person "of the greatest virtue this kingdom ever produced"; and Mr. G. K. Chesterton said about him that he was "more important at this moment than at any moment since his death, even perhaps the great moment of his dying; but he is not quite so important as he will be in about a hundred years time. He may come to be counted the greatest Englishman, or at least the greatest historical character in English history. . . . He represented at once a type, a turning-point and an ultimate destiny."[1]

William Tyndale, we can but fear, must bear, with Henry VIII and Thomas Cromwell, the initial responsibility for the English Reformation. Throughout life he was a lonely soul and, in his later years, Protestantism itself personified.

---

[1] *The Fame of Blessed Thomas More*, p. 63 (Sheed & Ward, 1929).

S

APPENDIX

A Note on the Death of Erasmus

THE last page of this book had been written, and the book itself was already in galley-proof, when a friend informed the writer that a recent article had appeared in Spanish entitled *La Muerte de Erasmo*, written by Father Villoslada, S. J.[1] and printed in volume iv of *Miscellanea Giovanni Mercati*, published in Rome at the Vatican Press in 1946. By the kindness of another friend the writer was able to obtain a copy of this most interesting and important paper, and what follows, he owes to the gracious permisison of Father Villoslada himself to make use of what he has written, and to set forth the substance of it as briefly as possible.[2]

Erasmus, after living at Freiburg-im-Breisgau for over six years from 1529 to 1535 made up his mind to leave it and make his way back to his native land. But he wished to call at Basle in order to put some finishing touches to his forthcoming treatise called *Ecclesiastes*, a small book on preaching which was published after his death, and to his new edition of Origen then almost ready for publication. But being in ill-health, he found the journey a difficult one; and when he arrived at Basle he became so disabled by that painful complaint arthritis that he was often obliged to keep his bed and for lengthening periods was unable to leave his room. Gradually it became clear to his friends and to himself that, now in his seventieth year, his death could not long be delayed.

Beatus Rhenanus, an intimate friend of his, has left two accounts of Erasmus's death, one in the preface to the edition of Origen's works, already spoken of, and dated the 15th of August 1536, shortly after Erasmus had died, the other in his dedication to the Emperor Charles V of his *Erasmi Omnia Opera*, dated July 1st 1540. From these accounts we learn that, after his arrival at Basle, Erasmus lodged with his friend John Froben, and later on in another of Froben's houses which was near St.

---

[1] Father R. G. Villoslada, S.J. Doctor of the Roman Gregorian University. Formerly editor of *Estudios Ecclesiasticos* and now a regular contributor. Sometime professor at Ona, the Collegium Maximum of the Castillian Province: now a Professor at the Pontifical University of Salamanca.

[2] Cf. also H. de Vocht, *Literae ad Franciscum Cranveldium*, Louvain, 1928.

Peter's Church and which had a little garden where he could walk in the evening sunlight, after the day's task was over. Here he worked with his usual and devoted industry, unless interrupted by recurring attacks of rheumatism; but these attacks grew steadily worse and more frequent. And so the time went on until his illness became so dangerous that a few days before his death he was visited by his old friends Boniface Amorbach, Jerome Froben and Nicholas Episcopius whom he playfully rallied because, as he said, unlike the three friends of holy Job, who had not been nearly as ill as he was, they visited him without their proper accompaniment of sackcloth and ashes. But he went on to speak to them in all seriousness of his approaching end. As he grew still worse, weakened by constant attacks of dysentery, he showed every sign of Christian patience and resignation, uttering such pious ejaculations as *"O Jesu, misericordia! Domine, libera me! Domine, fac finem, Domine miserere mei"*, and also in German, *"Lieber Gott!"*

Another letter written from Basle about the same time quotes among his last utterances—*"O Jesu, Fili Dei, miserere mei! Misericordiam Domini et judicium cantabo!"*

Father Villoslada, in his scholarly and careful study, after recording these sayings and circumstances of Erasmus's last moments, raises a question of grave and capital importance—Who was present at Erasmus's death-bed and assisted him in his last agony? And, we are glad to say, satisfies us with a clear and unequivocal answer. He tells us that he died in the presence, and with the spiritual assistance, of a Catholic priest, Lambert Coomans, a former protégé of his, some time his secretary, who, at the very end, performed the duties of his chaplain, and in whose arms Erasmus breathed his last.

Beatus Rhenanus, it is true, does not mention the presence of a priest at Erasmus's death-bed; but he may have taken for granted what was a well-known fact. This omission, if an omission, was taken advantage of by Erasmus's enemies who did not hesitate to suggest that he had died without Catholic assistance presumably because he did not desire it.

The facts about Lambert Coomans seem to be as follows: he was born at Turnhout in the Low Countries, and was therefore a compatriot of Erasmus. He studied at Louvain, and later became secretary to Cardinal van Enkevoirt. When the Cardinal died in Rome in 1534, he set out on his return to his native land, but called at Freiburg-im-Breisgau, in order to see his old master and friend, who was then living there. Erasmus persuaded him to delay his journey for a while in order that

they might travel together. When, therefore, Erasmus moved on to
Basle, in a very delicate state of health, Father Coomans accompanied
him, but his illness became so pronounced that the idea of going further
had to be given up; and so it was that his younger friend remained with
him to the end.

This evidence is borne out by a certain John Hoybergius, who, in his
notes on a work of John Latomus, writes as follows: "*His insuper decanus
(Lambertus Coomans) Desiderio Erasmo Roteradamo fuerat ab epistolis: cui
adeo fuit in amore et deliciae, ut illum secum esse voluerit usque ad extremum
vitae spiritum; et anno* 1536 *Basiliae, hujus Lamberti brachiis innixus in illis
verbis emisit,* 'O mater Dei, memento mei!' *ut ex illis viris fide dignissimis
intelliximus, qui haec ab ipso Coomans semel audiverat.*"[1]

Perhaps it may be said in all fairness that non-Catholic presupposi-
tions have played a considerable and often unconscious part in certain
descriptions of Erasmus's life and death written in this and in other
countries, between the sixteenth century and the present time. And not
only in Erasmus's case, but also in those, let us say, of Dean Colet and St.
Thomas More, all three of them, having often been described as what
might be called budding Protestants, who had they lived a little longer
would have been found on the side of the Reformers. This of course is
what, in present day phraseology, would be called "wishful writing."

But Father Villoslada probably keeps to the truth when he says
that "in Erasmus, in spite of all his modernity, there breathes a great
deal of the spirit of the Middle Ages and of respect for the Church".[2]
Time and again, as readers of these pages will remember, Erasmus made
the *ex cathedra* rulings of the Church his final court of appeal and accepted them in a true spirit of Catholic obedience. Nor are we surprised
when Father Villoslada writes that "when Erasmus saw death approaching, calmly and in the full enjoyment of a clear mind till the last moment having at his bedside a priest in whom he had entire confidence, it
is morally certain that he would not have neglected his obligations as a
Christian, nor would the priest (who was with him) have neglected his
priestly duty."[3]

[1] *Un theologien de Louvain assistant Erasme dans ses derniers moments; notice sur Lambert
Coomans de Turnhout*, en *Annuaire de l'Université catholique de Louvain*, 1852, pp. 251-5.
Coomans, after Erasmus's death, at once returned home and in 1559 was appointed Dean
of the Collegiate Church of Turnhout, where he died in 1583.
[2] Art. *La Muerte De Erasmo*, p. 23.
[3] *Ib.*, p. 24. A letter from Father Villoslada received after this was in print informs me
that he had not been able to verify the date of Coomans ordination as a priest. But the
presumption that he was a priest seems more than strong, as evidenced, for instance, by
the fact that he became Dean of the Collegiate Church of Turnhout, see note 1.

It is true that Erasmus, like St. Thomas More, was at one time uncertain whether certain practices of the Church were of divine institution or not. But as in More's case, so in that of Erasmus, his mind was
finally set at rest. In 1529, seven years before his death, we have his own
declaration that he would never dare to leave this life without having
confessed his sins to a priest; and the fact that he frequented the sacraments during the last phase of his life, and in confirmed ill-health, can be
inferred from the testimony of his own confessor, John of Breisgau
(Calceatoris) within fifteen days of Erasmus's own death–*"Fui illi dum
viveret aliquoties a confessionibus, in quo non nisi Christo dignam vitam depre-
hendebam."*[1]

Nor should it be forgotten that in a letter dated by Dr. Allen as written in 1523 on the occasion of the death of his friend Nevius at Louvain;
and with whom he had shared a room, when they were both there together, Erasmus is moved to some very serious meditation.

Such a sudden death, he writes, teaches us not to live in a state in which
we should not like to die. The terrible thing is not to die, but to die badly.
What greater folly than to put off the amendment of one's life until
the hour of death. Recourse to confession comes too late when the soul
departs with the last breath. "Grant me, Lord, contrition and sincere
confession before death", is the prayer of some people. . . . How much
more Christian is it to have no other care than to lead such a life that we
are not caught unawares at the last moment.

A little later he speaks quite frankly of his own spiritual dispositions:

I have had to wrestle with myself to show truly Christian charity towards those who have deliberately worked for my ruin; and I have succeeded not only in avoiding thoughts of revenge but also in not wishing
them any ill at all. . . .
I often think over these matters in my own mind and talk of them to
some of my learned friends. The wisest course seems to me to ask Christ
with prayer and good living for the grace of a good end; and then to
leave the result in His hands, putting, meanwhile, small reliance on one's
own merits and great confidence in His immense love towards us.[2]

No one, as Father Villoslada remarks, can doubt the sincerity of these
words used at a time of bereavement and when Erasmus, owing to his
own ill health, thought himself about to enter the valley of the shadow
of death.

Naturally a man of sensitive nature, he had much to discourage him,

---

[1] Allen, *Erasmi Epistolae*, tom. viii, 145. [2] *Ib.*, v, 238-50.

misunderstood and attacked as he was by enmities of a most virulent kind. On one occasion a false rumour of his death got about, and there was some unseemly rejoicing on the part of those who were more than unfriendly to him; and they are reported to have said that he died without the consolations of the Church, "*sine crux, sine lux, sine Deus*".[1] No doubt religious feeling ran high in those days; and this perhaps was an exceptional example of it. But it throws some light upon the nature and origin of many of the reports about Erasmus that seem to have been mistaken for the truth by a good many writers.

In 1524, the year following the period just referred to, Erasmus's health showed improvement, and much against his will he was persuaded to enter into controversy with Luther. But this step was a fortunate one for him and for the Church as a whole. He was quick to see that Luther's most vulnerable point was his contention that man had no free-will, and therefore had no sufficient incitement to virtue. But apart from its controversial value, "this was the decisive step in the Humanist's life, and also in that of many others who had been hesitating between Rome and Wittenberg, but no longer remained irresolute when they saw that the Prince of Humanists was going into battle against the heresiarch."[2]

But we must return to the last phase of Erasmus's life. In the autumn of 1534, when Paul III became Pope, he was anxious to enlist the services and advice of Erasmus at the Council he intended to summon, and made various approaches to him with that intention. But Erasmus, though personally gratified, knew only too well that he no longer had the physical strength to be of any practical assistance to the Holy See; nor had he, as we already know, any wish for high ecclesiastical preferment.[2] He writes, however, to Cardinal Cajetan; "What I place above all things is that which leads to the peace of the Church, rather than to my own honour. If I do the will of Christ, and if those who are like yourself approve of me, then I wish for no other honours."[3]

On March 11th, 1536, he wrote to his friend, Gilbert Cousin, who was a canon: "*Debilitor usque ad mortem*", I am sick unto death. And to another friend on the 17th of May: "Old age becomes daily more burdensome, and my illness increases. I am in no danger from the religious sects that surround me; but I don't like the idea of having any of them to see me." His very last letter was addressed to his intimate friend, Conrad

[1] Villoslada, *La Muerte De Erasmo*, p. 1.   [2] *Ib.*, pp. 9–10.
[3] Cf, Allen, *Erasmi Epistolae*, vii, 200.

Goclen, a canon of Antwerp, who was then teaching in the University of Louvain. It was dated June 28th, 1536, just two weeks before his death. He is overwhelmed with afflictions and despondency: there have been days when he could not even read. He had come to Basle with the intention of moving on; but his feeble health had obliged him to spend the winter there. The great Catholic Humanist, traveller and cosmopolitan, had a gentle longing to die in his own country. "*Ob dogmatum dissensionem, malim alibi finire vitam,*" he wrote, "there is so much contention here I wish to end my life elsewhere". But it was not to be. At Basle at about midnight on July the 11th or 12th, 1536, he breathed his last.

As soon as the news of his death became known, early on the morning of July 12th, the whole city showed its grief and respect. A great crowd hastened to pay its last respects to Erasmus's remains; and the body was carried to the Cathedral on the shoulders of members of the University, and there buried in the presence of the civil authorities, at the foot of the altar of our Lady.

"Frederick Nausea (Crawe), who later became Archbishop of Vienna and who died when present at the Council of Trent in 1552, wrote these words at the time of Erasmus's death: "*Nobis ex animo moerendum, lugendum, flendumque censemus, quod amisimus (heu dolor) amisimus amicum et longe maximum, non solum nostrae Germaniae, sed totius orbis ornamentum et decus, et inauditum pene seculis omnibus miraculum, cujus obitu nihil potuisset hoc tempore vel calamitosius, vel incommodius, vel tristius universae Ecclesiae, quam brevi per universalem Synodum repraesentatum iri speramus, evenire.*"[1]

---

[1] *Desiderii Erasmi Rot. viri incomparabilis vita et epitaphia quaedam, Antuerpia,* 1536, pages un-numbered.

BIBLIOGRAPHY

ACTON, LORD, *The Study of History.*
  Freedom and other Essays.
ALLEN, DR. P. S., *Erasmus Epistolae.*
  Proceedings of the British Academy.
  The Age of Erasmus.
AQUINAS, ST. THOMAS, *Summa Catholicae Fidei contra Gentiles.*
ARISTOTLE, *Politics.*
ATKINS, J. W. H., *English Literary Criticism.*
  The Renaissance.
AUGUSTINE, ST., *Against the Epistole of Manichaeus.*
  Against the Epistle of the Manichees called Fundamental.
  De Civitate Dei.
BRIDGES, J. H., *Essays and Addresses.*
BRIDGETT, FATHER, T. E., *Life of St. Thomas More.*
  St. John Fisher.
BRINKLOW, HENRY, *Complaynt of Roderyck Mors.*
BRODRICK, FATHER JAMES, *The Origin of the Jesuits.*
  The Progress of the Jesuits.
BURCKHARDT, J., *The Civilisation of the Renaissance in Italy.*
BURNET, GILBERT, *History of the Reformation.*
Catholic Encyclopaedia.
CHAMBERS, R. W., *Man's Unconquerable Mind.*
  Thomas More.
CHESTERTON, G. K., *The Fame of Blessed Thomas More.*
Chronicles of the Grey Friars in London.
Church Times, The (Feb. 3, 1928).
COOPER, C. H., *Annals of Cambridge.*
CRAIK, SIR HENRY, *English Prose Selections* (edited).
CREIGHTON, MANDELL, *History of the Papacy.*
DAVIS, MISS JEFFRIES, *Victoria County History of London.*
DEMAUS, R., *William Tyndale.*
Dictionary of National Biography.
DONNER, PROFESSOR H. W., *Introduction to Utopia.*
Downside Review (May 1932).
DRUMMOND, R. B., *Erasmus.*
ELLIS, SIR H., *Original Letters* (3rd series).
Encyclopaedia Britannica.
England in Henry VIII's Time.
ERASMUS, *Works.*
FISHER, H. A. L., *The Political History of England.*
FOXE, JOHN, *Acts and Monuments.*
  Book of Martyrs.
FROUDE, J. A., *Life of Thomas Carlyle.*
  History of England.
FULLER, T., *Church History of Britain.*
GAIRDNER, JAMES, *A History of the English Church in the Sixteenth Century.*
  Lollardy and the Reformation.
GASQUET, CARDINAL, *Henry VIII and the Reformation.*
GREEN, JOHN RICHARD, *Short History of the English People.*

Bibliography

GREENSLADE, *The Work of William Tyndale.*

HALL, F., *Chronicle.*

HUGEL, BARON F. VON, *Essays and Addresses,* First Series, p. 221.

JAMES, WILLIAM, *The Will to Believe.*

JEBB, SIR RICHARD, *Essays and Addresses.*

JOURDAIN, G. V., *The Movement of Catholic Reform in the Early Sixteenth Century.*

KEMPIS, THOMAS À, *Imitation of Christ.*

Letters and Papers of the Reign of Henry VIII, edited by J. S. Brewer, James Gairdner, R. H. Brodie.

LUPTON, J. H., *Life of Dean Colet.*

The Influence of Dean Colet upon the Reformation in the English Church.

MACAULAY, LORD, *Critical and Historical Essays.*

MAYNARD-SMITH, H., *Pre-Reformation England.*

MORE, CRESACRE, *Life and Death of Sir Thomas More.*

MORE, SIR THOMAS, *Works.*

MOZLEY, J. F., *John Foxe and His Book.*

" Tyndale's Supper of the Lord," article in *Notes and Queries,* Nov. 21, 1942.

William Tyndale.

MULLINGER, J. B., *The University of Cambridge.*

NICHOLS, F. M., *Epistles of Erasmus* (translated).

Erasmus on Dean Colet (translated).

NOLHAC, P. DE, *Erasme en Italie.*

O'SULLIVAN, RICHARD, " The Social Theories of Sir Thomas More," article in *Dublin Review,* July 1936.

Oxford Studies in Legal and Social History, edited Vinogradoff.

PASTOR, L., *History of the Popes.*

PLATO, *Republic.*

POLLARD, A. F., *Henry VIII.*

Thomas Cranmer.

Wolsey.

POPE, ALEXANDER, *Essay on Criticism.*

POWICKE, F. M., *The Legacy of the Middle Ages.*

READE, CHARLES, *The Cloister and the Hearth.*

ROPER, WILLIAM, *Life of Sir Thomas More.*

ROUTH, E. M. C., *Sir Thomas More and his Friends.*

RUPP, E. G., *The English Protestant Tradition.*

SAVINE, *Studies of Monastic Lands before the Dissolution.*

SEEBOHM, FREDERIC, *Oxford Reformers.*

STRYPE, J., *Ecclesiastical Reformers.*

STUBBS, W., *Essays on Mediaeval and Modern History.*

SWIFT, DEAN, *Works.*

THOMPSON, FRANCIS, *Selected Poems.*

THOMSON, J. A. K., *Social and Political Ideas of the Renaissance and Reformation.*

Times Literary Supplement, June 4, 1925.

TYNDALE, WILLIAM, *Works.*

Doctrinal Treatises.

VILLOSLADA, REV. R. G., " La Muerta de Erasmo," article in *Miscellanea Giovanni Mercati,* 1946.

VIRGIL, *Aeneid.*

Eclogues.

VOCHT, H. DE, " Erasmus," article in the *Clergy Review,* July 1936.

WESTCOTT, B. F., " Dionysius the Areopagite," article in *Contemporary Review,* May 1867.

WORDSWORTH, C., *Ecclesiastical Biography.*

INDEX

n indicates footnote.

H

Hadley, William, 19
Hallett, Monsignor, P. E., 262
Hall's Chronicle, 181–2
Hegius, Alexander (of Deventer), 60
Henry VII, King of England, 33, 40, 49
Henry VIII, King of England, 56, 84, 227
  More and, 90, 261
  Tyndale's books banned, 108–10
  Obedience of a Christian Man, interest in, 112 *et seq.*
  head of Church, 113, 178, 183–4, 188
  confiscation of church property, 155, 158, 160, 172
  Supplication for the Beggars, interest in, 156–7
  Simon Fish protected, 156
  divorce from Katherine of Aragon, 175–7, 180, 182, 186–7, 242
  relations with Parliament, 177–8
  Tyndale recalled from exile, 192 *et seq.*
  marriage to Anne Boleyn, 242
Henry of Bergen, Bishop of Cambrai, 28–9
Henson, Dr. Hensley, 112
Hertogenbosch, Erasmus at school, 27
Hilton, Walter, *Scale of Perfection,* 240
History of the Passion, See More, Sir T., *Works.*
Holbein, Hans (the younger), 56, 68–9
Holy Maid of Kent (Elizabeth Barton), 243
Houghton, John, prior of the Charter-house, 253
Hoybergius, John, 276
Hunne, Richard, 148, 163
Huskin, John, 222
Hutten, Ulrich von, 67, 70, 79
Hutton, John, 270
Hyperaspites. See Erasmus, Desiderius, *Works.*
Hythlodaye, Raphael, 84, 86, 89–94

I

Ignatius, St., 39
Imitation of Christ. See Kempis, Thomas à.
Inghirami, Tomasso, 48
Institute of the Christian Prince. See Erasmus, Desiderius, *Works.*
Institution of Christian Matrimony. See Erasmus, Desiderius, *Works.*

J

James IV, King of Scotland, 47–8
Jebb, Sir Richard, 56, 233
Jerome, St., 62, 65, 70, 76, 98, 232
John of Breisgau, 277
Johnson, Dr. Samuel, 97, 127
Julius II, Pope, 42–3, 45, 52–3, 66

K

Katherine of Aragon, 110, 121, 176, 179, 232, 242
Kempis, Thomas à:
  Imitation of Christ, 39, 240
Ker, W. P., 16
Kingston, Sir William, 259

L

Lady Margaret foundation, 59–61
Lambert, John, 105
Lamentations of a Christian against the City of London. See Brinklow, Henry.
Lange, Rudolph, 60
Latimer, Hugh, Bishop of Worcester, 59, 101, 104
Latimer, William, scholar, 45
Lawrence, Robert, Prior of Belleval, 253
Laws and Germania, See Tacitus.
Lee, Edward, Archbishop of York, 59, 108
Leo, X, Pope, 48–9, 55, 62, 66, 70, 103
Leonardo da Vinci, 19
Leontorious, Conrad, 68
Letter against Frith. See More, Sir T., *Works.*
Letters and Papers of the Reign of Henry VIII, 14
Life of Christ. See Bonaventure, St.
Life of Thomas Carlyle. See Froude, J. A.
Life of Sir Thomas More. See Roper, William.
Lily, William, 23
Linacre, Thomas, 19, 23, 45
Lollards, 59, 109
Lupton, J. H., 17, 19
Luther, Martin, 13, 38, 48, 77, 103, 107–8, 111
  New Testament translation, 62
  public burning of works, 100, 105, 109
  theses posted on Wittenberg Castle Church, 104
  More and, 148–52, 220–2
  Works:
    Babylonica, 220.
    Man's Will not Free, 230

M

Machiavelli, Niccolo, 19
Man's Will not Free. See Luther, Martin, *Works.*
Mantuanus, Baptist, 21
Manual of the Christian Knight. See Erasmus, Desiderius, *Works, Enchiridion Militis Christiani.*
Manutius, Aldus, 44–6, 51, 55, 68, 85
  press mark, 47
Maria, Francesco, Prefect of Rome, 43
Matsys, Quentin, 89